*f*P

SMART BUSINESS

How Knowledge Communities Can

Revolutionize Your Company

DR. JIM BOTKIN

The Free Press

THE FREE PRESS
A Division of Simon & Schuster Inc.
1230 Avenue of the Americas
New York, NY 10020

THE FREE PRESS and colophon are trademarks
of Simon & Schuster Inc.

Designed by Carla Bolte

Manufactured in the United States of America

10 9 8 7 6 5 4 3 2 1

Library of Congress Cataloging-in-Publication Data

Botkin, James W.
    Smart business: how knowledge communities can revolutionize your
company / Jim Botkin.
        p.   cm.
    Includes bibliographical references.
        1. Knowledge management.   2. Information technology.   3. Strategic
planning.   4. Organization.   I. Title.
    HD30.2.B676   1999
    658.4'038—dc21   99-17727
                                                                         CIP

ISBN 0–684–85024–9

Illustrations by Gary Lund.

Contents

An Economy of Ideas

Alan M. Webber

Fast Company

Boston, MA

We are living in an economy of ideas.

Just look around you, at the companies that are dominating today's headlines, at the organizations that are commanding our attention, at the people and teams that are capturing our imaginations. What we are witnessing is the creation of a new world of business, a place vastly different from that of the past. The old ways of keeping score—measures of tangible assets, factors of production such as land, factories, equipment, office buildings—are giving way to new metrics: The team with the best ideas, the best people, the most integrated way of working, the greatest passion, the closest relationship with the customer, the most out-of-the-box business model, the best execution, that's the team that wins. Soft assets matter most today. Ideas. People. Teamwork. Communities. Passion. Values. And knowledge.

That's the world that Jim Botkin and this book seek to bring to life. It is the new world of work, an exciting, exacting, creative place, populated by men and women with fresh ways of thinking and purposeful ways of working.

1

It is, importantly, a post-reengineering world. For most people and most companies, business process reengineering is a troublesome memory, a "Why did we do that to ourselves?" experience that today awakens feelings of organizational trauma and human distress. The recollection of downsizings, outsourcings, and other slash-and-burn tactics that celebrated business processes before business people, has left people wondering what that original belief actually was. Did we ever really believe, as serious business people, that we could cut our way to greatness? Did we truly think that lopping off organizational limbs was a way to run faster? Did we really expect that shedding people, and with them their expertise and capabilities, would build business operations capable of creativity, innovation, and growth?

These questions provide the backdrop to this book, and to Jim Botkin's work. Before I say a few words about the ideas in this book—important ideas in an economy of ideas—I think it first necessary to say a few words about Jim. It's another legacy of reengineering: When you're evaluating the quality of an individual's ideas, it's important to evaluate the character of the individual.

What I know about Jim Botkin is this: He is an individual of rare intellectual and personal integrity. He has been working hard in the vineyard of business and organizational thinking for decades, examining how systems work, how change can be made to happen, what makes for good and healthy organizations, and how people work together in communities of interest to get things done. He brings to his work and his writing a gift: He is both down-to-earth and open-to-wonder. I've found in my conversations with Jim that this is the perfect combination for a thinker-doer in an age when we are all looking for fresh, new ways of looking at business and work, and yet are mindful of the need for pragmatic results and serious competitive outcomes.

Jim is a believer in a workplace that exudes serious fun. And if that is an oxymoron, all the better, since it accurately reflects the mental composition of our present radical-conservative business world. What Jim's past experience and future orientation tell me is that this is exactly the kind of guide we need at this time, a playful mind and a trusted companion who can take us into a future where the old maps don't pertain and the only compass available is inside your head and heart.

If you choose to follow Jim Botkin into this exploration of a new business frontier, you will very quickly encounter some compelling questions that challenge most of your deepest-held assumptions about how business works. Take, for example, the question, Where do good ideas come from? This, it seems to me, is an elemental question, one that sits very close to the heart of the new economy. There is, of course, an old economy answer to this question. Good ideas—often more formally masquerading as "innovation" or "creativity" or "strategy"—come from the top. They come from the CEO, the boss, the corner office. After all, the big dog at the top is the one person in the organization, with all the answers, right? Or maybe, in some organizations, good ideas come from the duly constituted Department of Good Ideas. These are the professionals who have all the credentials necessary to think big thoughts, do strategy, manage the innovation process, and marshal the organization's resources to develop a breakthrough product or service. Coming up with good ideas—that's serious business, right? The kind of stuff best left to the pros.

Or so it went. But, as most of us know about life in the new economy—an economy that runs on ideas—the old sources are running dry. The big boss in the corner office is too far away from the fast changes in technology to know what's really going on. Customers are too fickle, competitors too slippery, markets too dynamic. And as for those pros in the Department of Good Ideas, they spend too much time talking to each other to have much of an idea of what's happening in the real world. They're playing by the old rules, and that's like dancing the minuet to rap music.

No, good ideas come from the heads of the people in the organization. Good ideas come from the trenches, where people are closest to the action. Good ideas come from your customers—if you're close enough to listen to them, and humble enough to pay attention. Good ideas come from your most recent hires—the Young Turks who are least likely to accept, as a valid response to their probing questions, the lamest of answers: "Because that's the way we've always done it." Good ideas are resident everywhere in the organization, at all levels, in all functions. They are in the dirty fingernails of the factory workers, the laptop notes of the sales force, the service notes of the telephone operators, the repair records of the tech reps in the field. In other words, as this book makes clear through anecdote and analysis, good ideas are the inchoate stuff that organizations carry around with them in the brains

3

of their people. Good ideas are knowledge waiting to be tapped, and it's the trademark of a smart organization—a fast company—that it knows how to honor and legitimize the tacit knowledge that its people have stored up in their work practices and make it visible.

They do this by answering a second question: How do you capture good ideas? Like the first question, Where do good ideas come from, this one is important because of the stark comparison between thinking in the old and in the new economy. In the old economy, good ideas were treated as a scarce commodity. For all the resources devoted to strategy, innovation, and new product development, you could never be sure when a good idea would emerge—or an idea good enough to warrant mobilizing major corporate backing for it (much less risking your next promotion or your career). As a consequence, good ideas were accidentally generated—and just as accidentally lost.

In the new economy, there is less of a gap between coming up with an idea and trying it. It's a part of the idea economy. Thinking and doing are lightning-fast and linked. So capturing good ideas and executing them— quickly, decisively, and curiously—is a key capability. Just as we've learned that knowledge is seeded throughout the ranks of a company's people, the ability to tap that knowledge is vested in communities. It is, in part, an unanticipated feature of the Web: like-minded people use information technology to cross boundaries, share ideas, engage in dialogue, and generate good ideas. Or they use coffee bars to do it—either way, they are creating the kinds of new communities of interest that form and re-form constantly, talking their way into new ways of working, new ways of competing, new ways of creating value.

Knowledge and communities, good ideas and fast execution, smart conversations and short feedback loops—this is the stuff of a business revolution. It is the stuff of exciting times in which to live and work, a time of individual liberation, personal challenge, great opportunity, uncharted possibilities. It is the stuff of a dynamic new world of work life and personal life—and it is the stuff that Jim Botkin has clearly focused on and made sense of in this book. Read it, think about it, talk about it, share it. Take it seriously and have fun with it—and remember: You're in good hands with Jim.

The Wisdom of Nature

RENEWAL, REVOLUTION, AND OTHER BLESSINGS

When Nature wants renewal, she sends fire, lightning, and destruction. Her strikes aren't pickets with placards and her speeches aren't soothing to stockholders. She strikes with lightning, and she thunders with a power so palpable that every creature trembles and scurries for cover. Despite all our satellites, simulations, and sensing devices for predicting storms, we nevertheless are subject to their force as part of the cycle of renewal.

Many of our major companies today are scurrying for cover in the face of a storm of our own human making. An explosion in knowledge threatens to prove the rule that success is the worst enemy of renewal. How can we make old-style firms, designed for the industrial world, ready for a different world? How can we take old stalwarts like Honeywell, GM, Prudential, or Volvo, all founded nearly a hundred years ago, and transform them into "smart business"—companies that engage the knowledge revolution and grow from it? How can smaller businesses, even recent ones, transform themselves from "postindustrial" to knowledge-based?

Currently, more than half the employees of traditional firms have emotionally disconnected from their workplace. As GM's Wayne Townsend puts it, "they've quit but are still employed." What will it take for companies with a legacy of prior success but reluctant to change to arouse the passion of people rather than their cynicism?

The premise of this book is that they must build "knowledge communities," groups of people with a shared passion to create, use, and share new knowledge for tangible business purposes. When they do, they will experience a transformation that powers their knowledge business and inspires new models of networked management.

To think about change requires a change in the way we think. My change agent was tiny but profound: I was stung by a bee and experienced an anaphylactic shock. My eardrums swelled up, and I lost my balance. The attack wreaked havoc with my heart, stomach, and digestive system. My throat closed up, my lungs shut down, and I could barely breathe. I had only enough air left to tell the emergency room nurses what happened before I collapsed in a heap at their desk.

I saw four people hovering above me, a doctor, two nurses, and an orderly. I heard the words "We're losing him. Double dosage! Now!!" Semiconscious but super-focused, I was acutely aware of the doctors and nurses working together frantically but effortlessly to counter my allergic attack. One was operating the computer, two others were holding me down, another was injecting antidotes—all the while barking orders and telling stories to each other. With only the slightest of signals, they seemed to know what to do now, what to do next, and what to do "after-next."

They operated like a well-synchronized team one would associate with a winning basketball or soccer squad, but their behavior went beyond that of teams. By computer, they tapped into a wider community of doctors and specialists with knowledge specific to my case. They wanted to know who my regular doctor was and where they could see my medical records to ascertain if the danger of heart attack was severe or unlikely.

In a blinding flash before slipping into darkness, I realized that modern medicine is a model for how knowledge could operate in business. This was a knowledge community in action. From then on, my work on knowledge communities had new purpose and meaning.

After I was released from the hospital, I returned to studying knowledge communities with an immediacy and practicality I had not previously shown. Nearly ten years before, I co-founded InterClass—the International Corporate Learning Association—a consortium of Fortune 500 companies seeking to improve their organizational learning and enhance their knowledge as a business resource. At first we had been exploring learning but later had expanded to include the impact new knowledge was having on business. From our conversations over many meetings, a formulation emerged of what knowledge communities are. Executive Vice President of Prudential Michèle Darling, Chairman of InterClass Eric Vogt, and Global Vice President of RR Donnelley Tom Trezise helped me and our group to define their business rationales, the technologies that enable them, and the cultures that enhance or inhibit them.

The ideas, concepts, and emerging practices presented in this book are designed to build on the work of many InterClass managers from more than twenty firms who aspire to unlock the power and potential of knowledge communities to enable business to lead in a knowledge revolution. This is the work of people using knowledge to grow and to restore meaning to their lives.

Many people, especially executives in business, feel their lives are out of balance. Hopi Indians have a word for this: Koyaanisqatsi, a state of life that calls for another way of being.[1] Many businesses today are in a state of Koyaanisqatsi. Knowledge communities not only are productive and competitively essential; they also can give new meaning to their participants. This is why I consider the bee's gift a blessing. I see more clearly now the meaning and purpose of knowledge communities, and I'm proud their outlines were sketched and continue to be expanded by a knowledge community of contemporary business people.

THE FIRST KNOWLEDGE COMMUNITY

The first knowledge community emerged from the medical profession as far back as the time of Hippocrates, the greatest physician of antiquity. Others came from modern sciences, especially as they unfolded during the Enlightenment. There are, of course, many more: religious, agricultural, and so on. So shouldn't development of business knowledge communities simply be a case of transferring principles and ideas from medicine, science, and other fields to business?

A tempting process, but a trap. Business does not yet have the cultures, the traditions, and the shared values that allowed medicine and science to form communities based on knowledge. But they will need them. In the past, companies developed ways to manage the traditional factors of production like land, labor, and capital. To grow in the future, they must learn to leverage *knowledge* as a new factor of production.

There is a further problem. We know how fast knowledge is changing in medicine and science; it seems there are new discoveries announced every day. But at least those professions are set up to handle the explosion of knowledge. Business, on the other hand, is not a specialized and specially trained minority of the population. It comprises a vast majority of people in every country and society in the world who are less well prepared for the deluge of data and information that underlie the knowledge revolution.

A major storm is looming in the business world, a huge inundation which will follow the merciless methods of Nature. Lightning, thunder, and deluge will challenge all companies more than the flood challenged Noah's ark. The only companies that will survive the tidal wave of data and information are smart businesses. Their calling is to engage the knowledge revolution and to grow from it. They can do so best by focusing on knowledge communities. Launching, building, and managing these communities will be key variables that allow some older companies to thrive on knowledge while others drown in data.

Leading smart business will take a lot of what the ancients call "rage of the heart" or courage. Some two hundred years ago, the Western world experienced a period, led by the French, when heart-rage or courage[2] took center stage. That was the period known as the Enlightenment. But the systems of knowledge developed then—Cartesian logic, Newtonian mechanics, and Rousseau's social contract—describe a world that no longer exists.

Social contracts between employers and employees have been superseded by entrepreneurship and self-employment. Newton's cause and effect physics is bowing to quantum sciences, where great leaps and dramatic changes replace incremental processes. And Cartesian logic is giving way to wider and more diverse ways of thought, emotions, and feeling. "I think, therefore I am" is becoming "I link, therefore I am" in a world where everything is being connected to everything else by the Internet, by new business partnerships and alliances, and by the ultimate "connection machine"—the knowledge community.

THE BLESSING OF THE BEES

In an effort to make bees allies rather than adversaries, I read everything I could about them. The honeybee and bumblebee have become my guides through the new world. I honor the bees for their pollinating ability, for their cooperative and productive behavior, for creating new honey out of a vast myriad of resources, for nurturing more than one-third of the world's total food supply, for developing their unique language of dance that provides information to hive-mates on where the best flowers are in relation to the sun. Sharing information and knowledge is smart business, and bees know it better than business does.

Knowledge is information put to productive use. Bees take information provided by dances and put it to productive use by flying directly and unerringly to the advertised flower patch. They balance the supply and demand of honey for their hive without any higher authority, other than Nature herself. And the elegant processes they have developed for energy efficiency, population control, and environmental protection have succeeded for millions of years, thriving longer than humanity has existed. Next time you hear a swarm of bees flying by to establish a new beehive and colony, remember they will be around a lot longer than most Fortune 500 companies like Microsoft and others creating such a buzz in the news.

I also asked a talented artist, Gary Lund, from my former home, Santa Fe, New Mexico, to do drawings of bees that illustrate the main topic of each chapter. For example, to start the chapter "Leadership Is Creating a Future for Your Community," Gary has sketched a picture of the one time bees exhibit leadership; namely, when an old queen leaves a crowded hive to start a new colony. My favorite is the one that starts chapter 6, "Learning to Lead the Knowledge Revolution." It shows the inside of a beehive where the bees are whimsically wearing night goggles since "you can't see inside of a beehive because it is dark." The quote comes from bee stories in "Mrs. Clark's Fourth Grade Classroom," a site on the Internet.

THE FIRST KNOWLEDGE BUSINESS

The first companies that explicitly organized themselves to value and market knowledge were the consulting firms. For companies like McKinsey, Booz • Allen, or KPMG and its sister professional services firms, knowledge is all they have, and all they've ever had. This is why it's not news when a particular consulting company appoints a Chief Knowledge Officer. The news is that it took them so long to do it.

The second knowledge businesses stemmed from the computer industry. For both hardware and software companies, knowledge is not a new resource. Among them are many young startup companies, including hundreds of service firms generated by and born on the Internet. It seems to me relatively easy to capture a reader's interest in these new startups. Like everyone else, I enjoy reading about them: how Compac's business plan was written on the back of a napkin, how Netscape went from zero to 60 million customers virtually overnight, and how Microsoft has a market valuation greater than GM, Ford, and Chrysler combined.

What I find disturbing is the fact that despite—or more likely because of—all their new business successes, these information age companies seem to be maturing with all the same ugly warts and whiskers of the industrial heroes of yesteryear. Microsoft may be a better stock buy than GM, but I find Bill Gates and his hierarchical organization less inspiring and less instructive than GM's Saturn Corporation and its men and women who work against all odds to keep Saturn's unique culture and mission alive in good times and bad.

In this book I focus on the GMs and Saturns of the world and how the knowledge revolution is pressuring them to transform. Saturn is an especially instructive case because it straddles two worlds—one of its new knowledge-based founding and another of its industrial parent in Detroit. It is at once both revolutionary and traditional.

I focus on traditional firms because they are, after all, the majority of companies in existence today. They are by and large the firms I work with in InterClass. Since its founding, more than two dozen companies have been members of InterClass. With the exception of Saturn, IRL, and CSC, all were started more than fifty years ago, and some one hundred or more years ago—BC, or "before computers."

They include companies like AT&T, Chevrolet, Honeywell, KPMG Peat Marwick, Prudential Insurance, Volvo, Xerox, and the World Bank, as well as IRL—the Institute for Research on Learning, a small and special InterClass member. I'll also refer to some earlier members: American Express, Chevron Oil, Du Pont, and Marriott International, as well as others with which I've worked: 3M, Motorola, Boeing, and Statoil, Norway's big oil company.

Other members I'll use as examples throughout the book include CSC (Computer Sciences Corporation, premier technology consultants), Canadian Imperial Bank of Commerce (one of Canada's big six banks), Skandia (the innovative Swedish insurance firm), RR Donnelley (world's largest commercial printer), Los Alamos National Laboratory (site of the World War II Manhattan Project), PIPSA (Mexico's largest paper and pulp company), and Sweden Post (the country's letter delivery service and, like many European postal offices, one of its largest and oldest banks as well).

Companies like these and their counterparts in other industries are the strongholds of employment and basic life services. They are the places where the vast majority of people work throughout their lives. What happens, or fails to happen, in such traditional legacy companies will tell us more about our future, our society, our quality of life—or lack thereof—than all the promises, prospects, and primers on the Internet.

NEW LIFE FROM NEAR DEATH

Many if not all of the companies mentioned share another common trait, which I knew about even before receiving the blessing of the bee sting. They've had a near-death experience. AT&T was broken up twice, once by court order and once voluntarily; General Motors flirted with bankruptcy in the years when its competitor, Chrysler, had to borrow government money to avert it; and Honeywell shrank to one-third its size after it divested its computer and military arms some years ago.

After the Cold War, Los Alamos completely changed its mission from nuclear weapons design to reducing the global nuclear danger; KPMG completed its fifth consecutive restructuring in about the same number of years; Marriott split in half and sold its catering business; and Sweden Post, the country's national post office, which reported to the King of Sweden for 350 years, is being deregulated. It has lost its monopoly and now faces competition. The list and stories could go on.

The point is that the companies mentioned in this book are those which, like me, had a near-death experience and survived. In their quest to incorporate knowledge as a business resource lies their greatest hope for new life. The real news will be when those mainstream companies become workplaces that leverage the economic value of knowledge and engage the passions of their people.

Legacy companies face a special challenge. Prior success is the worst enemy for current renewal of a mature company. There are many examples of well-known firms that went to the brink of bankruptcy shortly after their peak. Remington Rand in typewriters, RCA in televisions, American Motors in cars, even IBM had a brush with death when the PC first appeared, and DEC (Digital Equipment) didn't make it. At the time of this writing, Motorola and Boeing, long believed unassailable, are the latest sweethearts turned sour.

Why should we care? Beyond the obvious fact that people, probably friends and family, would suffer pain and loss, why should any of us care if all these companies became extinct? Isn't death a natural process of Nature? The environment changes, the old dinosaurs die, and new species—maybe birds—appear.

For me, the difference is that I accept the inevitable when it's from Nature's natural causes. When Nature decides to render a species extinct, I regret but accept. But when the cause is man-made, perhaps a human frailty or even stupidity, that's something else. When we lose some of Nature's biodiversity to uncontrolled growth of the human habitat, I'm outraged. When rhinos and elephants no longer have a place in East and southern Africa—or the wolves, bison, and bears in North America—then we are all the more impoverished because we, the human species, are not only the problem but also the potential solution. If all the companies on the endangered species list were to disappear—and it would be a big chunk of our economy as we know it—we would have the economic equivalent of biological disaster.

DEATH OF A SALESMAN,
BIRTH OF A KNOWLEDGE COMMUNITY

In the classic story *Death of a Salesman,* Arthur Miller portrays the hapless Willy Loman caught up in business dynamics at the end of the Industrial Economy in the late 1940s. What choices would Willy face today in an economy based on knowledge?

> Willy, Ora, and Maura all work in mid-management jobs for competing insurance companies. They are responsible for sales to large corporate accounts in the telecommunications area. Willy is a conscientious sort; this morning like every other when he arrives at work, he picks up the *Wall Street Journal,* removes it from its plastic protective bag, and promptly begins scanning for the news of the day. His trained eye looks for any articles on insurance and telecommunications companies. Having thoroughly scanned the paper by 10:00 A.M., Willy felt ready to start another day of client sales calls.
>
> Ora, who works not a mile away at a company Willy considers his arch-competitor, also reported to work that same day. She missed the familiar *Wall Street Journal,* the feel of the paper, the smell of coffee at her side. Instead, she logged on to her customized "newspaper," which scanned the Dow Jones news-feed, Reuters News Service, the AP wire, and the *Financial Times.* It also picked up hour-by-hour feeds from NewsAlert Inc., which has its own insurance industry sources plus those from A. M. Best, considered the best in the insurance business. Other services were also scanned—Information Inc. and Phillips, content providers for the insurance industry, and TRI, a content aggregator for the telecommunications industry. Ora's system also checked her firm's internal library for any new reports or other morsels of information someone else in the firm might have entered since she last logged on. By

10:00 A.M., she was ready to hit the road to visit her major accounts. To her surprise, her path crossed that of Willy, an old friend and competitor.

"Willy," she called out. "What's up? What do you make of the hurricane damage reports coming out of Florida?"

"Oh those," he said uncomfortably. He'd read about Andrew, one of the most murderous storms of the century, but hadn't seen any damage reports yet. He knew about Ora's personalized paper. He secretly envied her, because he knew that the number of papers and reports she'd scanned in an hour would have filled his entire office from floor to ceiling with useless data; she'd gotten more information in a morning than he could get in a decade. Exercising his old "competitive advantage" as a good ol' boy, he invited Ora to have a cup of coffee. She, feeling good (was she even sensing smugness?), accepted.

When they entered the coffee shop, Ora froze. Her smugness and sense of well-being vanished. Her arch-rival Maura was there, working on her laptop. Damn! She'd already finished her coffee and was standing up to leave. When Maura saw them she looked up, smiled, and came over to where they were sitting.

"Hi, how are things? Would love to get together and catch up," she said buoyantly. Ora, visibly tensed, said, "Well, I'm so busy I don't know when that would be." Ora knew her rival had not only the latest upgrade of knowledge management software, which creates the individualized newspaper, but all her co-workers and customers were organized into an online knowledge community. Her current clients and agents had conducted an hour's dialogue on the problems and prospects the storm had caused. They had already jointly analyzed the vital statistics generated by top experts in the weather, telecom, and insurance industries; traded views on what steps the telecom industry would be likely to take; and proposed what role insurance companies could play under different future scenarios. Armed with those insights, Maura's firm had created mass-customized sales proposals individually tailored to meet the concerns of each division for all the telecom offices in the city. Willy watched Maura depart with a blank stare; Ora had ice in her veins.

"Hmm," said Willy, who'd never heard of a "knowledge community" before but whose trusting nature prompted him to say, "She seems nice, maybe it would be good to see what she's doing to make all those sales."

"Whatever," sighed Ora as she sat down to her coffee.

Like Willy Loman in Miller's original, our Willy doesn't even know he's been beaten. Ora does know it. Knowledge sharing isn't in her company's culture, which leaves each individual agent to fend for him- or herself. Like Florida during the hurricane, she's buffeted by the knowledge revolution. Her choice is either to read the damage reports or to join forces with a firm like Maura's, more attuned to the new rules of knowledge economies.

Many people in business face choices like these: Whether to stick it out in a firm that's behind the times, move on to a new situation, or commit to a transformation effort can be a difficult choice. Yet new life from near death can be, as we've seen, a blessing.

Why are communities the key to unlocking knowledge? There are too many variables for any one person, no matter how gifted, to comprehend. In the storm story above, no one agent can know how the present storm impacts cellular versus satellite versus landline communication equipment, much less the secondary effects on budgets, spending, and pricing for multiple divisions of many telecommunications firms—where there used to be only one company, then seven, now hundreds, not only of phone companies but of cable television firms, satellite TV connections, Internet service providers, and Iridium satellite users. Let one satellite be blown out of orbit and half a million pagers go down with legal liabilities and consequences the lawyers can't even decipher. And it's all changing, day by day, sometimes hour by hour.

Being in a community where all those different perspectives are given voice doesn't necessarily "solve" the problem, but who would you rather be— Willy who's isolated, Ora who's connected only to her PC, or Maura who's connected to a whole community of experts and colleagues?

THE POWER OF SIX

Boeing, when it builds its 747s, uses a construct called "honeycomb construction" inside its wings because an elongated hexagonal structure is super-strong. I've used the honeycomb as a guide to organizing this book, because it highlights the interconnectedness of the six main parts of the book: business, organization, management, culture, learning, and leadership. Each gives a different perspective on the complex, multifaceted, and changing role of knowledge in business.

I've constructed the book so that you can read the six parts in any order. Jump right away to the ones of most interest to you. Be aware, however, that—like constructing airplane wings or honeycombs—building knowledge businesses, knowledge communities, or knowledge management systems requires attention to all six sides, or else they are compromised and may fail to work as intended.

Both the bee sting and the decision to write a book came at a time when knowledge as a resource in business was barely recognized. When I started to write this book, I did a search on the Internet for "knowledge and business." It yielded nothing. A short eighteen months later, the same search produced thousands of matches! Only FAST with capital letters can describe how changes are outracing our capacity to cope with them.

I'm all too aware that the cycle of new ideas turns faster than books are published these days. For that reason, I concentrate wherever possible on what in systems thinking are considered basic dynamics and relationships as opposed to citing a list of current events. I also have a web-site[3] to invite your participation with your own ideas as well as to update my thinking as it changes. I see this book as an interactive process. I've found a ground rule we use at InterClass to be helpful here: "Hard on ideas, soft on people." Share with us and with others your perspectives on the ever changing suite of knowledge and its role in business life. Do it not only with passion but also with compassion.

I cannot take credit for many of the ideas unfolding in the coming pages. Literally hundreds of people have been involved in their creation, articulation, and implementation. For ten years I have organized and led nearly fifty Inter-Class meetings for two thousand business executives from some thirty leading companies in every imaginable industry. Our inquiries delved into a dozen subjects: leadership and executive development; innovation and change management; futures and future business paradigms; knowledge management;

coaching; intellectual capital; virtual organizations; workforce development and diversity; globalization; partnering and alliances; learning organizations; and systems thinking. At the Salzburg Seminar and Club of Rome, I've also been able to absorb some of the best ideas and to learn from failures (including my own). As Woodrow Wilson once said: "I use not only the brains I have but all I can borrow." My hope is that the ideas, concepts, and emerging practices presented here will generate a deeper dialogue around basic questions that good executives ask about the new role of knowledge in business.

Chapter One

Why Knowledge Shared Is Power

*"Minds,
like parachutes,
work better when they're open."*

—Anonymous

The Nobel Prize was awarded to Karl von Frisch for deciphering the
dance bees use to communicate and share knowledge.

Thomas D. Seeley, *Wisdom of the Hive,* Harvard University Press, 1995

THE CHALLENGE IS TO SHARE KNOWLEDGE

Knowledge is power. But managers in most traditional companies still believe
the unspoken and tacitly held corollary: "Knowledge *withheld* is power."

After all our experience with teams and the need for cooperation, why do we still cling to this outmoded belief?

As children most of us are taught to share toys. But when we enter school something changes. The spirit of competition is instilled and linked to our individual performance. To get an A, we're taught, sharing answers is wrong; peeking at someone else's exam is cheating; borrowing another's idea is discouraged.

Values we learn at school become deeply rooted. Few of us are willing to share our ignorance. And when we do know something useful, we may be reluctant to share important insights.

That instinct is reinforced by a political past where accumulation and control of economic resources like capital, land, and labor did indeed result in power. But knowledge is different from those traditional factors of production. It has a unique characteristic in that the more it's shared, the more it grows, or as RR Donnelley's Senior Vice President John Greco puts it, "Shared knowledge is an engine of growth."

Therefore, companies or organizations where knowledge is shared freely have a great advantage over those that hoard or hide knowledge. They become flexible communities of men and women united to cope with change rather than organizations of experts divided by their egos and vainly seeking to master or control change. For example:

- PIPSA, the former paper and pulp monopoly of Mexico, uses "tri-generational learning cells" as knowledge communities that create new production techniques shared via satellite with all workers across its diverse paper mill sites. This obsoletes the notion that a developing country bases its competition solely on inexpensive labor.
- The World Bank is becoming a knowledge bank so that a health worker in Zambia can log onto the Bank through the Internet for immediate help to stop an outbreak of malaria. Yet there are people threatened by this capability, called by the Bank "internal knowledge brokers"—including both medicine men in African tribes and medical experts at the Bank.

- AT&T has developed six marketing and sales knowledge communities around services they offer: data, corporate networks, wireless, call centers, international and local services.[1] The company's ability to connect more than three thousand managers via IKE©, the Information and Knowledge Exchange system, which community members access an average of an hour a day, is credited with enabling a doubling of their annual revenue growth among their top 2,600 corporate clients worldwide.

The challenge for all is to stand firm against those who believe that knowledge withheld is power. Those companies that can maximize their knowledge resource will profit from a new economy driven by the force of a knowledge revolution; those that can't will be mired in data, the "sludge of the information age" as a former Bell Labs director put it.

Let's look further at the obstacles to sharing knowledge.

WHAT INNOVATION TELLS US ABOUT KNOWLEDGE

Everett Rogers, formerly of Stanford and now the University of New Mexico, says in his classic book *Diffusions* that innovation is a product, service, or process that is perceived as new. To be successful, it has to have a value greater than the present product, service, or process. 3M, the world's most successful example of large-scale industrial innovation, defines innovation as the practical application and use of creativity. Innovation can also be seen as the process of creating new knowledge with the application of imagination.

Rogers is best known for his classic "S" curve, which covers the four stages of birth, growth, maturity, and renewal. He plots the number of innovation adopters over time, and gets the curve shown in our first graph.

To be successful, innovations have to be adopted by five types of people: the innovators and early adopters, who are the quickest in a population to use the innovation; the early majority and late majority, who are slower to take it on; then the laggards, who finally adopt when the once-new innovation is already old hat.

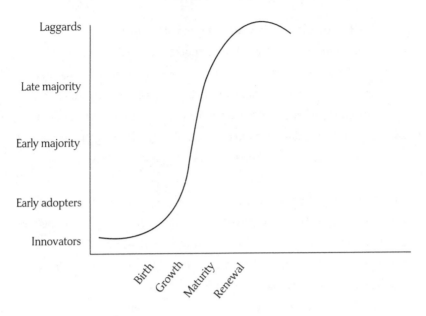

Innovation Life Cycle Curve

Adapted from Everett Rogers, Diffusion of Innovations.[2]

The Non-Diffusion Challenge

Knowledge follows the same dynamics as the innovation life cycle curve. To be successful, the value of shared knowledge has to be accepted by all five different types of people. Rogers calls this the problem of "non-diffusion." That is, large companies with tens or hundreds of thousands of employees face a major challenge of diffusing a new idea throughout their huge systems. Rogers uses the case of the demonstrably superior typewriting keyboard developed by August Dvorak to show how hard diffusion, even of great ideas, can be.[3]

When new ideas compete with old products, things get more complicated, as in our second graph. By showing two S curves, Rogers introduces the notion of discontinuous innovation or "discontinuities."

The discontinuities occur between the two curves. The first represents the path of a particular technology or innovation in current use. The second represents the path of a competing innovation. The problem is that very few

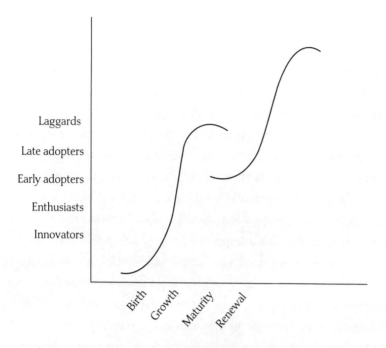

Laggards
Late adopters
Early adopters
Enthusiasts
Innovators

Birth Growth Maturity Renewal

companies are able to prepare for, recognize, believe, or transition from the original curve to the next.

The Invasion of the Radicals

A company may be chugging along the first curve, approaching its peak, when a competitor comes along in the second to displace it in "the invasion of the radical innovations," as the MIT innovation expert Jim Utterback calls this process. He compares it to the childhood game of "Chutes and Ladders," where one player is neatly climbing up the ladder when suddenly the other sends the first careening down a chute.

What is astounding, Utterback writes, "is the disturbing regularity with which industrial leaders follow their core technologies into obsolescence and obscurity. Firms that ride an innovation to the heights of industrial leadership more often than not fail to shift to new innovations."[4] Some examples:

- In the 1800s the Tudor Ice Company of Boston had a lucrative monopoly on *natural ice,* which it harvested from Walden and other New England ponds. In the 1850s its CEO and founder said, "We've been growing over half a century and we're just in our infancy." Though a patent for *machine-made ice* was issued in 1834—a full twenty-five years before that speech and fifty years before the peak of natural ice sales—Tudor failed to see any use for refrigerators outside the South. Tudor went bankrupt in the late 1880s. A decade before, there were 222 mechanical ice-making competitors chipping away at its natural ice-harvesting business. A decade after, there were nearly five thousand. Indeed, only years before the end, more than fifty new incremental improvements in harvesting ice with horses were made in a desperate attempt to fight rather than switch. Tudor's case remains a classic of a company blinded by success and unable to change. Similarly, in the mid-twentieth century the Swedish firm Tetrapak introduced a technology of aseptic packaging and "flash sterilization" techniques for milk. Its more efficient method of processing and packaging is successful with the food industry and consumers where refrigerator usage is limited. Even fifty years after the introduction of the product in Europe and elsewhere, American consumers with ample refrigeration remain largely unaware of or uninterested in its advantages.[5]

- Francis Cabot Lowell built the first textile mill in America in 1821 along the banks of the Merrimack River in a town that bears his name. His was the first of a string of textile, furniture, and shoe companies built in a chain of onetime water-powered industrial centers like Lowell, Haverhill, and Maynard, Massachusetts, stretching north to New Hampshire in towns like Nashua and Manchester, once the site of the world's largest textile mills. Operating profitably in New England in the nineteenth century, they all failed to adapt to the new weaving machinery and cheaper labor first appearing in the South of the United States and later in Asia. They stood by helplessly as their business migrated elsewhere, leaving behind empty brick factories alongside river-powered water wheels as lone sentinels testifying to the vanity of men, who for their time were the best and the brightest.

- Ken Olsen, founder of Digital Equipment Corporation, took over one of the Maynard mills as DEC's world headquarters just at the dawn of the information age. DEC was at first the industry leader in minicomputers, smaller and more flexible than IBM's mainframes. But when PCs came along to create a wholly different market structure, Olsen failed to recognize their value. Too late, he hastily built three different PCs, no one of which was compatible with the others or with the company's minicomputers. As if to underscore that failure, not only is the company's original headquarters a symbol of a defunct textile company, it is situated on the Assabet tributary of the Concord and Merrimack Rivers, where a pond is located from which ice was harvested even earlier by the ill-fated Tudor Ice Company! Toward the end of the information economy and the beginning of the knowledge age, Digital was acquired by Compaq, headquartered in Texas, once again testifying to the futility of men and women who still are some of the best and the brightest.

• Compaq in turn bought Digital in the same year that the first DNA computer—constructed not from silicon and electronics but from human DNA and genetics—solved the "Hamilton Path Problem," which can optimize airline routes and communications networks. Using Watson–Crick pairing techniques with a polymerase chain reaction, Leonard Adelman[6] created a DNA computer with a single gram of DNA genetic material that could hold the equivalent of one trillion CD-ROMs. One-fiftieth of a teaspoon of DNA analyzed 10^{14} possible flight paths in one second. This is approximately one hundred times faster than the fastest supercomputer known to humanity. If the menu for one-fiftieth of a teaspoon is so powerful, what will a tablespoon of the stuff do? Moore's Law states that the price/performance ratio of electronic computers doubles every eighteen months. But biologists see a more powerful DNA law that has dropped the price of sequencing a single gene by a factor of 2,500 to a dollar a gene by the turn of the millennium. If biologists in the knowledge revolution follow Moore's Law, which they consider "tame," then DNA computers will obsolete silicon-based computing even quicker than refrigerators demolished the ice industry.

Koyaanisqatsi. Life out of balance. A DNA computer is made from the stuff of life itself. The knowledge revolution has allowed us to harness our own cells and the DNA double helix for computation. Unless we keep up, we run the risk of repeating all the mistakes of the ice-king, the textile-barons, and the gremlins of silicon computer power.

Utterback and others give fascinating accounts of why companies at the top of the curve fail to innovate, but it all boils down to one thing: Leaders invested in current technology or ideas don't want to risk their own investment. Electrical engineers who spent university and graduate years to build their competence are overawed at the prospect of spending even more time to learn genetic instead of electrical engineering.

The Challenge of Crossing the Chasm

Building on Ev Roger's work, Geoffrey Moore[7] redrew the S as a bell curve to illustrate the market dynamics in the highly turbulent world of high technology. He renamed the customer types, calling them enthusiasts, visionaries, pragmatists, conservatives, and skeptics. Moore's "technology life cycle adoption curve" from *Inside the Tornado* is shown in our third graph.

Moore's curve highlights the special problem faced by high-technology companies, namely, "the chasm." The chasm consists of the great divide be-

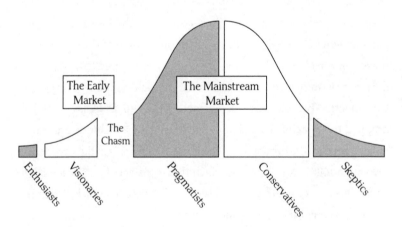

Technology Life Cycle Adoption Curve

Adapted from Geoffrey Moore, Inside the Tornado[8]

tween enthusiasts and visionaries on the one hand, and pragmatists, conservatives, and skeptics on the other. Crossing the chasm can be formidable. As Moore says: "Visionaries think pragmatists are pedestrian, pragmatists think visionaries are just plain dangerous." Sound familiar? It's sad but all too true in many companies.

Here we see a variation of the previous non-diffusion syndrome, which Moore calls the challenge of "crossing the chasm." The notion of knowledge in business is at present in the domain of the enthusiasts and visionaries. To be successful, it will have to cross the chasm to the domain of pragmatists, conservatives, and skeptics.

The very concept of knowledge as a new business resource—let alone the wisdom of setting up and managing knowledge communities—is likely to encounter the same challenges Tetrapak milk packaging does in the face of GE and Kenmore refrigerators and DNA computing does in the face of Compaq and IBM silicon graphics.

But it doesn't have to be that way. How many ice companies have to fail before we learn their lessons? How many textile mills do we have to build, only to watch them become lonely sentinels on the pathway to economic ruin? How many top silicon-based computer companies will we have to dismantle?

We can do better than that. If smart people and businesses can invent food packaging that needs no refrigeration and DNA computers that need no electrical wires, then surely we can practice the smart business of engaging the knowledge revolution and growing from it, rather than let large portions of our workforce become cynics and disbelievers.

WHAT "KNOWLEDGE" ARE WE TALKING ABOUT?

Our first challenge to understanding knowledge is definition. What kind of knowledge are we talking about? Visionaries want a noble and motivating definition, and pragmatists want to know exactly which are the specific bits of knowledge you want to capture, which ones can be ignored, and how to tell the difference between the two.

To get both groups started, I use a "waves to wisdom" model, pictured here.[9] It starts on the left with two stovepipes like the smokestacks on the *Titanic,* slowly sinking beneath the sea of the industrial era. Stovepipes, "silos" as they're sometimes called, represent the status quo of many legacy companies, referring to the narrow focus and dysfunctional state of functionally organized companies. Then come *data,* which are recordings of transactions in a system, and *information,* which are data arranged into a meaningful message. Then comes *knowledge,* which is information put to productive use. At the far right, on the horizon between sea and sky, is *wisdom,* the discerning use of knowledge.

Learning is the process of moving from one wave to the next, while training is instruction and mastery at any given wave. Since both learning and training have dynamic definitions that change in different cultures and times, we can define *learning* in business today as the process of acquiring knowledge, while *training* is the process of making sense out of data and information.

Later in the book I devote a chapter to what kind of learning is needed in traditional businesses, because it is not obvious. It's contrary to conventional wisdom. Following that, I'll initiate a dialogue on wisdom and address why and in what way wisdom will emerge as a serious topic for all corporations despite, or maybe because of, their knee-jerk reaction to resist.

The word "knowledge" encompasses both the content and the process of creating the content. That is, it refers both to a "thing" (what is known) and to

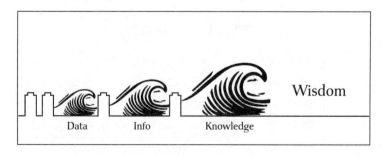

Waves to Wisdom

the process by which the thing was created (how it came to be known). This double meaning can lead to considerable confusion.[10]

When IBM's Larry Prusak says "Knowledge itself cannot be managed. You cannot manage what's in someone's head,"[11] he is referring to the process part. When McKinsey & Company says it has 12,000 documents in its knowledge management system with 2,000 requests per month,[12] it is referring to knowledge as a thing or an artifact. When managers say things like they need to "transfer" knowledge, it's useful to ask whether they're speaking of the content or the process. It's easy to transfer content. It's more difficult to transfer process.

Ikujiro Nonaka, Xerox Distinguished Professor in knowledge at UC Berkeley, introduces the Japanese concept of "Ba" (rhymes with "Aha!") as the space where knowledge is created, shared, and exploited. A company's Ba can be a physical lab, a mental model, or a virtual space—as in "cyber-Ba." A manager's new core task is to originate Ba through face-to-face socialization, to energize Ba through peer-to-peer interaction, to combine the Ba of individuals through group-to-group systematic collaboration, and to internalize Ba as a central ingredient of a company's culture. Nonaka uses this SECI model (Socialize, Energize, Combine, Internalize) with its concept of Ba to explain how all companies can develop their knowledge assets. These are concepts essential to the education of managers who aspire to succeed in a knowledge economy.

Nonaka's work provides a starting point to amplify the view of knowledge as information put to productive use. What about new knowledge, such as from the scientific Ba, that has no foreseeable commercial use?

Gary Glatzmaier at Los Alamos National Laboratory investigates how the earth's magnetic field is generated. The earth's inner core is a moon-size mass of solid iron that rotates faster inside than the earth itself does outside. Gary worked out the mathematical equations that simulate these dynamics. The simulation analyzes the last million years in packets of twenty days at a time. As Gary explains it, "we were running this simulation through the equations when suddenly the field spontaneously reversed itself. This was the first time any model had recreated what actually happens in nature."

This is clearly new knowledge that Gary has created.[13] He believes it has no practical or commercial use in the foreseeable future; his goal is purely to advance scientific understanding.[14] How do we include that knowledge in the definition of information put to productive use? The question is important for many organizations in the business of producing new knowledge, such as Bell Labs (formerly AT&T, now Lucent Technologies), Xerox PARC, and IBM's Watson Center, which are the business equivalents to Los Alamos and the other national research labs.

New knowledge is the high-value information on which a person bases his or her actions or strategic intentions. It is information put to productive use if that information contributes to our basic understanding of how the world works. Thus knowledge can be actionable information, even when its creators give little or no credence to its immediate practical use.

Skeptics will question whether the knowledge we're talking about isn't just old wine in new bottles—information masquerading under a new name. In many cases, it is. Knowledge is closely related to the information and data from which it is derived. Whether it is knowledge or information depends on how it is perceived by the individual. What serves as valuable knowledge for one person may be useless data for another.

In the next few pages, I shall summarize the challenges of what I call "the 3Ks of Knowledge," which are the three major ways knowledge pertains to business. They are knowledge communities, the knowledge business, and knowledge management.

WHAT ARE KNOWLEDGE COMMUNITIES?

Knowledge communities in business are groups of people with a common passion to create, share, and use new knowledge for tangible business purposes. Successful knowledge communities bond with a sense of belonging that comes with shared values or a common commitment. Members tend to trust one another and to open themselves up to creative brainstorming without fear of being ridiculed for ideas without immediate implementation.

Knowledge communities are closely related to "communities of practice," a term coined by the Institute for Research on Learning (IRL). These are the informal and often invisible communities that every company has. For example, IRL[15] has studied communities of practice in the airline industry. Pilots, flight attendants, and service personnel learn to work smoothly together as a community, responding almost unconsciously to signals. When the pilot turns on the "no smoking" sign, for instance, flight attendants know to prepare passengers for takeoff. Change a single signal in the community's established practices and you run the risk of upsetting the flow of work, which is why the no smoking light still is illuminated even in flights that prohibit smoking altogether.

Communities of practice are similar to knowledge communities in that they both describe how work gets done and how participation gives identity and meaning to their members' work. The difference is that communities of practice are informal groups, shaped by circumstances, visible mainly to social anthropologists. Knowledge communities are purposely formed—some, like those at AT&T, even have formal membership lists—and their purpose is to shape future circumstances. They are highly visible to every business person in the organization.

To clarify and better understand the dynamics of community, I created the "Waves to Community" model, which parallels the "Waves to Wisdom" one and is shown on the next page. Similar to the wisdom model, it starts on the left with two stovepipes that look like the smokestacks on the sinking *Titanic,* representing the present state or status quo of many legacy companies. *Sharing* is a description of behavior, and *cooperation* is a pattern of systematic sharing. *Community* is the organized use of cooperation, where the potential for conflict is high but actual conflict is low. At the far right, on the horizon between sea and sky, is the *common good,* which is community guided by wisdom.

Motorola uses a five-stage model, from which I've borrowed the idea of stovepipes or silos. They use the term "collaboration" instead of "cooperation"[16] and a step I've omitted for the sake of clarity, "reuse of knowledge."

For most companies, the initial wave of sharing represents a major challenge. Others, notably those with extensive alliances and strategic partnerships, need to tune into the new practices of cooperation. Bees learn this by going to their hive's dance floor; managers can learn the changing nature

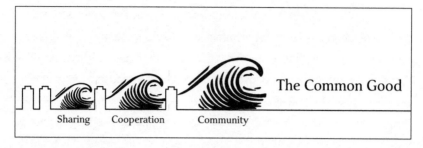

The Common Good

Sharing   Cooperation   Community

Waves to Community

of competition and cooperation by going to their customer's marketplace. The real challenge we've barely begun to consider is how businesses can surf the wave to community and whether that will result in the common good.

Knowledge communities can be understood as the next step beyond teams and task forces. A task force is a temporary group directed to accomplish a specific objective.

A team is a group organized to work together, presumably on the same side, though in some companies team members spend more time disagreeing with one another than they do working on the same side. Knowledge communities are larger than task forces and live longer than teams. They are like departments but are cross-functional. A check of *Webster's Dictionary* as usual helps. Community, in its general usage, is a group of people living in the same locality under the same government.

That broad definition does little to clarify what we mean by "knowledge community," though to the extent that locality refers to cyberspace, we are getting closer. Some business people, when they hear "knowledge community," think we are talking about "community relations." This is a worthy subject but not central to knowledge communities.

The second definition of community refers to "a group of people sharing common interests, as in the scientific community or the business community." Webster's further describes such communities as providing "identity as well as sharing, participation, and fellowship." This clarification has everything to do with the knowledge communities we are speaking of here. Identity, sharing, participation, and fellowship are all inherent to knowledge communities that excel.

Knowledge communities are more than just a next step beyond teams. Business-based knowledge communities represent basic building blocks for organizations focused more on networks than on traditional hierarchies. They are groups of managers and workers—"knowledge workers"—whose mission is to create, use, and apply the new knowledge in their industry for tangible business purposes.

AT&T has created six knowledge communities in its Global Services division. They took over two years to build and are formed primarily of marketing and sales personnel. One of them, the Data Community, has 550 members located virtually anywhere, and specializes in Data Networking. That means its members have competencies in high-speed packet-switching lines for huge data dumps—as banks do to take inventory at the end of each day. The purpose of the group is to accelerate the revenue growth beyond corporate targets for sales growth for the top 2,600 global corporate accounts. Every morning, all 550 members from Asian, American, and European offices log onto their community's home page on IKE©, AT&T's proprietary Information and Knowledge Exchange, to get the technical and client information they need to do their work that day. They log on again at the end of the day to submit what they've learned about their accounts. All told, they spend an hour a day on IKE, another hour a week on a conference call with Subject Matter Experts ("SMEs"), as well as four days a year devoted to face-to-face meetings of community members. Pat Traynor, Marketing Vice President for Global Services and architect of AT&T's knowledge communities,

---

The Nobel Prize was awarded to Karl von Frisch for deciphering the dance bees use to communicate and share knowledge. Years later, Tom Seeley describes the social behavior of honey bee colonies in his book *Wisdom of the Hive*, where he shows how nature allows bees to go from independent organisms to integrated societies. Cooperation applies to bees, he writes, "where the potential for conflict is high" (all worker bees have stingers) "but the actual conflict is low" (only virgin queens will kill their rivals).

—From Thomas D. Seeley
Wisdom of the Hive: Social Physiology of Honey Bee Colonies,
Harvard University Press, 1995

---

cites double-digit sales growth as the chief result of knowledge communities in data, corporate networking, wireless, call centers, international services, and client business managers.

The focus on "tangible business purposes" is all-important. For AT&T the purpose, in the words of Brad Hall, Division Manager of Knowledge Communities, is "sales, sales, sales." The tax services part of KPMG sees its knowledge programs as offering superior professional services to clients. Doug Izard, Director of Tax Knowledge Management, says his community's professional competency is superior to the IRS, where he used to work before coming to KPMG. Skandia AFS credits its intellectual capital communities with adding more than a billion dollars worth of new insurance business. Leif Edvinsson who instituted communities based on the concept of intellectual capital, also created the office of Comptroller of Intellectual Capital, held by Elisabet Mikkelsen, whose studies show return-on-investment (ROI) over 100 percent.

Such examples show the promise of the knowledge community concept applied to different industries. Whether those particular cases are enduring, or whether their exemplary results prove sustainable, is not the point. The main point of those and future knowledge communities is that they show solid business results as well as bring new purpose and meaning to their members' work lives.

Booz • Allen & Hamilton, in a *Strategy and Business* quarterly issue "Why Knowledge Programs Fail," cite reason number one for failure as "no specific business objective." A former Ernst & Young research director, Tom Davenport, in his *MIT Sloan Management Review* article "Successful Knowledge Management Projects," cites "link to economic performance" as the number one critical success factor.

Recalling the innovation bell curve at the beginning of this chapter, we are still at the early market stage of knowledge as a business resource. Not many companies beyond those cited above use the specific term "knowledge community" yet. It will become part of common business vocabulary only when the idea crosses the chasm and is accepted by the mainstream.

Knowledge communities encompass all the people-oriented, corporate culture factors that are essential to achieving business results. For knowledge initiatives to be successful, the corporate culture has to support them; otherwise, no amount of computer technology, powerful content, or astute management will yield positive results.

Successful knowledge communities are good at sharing knowledge. That is a far greater challenge than many people assume. There are lots of reasons why, despite good cause to cooperate, many executives and entrepreneurs do not. In some cases collaboration is illegal; it is, for instance, deeply embedded in antitrust law, or runs counter to lawyer–client privilege, as it does doctor–patient confidentiality. In other instances, it is foolhardy. Inventors and entrepreneurs who are first to the patent office win a window to develop a new idea into a successful innovation. That too is embedded in law and is a part of the business system, which, while surely modifiable, is unlikely to change any time soon. Later we'll address these and other issues around intellectual property rights, showing how they came from industrial thinking and need to be "tuned up" or more in tune with the "laws" of the knowledge economy.

As shown in the AT&T, KPMG, and Skandia examples, knowledge communities are usually internal to a company. But they can also be external and involve any number of partners, as is the case in most software developers with computer hardware suppliers—for example in the Microsoft-Intel strategic partnership. InterClass is a knowledge community embracing some twenty different kinds of companies from different industries.

"I'm willing to share my successes with corporate partners, but don't expect me to talk about any failures if a competitor is in the room," one GM executive says. An AT&T counterpart echoes: "I'll show 5 percent of my overheads if a competitor is there to see them; but I'm willing to share 100 percent if I'm guaranteed no competitors are present." An executive from Motorola University: "Here's the overhead we show the public," he says and pauses, checking the room. "And here's the actual situation we face."

Wherever a community crosses company lines externally, or even when it crosses functional lines internally, the value of sharing collides head-on with the competitive instinct to withhold. Such ambiguity about when to share knowledge or not is compounded by partnerships that seem collaborative and competitive at the same time. Cases in point are the General Motors partnership with Toyota in its NUMMI auto plant in Freemont, California, or Xerox's partnership with Fuji-Xerox in Tokyo. Both firms have trouble reconciling when to compete with when to cooperate. The subject of competition versus cooperation is ripe for further research and deeper inquiry.

Some knowledge communities are online. Esther Dyson in her book *Release 2.0: A Design for Living in the Digital Age*, says "community is the unit in which people live, work, and play." The benefit of the Internet, she says, is that it allows the formation of communities independent of geography. Yet she also adds there is no substitute for face-to-face contact: "You just can't share a sunset, a hot tub, or a hot meal over the Net."

While Internet technology has been a breakthrough in facilitating electronic dialogue and exchange of ideas, it usually has to be matched with person-to-person contact to sustain long-term deep-sharing knowledge communities. AT&T requires its knowledge community members to attend annual face-to-face meetings at headquarters as well as participate daily on an intranet home page and join in a weekly conference call. Tom Davenport, coauthor of *Working Knowledge* and Director of the Andersen Consulting Institute for Strategic Change, reinforces the need to meet in 3-D. "There are strong-tie and weak-tie networks," he says. " Electronic networks are weak tie." However, there are cases where electronic contact is the only possibility. For example, an acquaintance is disabled with health problems; Internet connection to a community of friends is her lease on life, and she tries to develop telephone "remote-receptionist" skills as a source of income.

Besides learning to share knowledge, the two most important challenges to make a knowledge community successful are the development of trust and mutual support for a particular type of learning I shall refer to as innovative learning—preparing people to act together in new, possibly unprecedented situations—which is the essence of a knowledge community's agenda. We'll explore issues of trust and learning in later chapters. First we need to clarify the context of business in our current economy compared with earlier ones and the emerging role that knowledge is playing as a new business resource.

WHAT'S THE KNOWLEDGE BUSINESS IN YOUR BUSINESS?

A knowledge business is one that embeds knowledge and learning into its products, processes, and services. Computer companies were and are in the knowledge business ever since AT&T licensed its transistor technology in the early 1950s (for only $20,000 per company—one of America's greatest gifts and worst pricing decisions of all time). IBM and other companies like UNI-VAC, GE, and RCA built computer hardware and software, created with the knowledge based on information sciences. Those companies were called "high-technology" or high-tech companies, a term becoming less in use as the knowledge economy develops. As computer chips become ubiquitous and widespread, what started as "high" tech is becoming "wide" tech. Soon they'll be called an important sector of "the knowledge business," which eventually will be referred to as just "business" when microprocessors become embedded in nearly every product and service in the world.

While IBM is the best-known knowledge business of the first half of the information age, Microsoft is at the top of the second half, highlighting the shift in importance from hardware to software. There are hundreds, thousands—if not millions—of companies built on information sciences. Hardware companies are examples of those that build knowledge into their products and software companies into their software, where the distinction between product and service has blurred. All are knowledge businesses because they embed new knowledge and learning into their products, processes, or services.

In the world of legacy companies—Chevron in the oil business, Du Pont in chemicals, AT&T in the telephone business, American Airlines in the travel business—it is not so obvious what the knowledge business is or even could be. We get a hint by examining the different types of new businesses companies have engaged in since 1945: the data business, information business, now knowledge business, and in the future, biotech business. In the fifty years since 1945, we have gone through a period of automation, with the application of computers to traditional businesses. Now we are entering a period not just of organizational transformation but industry transformation, which some refer to as "revolutionizing industries." The advent of DNA computing, for example, will revolutionize the silicon chip industry. This is the progression of the Wisdom Model in action: First data businesses provided the step for information businesses, which in turn set the stage for knowledge business. The cycle will then continue with the beginning of another economic revolution through the rise of the biotech business. As we'll see shortly, this entire hundred-year period can also be called "The Knowledge Age."

An example of a data business is one that provides family census history for genealogical research. This used to be done by sending cumbersome books or would entail traveling to the civic records of towns. Now that it's done by Internet, it has become one of the biggest data businesses ever.

Another example of data businesses is Dun & Bradstreet, which has an enormous data base on millions of companies in the United States. Other companies take its data and cull out specific industry segments. A Colorado firm, for example, provides detailed data on all high-tech companies.

Information businesses have had a special appeal for a number of legacy companies, ever since it was realized that they are often more valuable than the original core business on which they were based. For example, the OAG, the Official Airlines Guide, which experienced travelers carry, is a listing—a mere listing—of all the information about air flights for a month. When it was sold in the late 1980s, it was worth more at the time than triple the value of the Eastern Airlines Shuttle and only slightly less than the market valuation of US Air.[17]

In the TV industry, it was *TV Guide,* which when Rupert Murdoch bought it had a value greater than any of the major broadcasting companies, CBS, ABC, or NBC. It is surprising but true that in some cases information about the core business can be worth more than the core business itself.

These information businesses were built by applying principles of the value of information to older businesses. In the same way, it is possible to apply new principles of the value of knowledge to traditional business, which we call knowledge-based products and smart services, or more simply "the knowledge business." We'll examine the process more closely in the next chapter and propose some possible knowledge businesses for mature companies. While the progression of business logic goes from data to information to knowledge business, the accompanying organizational impact works quite differently. Information businesses that use computer technology to automate work *reinforce* the old industrial structures and cultures, whereas the new knowledge businesses *transform* the way companies work.

Gary Hamel, one of the world's foremost strategy consultants, points out that some companies transform the way they work ("organizational transformation"); others transform their entire industry ("industry transformation"). In our work with knowledge communities, we are especially interested in the former. In our work with the knowledge business, we are especially interested in the latter. One complements and reinforces the other.

Saturn, when it turned out its first cars in 1990, incorporated into the company "everything that was known about building small cars." It used the latest knowledge embedded in, for example, computerized painting for its bodies or lost-foam casting for its engines. It incorporated the innovation of no-haggle pricing into its services and the union–management partnership into its internal processes of decision-making. In short, it was a prototype of what can happen when new knowledge (about technology, customer focus, and human relations) is applied to an old industry (making, selling, and servicing cars).

Skandia AFS was an old-line insurance company based in Stockholm, Sweden. Founded in 1855, it sold conventional life insurance to conservative Swedish heads of families. It languished for years, growing about 10 percent a year, interrupted by World War II, then recovering to its former self. The firm continued until about 1970, when a new CEO, Jan Carendi, took over. He incorporated a radical new concept of "intellectual capital" into the company's strategy, headed by Leif Edvinsson in the early 1990s. New insurance products like unemployment policies that pay for retraining, new partnership arrangements with brokers, and direct relationships with customers transformed Skandia to one of the fastest growing most successful insurance companies in the business.[18] Intellectual capital analyst Scott Hawkins characterizes Skandia AFS as a knowledge company that just happens to be in financial services.

Other examples of knowledge products are the 800,000 soda machines that Coca-Cola has in Japan. Each one has a computer chip, which tracks full or empty, warm or cold, night or day, and a profile of its own sales record. Armed with this information and a software program, now the machine can engage in real-time pricing. If it's hot outside and supplies are running low at a peak buying time, the price inches upward. If it's a slack time, supplies are plentiful, and the ambient temperature is cool, the machine advertises a bargain price. This is a smart knowledge-based product that is a forerunner of how many product/services will be priced in the future—in real time, more like stocks and bonds, less like cars and cement.

Where's the knowledge business in your business? Are you looking for it? How would you know it if you saw it? Or would you, like the automotive companies, consider it simply a new enhancement of a core product—like the new radar-based cruise control that slows automatically when you approach a slower car? Would it be interesting to envision a car where every single part was "smart"? Smart mirrors that looked for the blind spot, smart brakes that told you when they were wearing out, smart alternators that sensed when they were going dead far enough in advance that they automatically ordered the replacement part that is sent to your "repair address of record" encoded in a profile you carry on your car's onboard computer.

WHAT DOES IT MEAN TO MANAGE KNOWLEDGE?

Many skeptics question whether it is possible to manage knowledge. But we have always managed knowledge. In business, it's called R&D; in medicine, it's called medical research; and in science, it's what the whole enterprise is about. "Knowledge management" is something we've always done in business unconsciously. The question is whether making it conscious, we can manage it better, differently, or any more wisely.

Consulting firms were early players in developing knowledge first for internal use and later as external offers to advise clients on knowledge management ("KM")—the process of capturing, sharing, and leveraging a company's collective expertise. Those elements are shown in the model here, illustrating the "flow of knowledge management." It can be seen as a flow because three different streams have to come together to form a fluid system.

That consultants have learned to manage and sell knowledge may be news in the academic world of management, but it's not surprising to the rest of the business community. To us, the news would be if the McKinsey's of the world did *not* do knowledge management. The really big news will be when AT&T, CIBC (Canadian Imperial Bank of Commerce), General Motors, RR Donnelley, Statoil, and the Swedish or U.S. Post Office do knowledge management and do it well.

Albert Siu, Dean of the AT&T School of Business and vice president of human resources: "We have some cultural elements that inhibit the sharing and leveraging of knowledge but others that promote it in our five principal sets of constituencies. These are shareholders, customers, our people, partners, and communities. Rather than measure knowledge, we are more keen to maximize its use for our shareholders and for our customers."

Wendy Coles, director of GM's knowledge network: "How do we use knowledge to halve the cycle time of a vehicle development program when half the engineers are in Tokyo and the other half are in Detroit? We want to learn from the Isuzu process compared to our standard vehicle development process."

Bruce McBratney, VP of management and organizational development for RR Donnelley: "We print nearly three-quarters of the documents in your home. We're just getting into KM. A lot of the more conservative folks are wary."

Gösta Hägglund, a deputy Senior Director at Sweden Post: "This idea of managing knowledge started first in the U.S. In Europe we are still hesitant

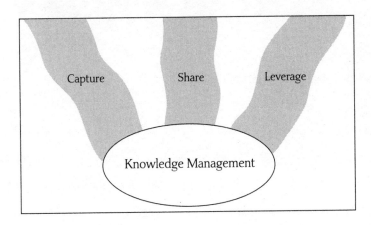

about the concept." The knowledge business, however, is something else. "The latest IDC analysis shows that almost 40 percent of Swedes use the Internet regularly. Of these, 13 percent shop frequently on the Internet, making Sweden the country with the largest number of online shoppers.

"Torget is Sweden Post's marketplace on the Internet. It has more than 250,000 visits a day and more than 100 shops where you can buy books, dish washers, jewelery, train tickets, underwear and cheap CDs."[19] This makes it possible for Sweden Post to provide solutions for parcel delivery, bank payments, and communications—in short, a new electronic knowledge business.

Ove Hjelmervik, Project Manager in the Exploration and Development arm of the Norwegian oil company Statoil: "We've named our knowledge management system 'Faros,' which is Norwegian for lighthouse. We think it will shed lots of light on our learning and knowledge assets." Norway is the number two oil exporter in the world.

We'll take up the subject of knowledge management in a later chapter. Now we turn to the knowledge business, which we examine next, and knowledge communities, which we examine after-next.

Chapter Two

The Knowledge Age—Opportunity for a New Enlightenment?

Everyone,
except the bumblebee itself,
knows that a bumblebee can't fly.
Its body is too big for such small wings,
making it aerodynamically impossible to fly.

—Entomology Notes no. 10, Michigan Entomological Society[1]

Every few
hundred years
in Western history,
there occurs a sharp transformation.

—Peter Drucker

THE OPPORTUNITY IS TO ENGAGE
THE KNOWLEDGE REVOLUTION

The science historian and writer Thomas Kuhn, in *The Structure of Scientific Revolutions,*[2] shows how paradigm shifts—changes in the way we see the world—are caused when anomalies appear that prevailing beliefs can no longer explain. Such shifts are almost always revolutionary. Indeed, both scientific and economic history can be understood as an ongoing series of radical innovations that form an endless double helix spiraling upward. Spectacular advances in knowledge linked to the unprecedented resources of business offer us that opportunity today.

You can learn a lot about the future through analogies with the past. The European century from the late 1600s to the end of the 1700s, popularly known as the Enlightenment, is the period most similar to our own in that "knowledge" is the key focus of both. Spearheaded by French thinkers like Rousseau and Voltaire, the Enlightenment also encompasses English greats like Adam Smith[3] and Americans like Benjamin Franklin. Their aggregate work—though some of it ended in the violence of the French Revolution—establishes the power of an age built on new knowledge. Today, an opportunity beckons for companies with research resources and financial power to lead a new revolution in the development of knowledge, this time peacefully transforming themselves and society in the process.

During the Enlightenment, scientists made many discoveries that required miniature paradigm shifts. Those were typically resisted by many. A good example is Priestley's and Lavoisier's discovery of oxygen.[4]

Fire is the process of combining materials like coal or sulfur with oxygen. Before oxygen was discovered two centuries ago, combustion was thought to be caused by "phlogiston," a hypothetical substance that could be burned up. According to phlogiston theory, everything that burned contained phlogiston. The faster it burned, the more phlogiston was consumed. That belief was so strong that when its skeptics showed that mercury becomes heavier when burned, phlogiston believers revised their theory to say that the phlogiston in mercury had negative weight.

When the English chemist Priestley first discovered the substance supporting combustion, he called it "de-phloginated air." The demise of the phlogiston theory was finally at hand when the French chemist Lavoisier isolated "air unto itself" in 1776. Nonetheless, it took nearly twenty-five years (until 1800) before it was widely accepted that oxygen, not phlogiston, was the food of fire. Mainstream scientists often initially fight rather than switch to new paradigms.

In this respect, most pragmatist managers are no different from mainstream scientists. The fact that knowledge behaves differently from other business resources is treated by many conservatives like mercury's phlogiston—they say it has negative weight. In a desperate effort to preserve their belief in hierarchy and divisions needed by capital and labor, we may well experience twenty-five more years until knowledge and networks become the basic building blocks of the corporate world, unless we become active participants in accelerating the process of transformation.

FIRE, PHLOGISTON, AND GENERAL MOTORS

The dynamics of the knowledge revolution are similar to those of the Enlightenment, just as the phlogiston theory actually made way for something much greater than a single theory: an entire new science. When the new idea of oxygen took hold, at a time of experimentation (the Enlightenment), it contributed to the new science of modern chemistry.

Today, in business, a new idea (knowledge sharing) is taking hold at a time of major change (the Knowledge Age) and leading to a whole new idea of enterprise: smart business. By the conclusion of the Knowledge Age, smart business will be known as "modern business" or simply "business"—the way all companies work, compete, and cooperate. Knowledge management guru Tom Davenport says that as companies mature, every business, function, and process becomes knowledge-intensive. Even general managers become knowledge managers. And the scarcest resource becomes attention.

The challenge, then, is to transform phlogiston—old-fashioned companies—into highly profitable enterprises based on knowledge networks and community sharing rather than hierarchy and divisions. Such transformation will not come easily. But once started, it will be hard to stop. A profitable General Motors based on knowledge will make the old GM look like a medieval theory, a system once widely shared, then ignored, and finally forgotten.

To anticipate how this process may work and to see how much more remains to be done, we need to learn how to apply several tools. One we already know: innovation life cycle curves, but this time applied to entire economies rather than single companies or technologies. Another is generation theory, which we'll explore shortly. Along the way we'll need to develop some new vocabulary to use throughout the book so that we can share a common terminology without resorting to words like "de-phlogenated air," "horseless carriage," or my favorite from Xerox, "digital document."

APPLYING INNOVATION LIFE CYCLES TO ECONOMIES

Innovation life cycle curves can be applied to entire economies, such as the agricultural economy, the industrial economy, or the present one—variously called the postindustrial economy, the information economy, or the knowledge economy.[5] As we'll see below, all three of these names are valid, but refer to different time periods.

Technological innovation drives our definition of economies. It was the new products like railroads, steel, and cars that gave the "industrial economy" its name. The cotton gin invented by Eli Whitney is an example of an industrial age product that transformed, and eventually enabled the senescence of, the entire basis of an economy: agriculture. Whenever we have cross-economy applications on a wide scale, the new economy revolutionizes the old

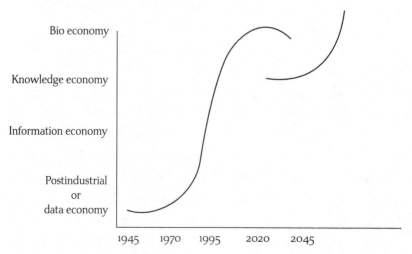

Innovation Life Cycle Curves Applied to the 100-Year Economy 1945–2045
A second truncated curve is shown, indicating the start of a next economy—the bio economy.

one. Today's analog to the cotton gin (and the McCormick reaper, etc.) is the biotech innovations that are transforming not only agriculture but the entire computer industry.

Most people date our current economy as starting shortly after World War II, when computers first began to be used in business. Following the innovation life cycle, only the technology enthusiasts and the visionaries first used computers. Somewhere around the late 1950s and early 1960s, computers "crossed the chasm" and were embraced by the mainstream market. That was the heyday of the IBM mainframe. The roughly twenty-five-year period starting in 1945 is what was known as the postindustrial economy. I call this early period the "data economy." It, in turn, gestated the seeds of the present economy. Today we can see that the second half of the information age is computerizing industrial businesses, producing a revolution in legacy companies just as the cotton gin revolutionized agriculture.

The IBM mainframe was followed a decade later by Digital Equipment Corporation's minicomputer, which in turn was followed a decade later by Apple's Macintosh and IBM's PC. The twenty-five-year period from roughly 1970 to 1995 was one of extraordinary growth and flowering of computer usage. It is understandably called the information economy or information age.

Today we are at the midpoint of the information age. How do I know? Admittedly no one can predict how long an economy based on a class of technology will last. What we do know is that the agricultural economy lasted thousands of years and the industrial economy several centuries.[6] We also know that cycle times are getting ever shorter. It is therefore likely that the economy based on computers and communications will be shorter than the industrial economy. If it is as short as a hundred years, we are literally at the midpoint.

Another technology is already gestating another future economy—biotechnology, genetic engineering, and molecular biology. Many of our leading thinkers see the turn of the millennium as a first turning point and the year 2020 as another.[7]

Those turning points, or "discontinuities," have traditionally served as signs that an economy is starting to mature. In the agricultural economy, one discontinuity was the switch from family farming with manual plows and hand-harvesting to agribusiness with irrigation, tractor-combines, and fertil-izer. In the industrial economy, a discontinuity occurred with the switch from railroads and steam to the automobile and petroleum. This time it's the switch from computers as number crunchers to computers as connectors, where the enabling technology is the Internet.[8]

The shift from crunching to connecting marks the commencement of the next twenty-five-year period, which is properly called the knowledge econ-omy. It is the time when knowledge management projects are the rage and when knowledge workers are enthusiasts in the process of mainstreaming. You can see them in companies in every industry. Nearly all AT&T and Saturn peo-ple, for example, can be described as "knowledge workers." AT&T uses the col-legial term "associates" for them; Saturn declines to use titles.[9] Unless otherwise specified, I will use the term "knowledge workers" to refer to the workforce of the "knowledge economy" which covers the twenty-five-year period from 1995 to 2020.

Looking beyond 2020 becomes even more speculative. The emphasis on knowledge is likely to continue and to accelerate, but the focus will probably shift to either biotechnology or possibly to space-based technology or per-haps both. Whichever turns out to be the case, I predict that the quarter-cen-tury after 2020 will see the waning of silicon computer chip technology and the gestation of a new set of technologies for a future economy. These conclu-sions are summarized in the accompanying tables.

THE HUNDRED-YEAR PERIOD FROM 1945 TO 2045 CAN BE CALLED THE KNOWLEDGE AGE

Years	Quarters	Name
1945–1970	Q1	Data Economy
1970-1995	Q2	Information Economy
1995–2020	Q3	Knowledge Economy
2020–2045 and beyond	Q4 of current cycle Q1 of bio-economy	Beginnings of Bio-economy

---

BUSINESS STRATEGIES IN DIFFERENT ECONOMIES

In the information economy (1970 to 1995), the best strategy was to overinvest in crunching power. Competitive advantage accrued to those who invested more than their competitors to process more data and information more quickly.

In the knowledge economy (1995 to 2020), the best strategy is to overinvest in connecting power. Competitive advantage accrues to those who invest more than their competitors to connect to more people and share knowledge faster and farther.

In the information economy, Moore's Law was the operative rule. Moore's Law says that the price/performance of computing doubles every eighteen months.

In the knowledge economy, Metcalf's Law[10] is the operative rule. Metcalf's Law holds that the value of a computer is proportional to the square of the number of connections it makes.

WHAT GENERATION THEORY TELLS US ABOUT OUR FUTURE

So far, we've applied life cycle theory to knowledge as a business resource and to entire economies—agricultural, industrial, and the information/knowledge economies. It also applies to us as individuals. When applied to individuals and their birth cohorts in society, the process is called "generation theory." It looks a lot like innovation theory, so it should strike you as familiar.

Like innovation theory, generation theory uses four stages. We all go through youth, adulthood, and midlife, and become elders. Gail Sheehy uses a similar construct in her book *Passages*. She calls the "seasons" of a person's life infancy, growing up, reaching maturity, and entering eldership or old age. More poetically, these four stages are the spring, summer, autumn, and winter of life.

The age ranges associated with these four stages vary with different individuals, but they can be summarized as in the accompanying table.

In their book *Generations*,[11] William Strauss and Neil Howe use four periods in a person's life similar to those above: youth, rising adulthood, midlife, and eldership. But they have extended the concept to cover entire cohorts of

Name of Life Period	Average Ages for the Period
Youth ("spring")	0–21
Young Adulthood ("summer")	21–45
Midlife ("fall")	45–65
Eldership ("winter")	65–95+

individuals, just as above we extended innovation theory to cover entire economies. Cohorts are groups of individuals born in the same range of years. For example, people born between 1943 and 1960 are part of the "boomer" generation. People born between 1961 and 1981 are part of "Generation 13" (Strauss and Howe's name), "Generation X" (a name used by older people who don't understand the younger), or "Generation Next" as the Pepsi ad says it.

Strauss and Howe identify four types of generations: idealists, pragmatists, heroes and silents.[12] Applying this lens of generation types over the last 500 years, they show how American history can be understood as the outcome of the interactions among the four types of generations as they all progress and mature, going through their four different stages. And they provide food for thought as to what this portends for the years ahead. Hence the subtitle of their book is *The History of America's Future, 1584–2069*.

Paradigm shifts occur when an idealist generation enters its period of maturity and approaches eldership. That is because idealists bring a new set of values, new social rules, and, in commerce, new businesses, which are then implemented and developed by succeeding generations. The present generation of idealists, the boomers, are crossing midlife, and the first wave of them are entering maturity. As they do so, they will bring with them a shift in the way we see the world. In business, this is the paradigm shift to knowledge; in economics, it is the shift to a knowledge economy. In society in general, I predict that this shift and period will become known as the Knowledge Age, though we'll know the actual name for sure only after more time goes by.

To understand generation theory no matter which generation you're born in, you have to think in one-hundred-year packets, which the Romans called "secula," from which we derive the word "century." A generation lasts roughly twenty-five years before its members give birth to children. Yet each generation lives for nearly a hundred years. To comprehend your own life, you need to look four generations back to your great-grandparents, or about a hundred years ago.[13]

The idealist generation in the last century was known as the "Missionary" idealists, who were born in the years between 1860 and 1882. The well-known business leaders Alfred Sloan, Henry Ford, and Pierre Du Pont were all part of the Missionary idealist generation.[14] They were contemporaries who ushered in the second half of the industrial age and established the organizational forms and norms still practiced today and still considered the model for modern management. Two other members of their generation were the Wright brothers, who invented and flew the first practical airplane. Together with Sloan and Ford, they were responsible for the transportation revolution.[15]

Contrary to conventional wisdom, the pace of change today is not very different from the last time we had idealist generations entering their maturity. But you have to look in sets of centuries to see the similarities. The invention of the automobile and the airplane represented just as great a change to our great grandparents as the computer and knowledge revolution poses to us today. The pace of change is similar (both are frantic!). What's different is what changes—a shift from how we move to how we think—but the pace and process are the same.

THE MANAGER'S CORE WORK

Family businesses often have three generations in them at once: grandparent, parents, and sons and daughters. As each succeeding generation comes to the top positions of power, the nature of the business often changes. LL Bean in the days of the founding generation was a small family woolen clothing business relying on word-of-mouth advertising; the second generation expanded to outdoor clothing in general and sold by mail order catalog; now the third generation is expanding again to outdoor furnishings for home and camp and selling via the Internet. The challenge for LL Bean is to keep its value of integrity and Maine backwoods honesty intact.

The larger and slower the company, the older the in-power leaders are likely to be. The chairmen and CEOs of many legacy companies are finishing their final years before leaders of the boomer generation become the ones in power. That is often a difficult transition—witness for example in politics the shift from President Bush (GI Joe hero generation) to Bill Clinton (first of the boomers).

Through the lens of generation theory, it is no surprise that so many boomers are taking early retirement. Boomers comprise statistically the largest segment of middle managers. They are easily frustrated with leaders they see as bureaucratic. Many either welcome early retirement if they have the chance or become "those who've quit but are still employed" and remain in the workforce.

It doesn't have to be that way. A manager's core work, no matter which company he or she is in, is to usher in and nurture the environments that promote continuous lifelong learning and continually advancing knowledge. It is a builder's role that fits naturally with nature's cycle of four seasons and humanity's cycle of four generation types. Managers acting like victims will need to transform themselves into the role of activists. People fed up with their jobs need to ask themselves how they're investing their lives. How are we investing our lives together? As Gary Hamel asks, "Which side of the revolution are you on? The movement or the establishment?"

CORPORATE WISDOM: FROM OXYMORON TO LEGITIMATE TRUISM

The biggest opportunity opened up by generation succession and paradigm shifts is the dialogue on wisdom. It has already started. Books on soul and spirituality in the workplace are examples. *Leading with Soul* by Terry Deal and Lee Bolman is an example of the wisdom of coaching that highlights the roles of different generations and genders in speaking their truths. Whatever we mean by "wisdom"—and there will never be uniform agreement (thank goodness)—it is a subject on the agenda of every generation as that generation approaches and enters eldership. This is the role of "elders" in American Indian tribes; it is the correct role of Boards of Directors in corporations; and it is a role for all those who aspire to "live in harmony and walk in beauty," as the Navajo in the Southwest say.[16]

The greatest significance of the focus on knowledge in business is that it will demand serious dialogue on wisdom in the corporation, where, at least initially, the discerning use of knowledge for the common good is the type of wisdom that will be engaged. This focus on questions around wisdom is important for every generation. Idealist generations, however, take it on with special energy. This is what Strauss and Howe highlight in their follow-on book, *The Fourth Turning*, which refers to the time when the idealist generation reaches its fourth life stage and its members become elders.

It is both fitting and proper that dialogue about wisdom be taken up in business. Indeed, it will become more essential as the generations complete their cycle. Idealists are prone to not only great achievements but also great catastrophe. The Enlightenment ended with the cataclysmic upheaval of the French Revolution, fought over political and social injustice. This time around the problem is more economic than political. The focus on economic inequity puts business at center stage for the coming discourse on wisdom, an uncomfortable and unprecedented role for business but also an unavoidable and essential one.

HONEYBEES FIRST APPEAR IN ROCK PAINTINGS NEAR VALENCIA, SPAIN, DATING FROM 7000 B.C.

The Greek god of bee-keeping is Aristaeus. Aristotle reported his findings about bees. Pliny wrote about them. Virgil wrote poems about them. They all extol the kingdom of bees. The second temple at Delphi was said to have been built by bees.

In 1609 the English author Charles Butler wrote *The Feminine Monarchie* in which he daringly asserted that the King Bee was no male at all but a female and must henceforth be called Queen.

—adapted from Sue Hubbell, *A Book of Bees*

At a time when Europe experiences persistently high unemployment rates, when America's growing wealth results in a two-tier third-world-like society, and Japanese and East Asian economies start to unravel their economic miracles, it is a time to take seriously the need for wisdom as a legitimate part of every business plan, economic strategy, and meetings of all kinds. "Corporate wisdom," currently an oxymoron, needs to become a legitimate truism.

It is a supreme historical irony that the Enlightenment ended in violence. It would be an unspeakable future ignorance if in the Knowledge Age we should permit history to repeat itself.

The business world that I know is woefully unprepared for its role. Most leaders today would vehemently deny this responsibility, claiming it more properly belongs to political, philosophical, or religious leaders. That threadbare excuse is beginning to fray. Until we embrace a dialogue on wisdom as a necessary condition for doing business ethically, generating new smart business will be little more than proliferating cold technological curiosities. The future we're looking for is a BOTH/AND future: BOTH economic success AND, at the same time, social justice.

Chapter Three

What's the Knowledge Business in Your Business?

*Honey bees pollinate
over $10 billion worth of crops each year
in the U.S. and over 90 crops are dependent
on the honey bee for pollination.*

—American Beekeeping Federation

An investment
in knowledge always
pays the best interest.

—Benjamin Franklin

THE KNOWLEDGE BUSINESS

Massey Ferguson's new tractor is linked to a the satellite-based Global Positioning System, which records the latitude, longitude, and yield of each square yard in every field. The data are automatically sent to the farmer's desktop computer, which generates yield maps showing where variations are above or below target. Armed with this information, the farmer can practice small-scale farming on a large scale, using fertilizers only where necessary and in the exact amounts needed. Farmers who use this new method comprise an emerging community of interest.

Suntek produces Cloud Gel, a new material that can prevent overheating when applied to window glass. When the sun is strong, Cloud Gel reflects rather than transmits 90 percent of the sun's rays; when more heat is needed at a specified temperature, Cloud Gel lets in more warmth. If all the world's annual 6 billion new square feet of glass used the product, energy consumption would drop by 17 percent and more than a billion tons of air pollutants would be eliminated. The users of Cloud Gel have not yet, to my knowledge, formed any bonds of support with one another or with other industries, but they'd be even more powerful if they did: Imagine car makers learning from greenhouse designers about how to avoid having your car heat up in sunny parking lots.

Coca-Cola, Unilever, and Tyson Foods all use the Hartness International Video Response System. The VRS has a camera, keyboard, transmitter, and monitor that enable expert technicians to view and diagnose machinery breakdowns at a distance minutes after they occur. Shutting down a bottling line costs $150 a minute. That's $216,000 over twenty-four hours, which is how much time it used to take for a technician to fly to the site. This new customer service has added more than $2.5 million in sales to the company. The Hartness technicians who operate the system and their customers who learn how to fix the machinery represent a community whose purpose is to share a smart service delivered in a new way.[1]

Those are all examples of knowledge businesses, because they embed new knowledge and learning into their products, services, and processes. They are also examples of potential knowledge communities where employees and customers could work more effectively together to use, apply, and extend the embedded knowledge, but as yet they haven't.

This is a tremendous opportunity waiting to be exploited. Because the knowledge business is both new and relatively complex, it can best be carried out not by a single leader or technical genius but by large numbers of people organized into knowledge communities. Thus, linking knowledge businesses to knowledge communities is a powerful strategy for growth and renewal. It is more than just organizational transformation. It is industry transformation.

To make the strategy work poses two main challenges for legacy companies. One is the threat that new knowledge products will cannibalize existing products; another is the fear that communities will dilute the power of old-timers in the hierarchy. The question is less whether the migration to knowledge products and knowledge-based organization will occur than whether legacy companies can learn the strategy before being forced out of business by powerful startups not constrained by industrial-age baggage.

LAUNCHING A NEW INDUSTRY— STRATEGIES FOR REVOLUTION IN THE BUSINESS

The business strategist, Gary Hamel, distinguishes among rule makers, rule takers, and rule breakers. Rule makers are companies that set the standard. An example in airlines is British Airways, considered by experienced international travelers to be at the top of the industry. A rule taker in this sector would be Air France, essentially a follower to the benchmark of BA. The rule breaker is Virgin Airways. On Virgin's transatlantic flights, "Upper Class" passengers can get complimentary chauffeur-driven sedan service and free massages on selected flights, and all passengers can use Virgin Atlantic's Drive-thru Check-in at London Heathrow's airport, the world's first.

Too many companies are interested in benchmarking. They want to know how they stack up against competitors or what they can learn from "world-class" service, quality, or other processes. Not enough companies think of setting their own benchmarks. Inventing your own benchmarks are how you can lead a knowledge revolution. More radical still, write the benchmarks for a whole new industry. That is what Virgin is doing in airlines, The Body Shop in cosmetics, and Charles Schwab in brokerage services.[2]

Legacy companies need to ask themselves, "Are we living off a legacy or building a new one?" Going into the knowledge business is all about building a new legacy.

So many opportunities exist for knowledge businesses it's hard to know where to start. Have you looked in the National Geographic Society's gift cat-alog lately? How about the laser-tipped pen that, when you run its light over a foreign menu, shows the translation at your fingertips? Or how about 108 years of National Geographic on CD-ROM—it's spicier than the Encyclopae-dia Brittanica. Products like those are not rocket science, but they're new, imaginative, and different. Note that while they are offered by an organiza-tion over a hundred years old, they do not compete with or cannibalize its main business, supporting and reporting geographic exploration. The Na-tional Geographic case is a success story because the society has created a fledgling knowledge business and a method of distribution that complements its existing capabilities. Now its challenge is to develop an organizational form that can enable more complex, possibly networked, knowledge products—that is, the National Geographic Society needs to organize as a Virtual Knowl-edge Community.

In the automotive field, how about cars that send a signal to your key ring when you've forgotten where you parked? How about public parking garages where your place is assigned when you check in so you don't have to search for the one empty parking space at the airport when you're in a hurry? Com-panies are already developing the GPS Never-Get-Lost system that puts a map on your dashboard with voice directions teiling you where to turn. Why not connect it to traffic reports on radio stations so your computer can route you around traffic jams? As in the National Geographic case, those are oppor-tunities that can complement General Motors' existing line. Why not organize it more aggressively as a new line of business? To do so will require large-scale reorganizing—not immediately, but inexorably.

As in the case of the Coca-Cola vending machines mentioned earlier, the goal of many knowledge products and services is real-time action: real-time pricing, real-time traffic reports, or real-time catalog services. Think of every single component or product as having a computer chip and transmitter. Ten-nis racquets that glow where the ball strikes, diapers that notify when wet, au-tomobile parts that signal when they're wearing out, or milk cartons that sense whether the milk is fresh (Tetrapak is working on that one).

During the Cold War, every computer mainframe made in the United States contained a chip and transmitter to prevent its export to Communist countries. Millions of dollars were spent in the name of national security. Now when Russian and former Warsaw Pact people regularly visit Los Alamos and other computational centers once considered off limits, why can't we turn our attention to the other national security issue, guns and violence in the public space? Smith & Wesson makes a smart gun that fires only in the hands of an authorized owner so that teens can't use a parent's gun. Why not a purse with a chip and transmitter that can give purse-snatchers pause?

Not only has the nature of war shifted to smart weapons, but the quest for peace and conflict resolution has strengthened.[3] Communities forming around the Internet and fax machines have been able to topple repressive governments unresponsive to the new knowledge and power of common purpose. New technologies have also moved the debates on human rights away from smoke-filled rooms of central committees to the global cyberspace of knowledge communities.

FOUR STAGES IN THE KNOWLEDGE BUSINESS

Historically, the hierarchical model of conducting industrial business did not emerge until more than halfway through the industrial economy, when Alfred Sloan, Henry Ford, and Pierre Du Pont created it in the early 1900s. That is, the business comes first, followed by the organization that enables its profitability. This pattern is repeating itself today. Halfway through the knowledge age, we are glimpsing the organizational forms that can make the knowledge business profitable. I believe that form is the knowledge community. To understand this dynamic better, we turn again to innovation theory, which provides us with a tool to investigate the stages of the knowledge business.

The first two stages were the data business, like the airlines SABRE system, and the information business, like the Official Airlines Guide (OAG). Those occurred during the fifty years following World War II. The application of IT, or information technology, during that time was for the primary purpose of automation.

Automation has the effect of freezing into computer hardware and software the basic business processes that have already been done for a long time.

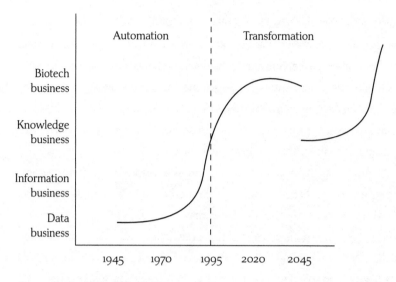

Stages in the Knowledge of Business

Such a use of technology allows people to do what they've always done before, but faster and cheaper. It reinforces the old ways of doing business.

The following two stages of the knowledge businesses are those based on the technology of computers and communications and those based on biotechnology. This is the business just gestating and are marked by the partial curve at the right in the accompanying graph.

The computer/communications and biotech processes applied to other business have as their fundamental purpose not to automate existing processes but to create entirely new enterprises—the former in the businesses enabled by connecting people and technology into new arrangements (such as virtual stock markets that directly link buyer and seller),[4] and the latter by revolutionizing silicon-based technology and replacing it with genetically enhanced processors (such as DNA computers) whose business opportunities are yet to emerge. Where some examples exist already, I'll refer to them later on.

LOOKING AT THE KNOWLEDGE BUSINESS, STAGE BY STAGE

To understand the power of the knowledge business, let's review the four stages of the journey stage by stage.

Database Days

In the 1950s and 1960s data were the rage. "Databases" could be bought and sold. Database management was a specialty taught at the best business schools. Data, especially their integrity and accuracy, are still as important today as they ever were, but we tend to take data for granted. We take them for granted until they are wiped out by a power failure or other malfunction.

An example of the data business is an airline reservation system like SABRE, built by American Airlines in the early 1950s. The SABRE system keeps track of huge amounts of data—names, dates, flight numbers, prices, routing, special meal requests, and so on. Systems like SABRE constituted one of the first important applications of computer technology to automate business processes. During the years when high jet fuel prices caused losses in operating profits, American and other airlines seriously considered spinning off the profitable parts of the system, namely the data-based reservation systems, which were consistently more valuable than the flying operations they supported, and indeed they have all done so.

That automation process froze into computer code the basic ways the airline business had already been done for a long time. It strengthened the system of an airline company served by authorized travel agents and priced by a team of experts skilled in airline routes and loading factors. But it was still a tool for a world of fixed prices (albeit a huge number of them targeted to different market segments). Today the Internet promises to change the system much more radically, to allow customers to *bid* on prices. Initially, one proposed system just matches your bid to the hundreds of preselected prices each airline has developed. But eventually those prices will fluctuate each day or hour depending on flight loads and prior histories. In those conditions, a bid-and-ask system makes sense.

In the twilight of the database days in the late 1960s, I started my doctorate at the Harvard Business School. Harvard had just created its first degrees for information—Management Information Systems (MIS)—and I was among its initial graduates. One of my first jobs was to automate Harvard's Case Clearing House. That consisted of building a database of all the cases—name of author, title, company, topic, and so on.

That automation process left the small but cohesive Case Clearing House just as it had always been: a library with supplies of printed cases, filed by clerks, and sold via unsolicited telephone orders. Contrast that approach of the 1960s with the move in the 1990s that put the whole database on the Internet. This move has fundamentally changed the way the business is done by allowing customers direct access to cases and an ability to review and, with proper payment arrangements, download them online.

Information Businesses

In the 1970s and early 1980s, information rather than raw data was the focus. That was the era when management information systems were being built. Computers were kept and operated in centralized "data centers" in air-conditioned rooms behind glass walls separated physically and psychologically from normal business operations. Typically, each department in the company would make up a list of projects they wanted to computerize: software they wanted the information processing professionals to write for them. Managing that process was a difficult and frustrating task, because it was a centralized or even decentralized staff trying to deliver a service that was inherently networked (an issue we'll take up later).

When personal computers arrived on the business scene they were seen as threatening to many managers of information processing, because they undermined their power and made their job of managing technology much more difficult. Many companies created a position of Chief Information Officer (CIO), to which the best of the MIS managers migrated.

Personal computers, distributed access to mainframes, and creation of CIO positions enabled enterprising groups to start "information businesses." Most common were internal services to top management. DSS, or decision support systems, are one of many examples. Here a top management committee and its support staff receive a program (like a Lotus 1-2-3 spreadsheet) to manipulate data and create scenarios for the future under differing assumptions. Those were very restricted internal markets, in which only top managers could take advantage of data-manipulating software to create knowledge. They were not for everyone, or even most people.

STAGES OF BUSINESS DEVELOPMENT

	Data	*Information*	*Knowledge*
Business	Database business	Information systems	Knowledge business
Example	SABRE	Decision support systems	Smart tractor
Technology	Mainframes	Minis/PCs	Miniaturized chips Telecom connections
Market	External Customers	Internal Services	Customers direct
Focus	Centralized	Distributed	Networked
Organization	Task force	X-functional teams	Partnerships/alliances Knowledge communities
Leader	DP head	CIO	CKO

The degree of your company's readiness to move into the knowledge business depends in large part on where it is in its stage of business and technology development. The experience across several different dimensions is summarized in the accompanying table for the data stage, the information stage, and the next stage, which is knowledge.

Most businesses have completed the move from the data business to information services. Just as for the stages of an economy, however, it's important to remember that the old data and information activities won't disappear. They continue to exist and may be highly important financial or service contributors. They do not, however, represent the latest management thinking, just as the agricultural economy and the industrial economy no longer represent the mainstream or future developments of the majority of businesses.

The table shows the businesses across a horizontal axis of data, information, and knowledge and their six supporting components listed here:

- The example of "lines of business" are SABRE, DSS, and Massey Ferguson's smart GPS-linked tractor.
- The technology has moved from mainframes to minicomputers and PCs

to palm-pilots or miniaturized chips and telecommunication connections like the GPS and the Internet.

- The market has moved from external customers to internal services for executives and managers, and then to direct contact with external and internal customers.
- The management model has gone from centralized systems to distributed ones and is moving to networked arrangements.
- The supporting organization has moved from task forces and cross-functional work teams to partnerships, alliances, and knowledge communities.
- Leadership—or at least its titles—has gone from the Head of DP (data processing) to CIO (Chief Information Officer), to CKO (Chief Knowledge Officer).

Pulling all these different dimensions (business, technology, market, management, organization, and leadership) together into a whole that is coherent and consistent for a particular company is what businesses need to do to innovate their strategic thinking process.

IDENTIFYING KNOWLEDGE-BASED PRODUCTS AND SMART SERVICES

It's easy to identify the business opportunity in the companies that by their very nature are knowledge businesses—consulting firms and computer hardware and software companies. Identifying the knowledge business in companies that do not have a history or experience of knowledge as a business is a more challenging task. Take a clothing manufacturer. What's the knowledge-value a producer can embed in clothing, say, in a jacket or sweater? What's the knowledge-value a customer of such a product can extract from it? (I'll show you an example below.) Or what's the knowledge business that could be created for a food company? (With genetic advances, there are going to be a lot of them, but I'll propose one below based on electronics rather than genetics.) How should a company like General Motors, which thinks of itself as a producer and seller of cars, approach the knowledge business? (It's already in the business, but it calls it something else.)

The mainstream of pragmatic managers finds the search for their company's knowledge business to be a daunting if not nonsensical task. It is often culturally new; it requires suspending judgment and adopting a new mindset. But it's not as difficult as it might seem at first glance. Indeed, the automotive companies have one of the largest knowledge businesses going—they just don't use that name for it.

Here's a process I use to generate ideas of what is a possible knowledge business inside your company. First, an actual case—a business service currently operated by General Motors.

1. **Business Need:** Start with a current product or service your company currently makes or provides in which you already have some know-how.

GM has a service to train mechanics to diagnose and repair its cars, especially the new electronics-intensive engines and other computer-controlled devices. (There are more processors inside a car today than inside a PC!)

2. **Business Example:** What new service could we create that could be based on new knowledge or a new way of connecting to the user or customer?

CAMS, the Computer Aided Maintenance System from General Motors, is a knowledge-based service that can get your car fixed by helping mechanics diagnose and repair even the most sophisticated new cars.

3. **Technology:** Apply the new knowledge to it—miniaturized computer chips and wireless communications—or what we call a "magic computer (MC)." Imagine that the MC has enough intelligence such that it can readily understand you and respond. Imagine what the product would do if it had a magic computer inside. Suspend your judgment that it might be a stretch to put the MC into your product or service since it's not been done before.

Each mechanic who makes a successful repair adds the example to the system. Since all CAMS terminals in garages are connected to a central home base, each mechanic becomes the beneficiary of the combined skills of all the other mechanics on the system.

4. Market: Ask yourself what it might do differently from the old methods and to whom this would appeal.

Designed initially to allow novice mechanics to diagnose and repair cars, CAMS has evolved into something more: It has become a trainer for mechanics, enabling them to develop their own expertise repairing electronics-based auto engines.

5. Focus: Is this something that is centralized, distributed, or networked?

CAMS is an internal service that is distributed among dealerships. It has a central database tied together into multiple sites. It is not yet a "networked" system, tying one mechanic directly to any other, but it would not be technologically difficult to grow this ability.

6. Organization: Is this something that implies partnerships, alliances, communities?

CAMS is an important part of the company's partnership with its dealers. Dealerships are currently at arm's length from the auto producers. Anything that could make them feel more of a community rather than second-class citizens would benefit both parties. CAMS provides a beginning in this direction.

What makes CAMS a knowledge business? What's the knowledge part? The more the system is used, the smarter it gets. CAMS teaches the person how to become a good mechanic; good mechanics teach the system how to become a better teacher. The more the knowledge to maintain a car is shared, the more it grows. It grows up rather than gets used up.

New cars from nearly every major manufacturer are beginning to be packed with knowledge. In some cars, stepping on the brakes doesn't cause a mechanical reaction that pushes drums or discs against the wheel. Rather it signals a computer chip to sense the road conditions and then apply brakes in a system known as ABS. "With ABS," says an industry spokesperson, "you can make a typical driver perform like an expert." Take it to the next level. If ABS can avoid skids, it can also compensate for drivers who try to take a curve too fast. Yaw and pitch sensors intervene to prevent fishtailing or oversteering.

Optical imaging chips on the bumpers can aid in parallel parking. They can also peer beneath large trucks you want to pass to see better than the driver can whether passing is safe or not. The ESP—Electronic Stability Program—invented by Bosch, can safely swerve your car around an unexpected obstacle. The system is good enough to pass Sweden's so-called loose moose test, where moose are frequent interlopers on Arctic roads.

New cruise controls are on the way. They don't just maintain a set speed any more. They use radar to gauge the speed of slower-moving vehicles ahead and automatically slow your car to the same speed until you decide to pass. Such adaptive controls are already available on some Mitsubishi and Jaguar models.

Infrared sensors can now register the heat of a car in the blind spot and warn you if you turn on your blinker to pull out at the wrong time. Based on work at MIT, chips sensitive to stress and mood can determine if you're drowsy and can sound a signal. Pulling into a crowded passing lane will also be easier, because your car's computer will alert adjacent cars, which will let you move in because chips don't practice aggressive driving. Car-based cell phones will download traffic reports from the Internet in real time, allowing you to reroute your journey with your onboard computer.[5]

> One bee would have to fly the equivalent of three orbits around the earth in her foraging flights in order to produce a single pound of honey. Ironically, beeswax is worth more money per pound than honey! It has many uses besides candles: a component for polishes and waterproofing; a base for ointments, creams, and cosmetics; and an ingredient in adhesives, crayons, and chewing gum. Its chief value is to beekeeping supply companies, which remelt it and mold it into new frames to sell back to beekeepers.
>
> —adapted from Sue Hubbell, *A Book of Bees*

Reflecting on such examples makes one pause to ask: Is this really knowledge? For people, we define knowledge as information put to productive use. The more novel the action, the more we accept it as knowledge. Is it knowledge nonetheless when the actor is a machine, a computer chip? Artificial intelligence answered that long ago. Yes, it is human knowledge embedded in an electronic device. What about the cases in nature of animals, insects, and bees? When a worker bee communicates information on the location of flowers by dancing and her hive-mates fly off for the nectar, is this information put to productive use? Yes it is, but here the bee is operating by instinct rather than intelligence. But if a computer can exhibit knowledge when preprogrammed by humans, then surely we can grant bees knowledge when preprogrammed by Nature.

Let's try another example. Let's repeat this process for a hypothetical food company. I'll use the name Kellogg's, but it could be any producer of breakfast cereals.

1. **Business Need:** Start with a current product or service your company currently makes or provides in which you already have some know-how.

Kellogg's has a cereal that goes "snap, crackle, and pop." The product has had a long and successful past, but children today are getting more sophisticated. Kellogg's needs something new to distinguish it from competitors.

2. **Business Example:** What new product could we create that could be based on new knowledge or a new way of connecting to the user or consumer?

Smart Cereal! It listens to you while you eat and can be "trained" to repeat what you say to it. Endless hours of fun—and laced with nutrition while it improves your pronunciation! Your kids will love it.

3. **Technology:** Apply the new knowledge to it—miniaturized computer chips and wireless communications—or what we call a "magic computer" (MC). Imagine that the MC has enough intelligence that it can

readily understand you and respond. Imagine what the product would do if it had a magic computer inside. Suspend your judgment that it might be a stretch to put the MC into your product or service, since it's not been done before.

Computer chips can be made so small and inexpensively that we embed a chip in each piece of crispy rice. The new "Varadon" electronic tongue developed at the University of Pennsylvania would be a good candidate to perform this task. When the chip senses milk, it could send a signal to the cardboard box, which would turn on its mini-microphone. Whatever it hears, it would speak back. If the word was mispronounced, the parent would say it correctly, and the cereal would respond with the correct pronunciation.

4. Market: Ask yourself what this might do differently from the old methods and to whom this would appeal.

It would appeal to parents who want their child to get better nutrition and a better speaking vocabulary. It would appeal to kids, who would find endless things they wanted their cereal to say—to them and to their friends! This would engage even more consumers.

5. Focus: Is this something that is centralized, distributed, or networked?

Smart Cereal would first be a "distributed" system, but it's not hard to imagine it networked to the family personal computer. If the PC were linked to the Internet, the parent could coordinate it with a lesson program geared to the child's age.

6. Organization: Is this something that implies partnerships, alliances, communities?

This suggests a business partnership between Kellogg's and Intel—as well as involvement of teachers from the educational community.

What's the knowledge part? The more the cereal is used (eaten), the smarter the consumer gets. The more the child uses new words, the smarter the system gets. The beneficiary is the ultimate consumer (child and parent) as well as the Kellogg's Cereal Company.

EXAMPLES OF KNOWLEDGE BUSINESSES

Here are some examples of other knowledge businesses that exist already or, in the case of the "electronic tongue," are close to commercialization:

NeverLost is Hertz's system that places electronic maps on your dashboard. You enter your destination and a map appears that tracks your progress in real time. You see your car move along the map's roads, which are as accurate as the professional maps you buy at the gas station, except that they are always up to date. The guts of the technology are the twenty-four global positioning satellites (GPS) that the U.S. military uses. The car's GPS antenna uses as many as six satellites to fix the vehicle's location by triangulation. Combined with digital maps, electronic databases, and sensors that monitor the vehicle's speed and direction, the systems display maps on a small dashboard monitor that can zoom in or out for more detail. Oldsmobile has a similar system called Guidestar, and Rockwell's is named Pathmaster. Advanced versions of the system can adjust to your preferences—whether to take the scenic route or the most direct one. Combined with real-time police monitors, the guides could also route you around accidents, construction sites, or traffic problems. The more customers use this system, the smarter they get about driving routes. At present, no single company has emerged as the chief purveyor of this smart product.

Security First Network Bank started in Canada via the Internet. It performs all the functions of traditional retail banking. It accepts deposits, makes loans, provides letters of credit, enables home banking and electronic bill payment, and so on. But except for a single physical office required by Canadian law, it has no branches or personnel. It's a virtual bank built on software and multiple partnerships with a whole series of "real" banks, each of which performs the individual functions. Its startup cost of $40 million is a fraction of the cost it normally would take to establish a traditional bank with multiple branches. While most traditional banks today are available twenty-four hours a day, seven days a week through their ATMs or through their home banking facilities, Security First is truly independent of time and space. About the only thing left with physical reality is cash. But a recent spate of bank robberies in Belgium has given a boost to another related knowledge business, a smart cash card where individuals can make transactions without resorting to cash.

The Varadan Microsensor "electronic tongue" is the technology for a future smart business of putting chemical sensors inside of milk cartons, juice bottles, or any agricultural products where customers want to know quickly and easily the extent of any spoilage. A small dial built into the milk carton will tell you at a glance if the milk is fresh, just as the same sensor on the inside of food processing vats can detect the growth of unwanted bacteria. The technology is made from silicon, quartz, and aluminum and is wireless. Unlike biological assays, the Varadan tongues can detect chemical signals without performing any chemical reactions. They sense changes in viscosity, the stickiness of fluids, and changes in their electrical properties. The product is named after Vijay and Vasundra Varadan, a husband-and-wife research team at the University of Pennsylvania. This example is part of a steady process of endowing miniature computer chips with all the senses available to humans—sight, hearing, touch, smell, and now taste. Combined with the right business product, they can provide a competitive edge for very little additional cost.

Micro PCMs, or Phase Change Materials, are genetically engineered particles that have the unusual property of turning warm when they sense cold and vice versa, cooling down when the ambient temperature is warm. This knowledge-based product, developed by Outlast, Inc., of Boulder, Colorado, has the property of adjusting itself to your requirements. When woven into cloth, it can produce a ski jacket that turns warm when it senses cold or cools down on sunny ski days. The same micro-PCMs can be embedded into car seats, for example, or even into wallpaper. Outlast has concluded partnerships with Biddeford Textiles (blankets), Hardcorps Sports (skiwear), Manzella (outdoor gloves), Mason Shoe (hiking boots), Wells Creek (fishing outerwear), Wigwam Mills (gloves, caps, and socks), Nordica (the Italian ski boot maker), and Eddie Bauer in Canada for its EBTek™ Extreme Gear Parka. Not based on any computers, communications, or electronics, it represents a

SIX TOP ATTRIBUTES OF KNOWLEDGE PRODUCTS AND SERVICES

Learn	The more you use them, the smarter they get. The more you use them, the smarter you get too.
Improve with use	Enhanced rather than depleted when used, they grow up instead of being used up.
Anticipate	Knowing what you want, they recommend what you might want next.
Interactive	Two-way communication between you and them
Remember	Record and recall your past actions to develop a profile
Customize	Unique configuration to your individual specifications in real time at no additional cost

preview of one type of smart product that comes from an emerging bio-economy.

SIX ATTRIBUTES OF KNOWLEDGE PRODUCTS, PROCESSES, AND SERVICES

Those examples and hundreds more led Stan Davis and me to develop a series of attributes that characterize knowledge-based products and services. Many of them were published in one of the first articles in the *Harvard Business Review* on the coming of knowledge-based business, which he and I contributed. The article describes many products now on the market.[6] The six top attributes of knowledge products and services are shown in the adjoining table.

LAWS OF THE KNOWLEDGE ECONOMY

Older firms understood and mastered the dynamics of the industrial economy in order to succeed. Those dynamics, or "laws," emphasize long production runs and economies of scale; relatively long periods of economic well-being followed by slowdowns in growth; the law of diminishing returns (a yield that beyond a certain point fails to increase in proportion to additional investments of labor or capital); and the belief in vertical integration (do everything in-house). In the knowledge economy, many of those long-held beliefs no longer hold. Now companies have to learn and tune into the dynamics of a knowledge economy.

Mass Customization

Flexible technology systems make possible the ability to customize each unit on the production line. Nowhere is this clearer than on modern automobile assembly lines, like Saturn's but also like many others, such as the Corvette plant in Bowling Green, Kentucky, or the NUMMI plant in Freemont, California. On the Corvette line, you can read the name of the buyer for a special production car that is made right alongside the standard shipments.

This holds true for other industries as well. RR Donnelley has the ability to print catalogues by the millions. It can also customize the catalogues for a particular geographic region or for particular zip codes and to imprint your name onto certain products like T-shirts or sweaters. For important customers, the printing process can be set up ready to go, but then can insert last-minute price changes with less than twenty-four hours' notice. That means Toys-R-Us can wait until it sees the prices from Fisher Price before making a final decision on its own.

Thus while long production runs are still valued, each item in the production run can be customized to individual specifications at virtually no extra cost to the customer. The goal of such mass customization is a production lot size of one. The technology that makes this possible is the application of the new knowledge of miniaturized chips and wireless communications to the manufacturing process.

Boom and Bust

The knowledge embedded into products, processes, and services can be of two types. Some is general knowledge, unpatented or unpatentable, and is generally available for competitors to copy or enhance. Other knowledge in the form of patents is protected. It is intellectual property designed to protect entrepreneurs and reward them for their ideas.

In both cases, however, it is increasingly difficult to prevent competitors from using key ideas that bestow an advantage. Microsoft's Windows operating system, for example, has the look and feel of the proprietary Macintosh system. Court rulings, however, in this and other similar cases, have gone against the original designer. It is conceptually difficult to grant even a temporary monopoly advantage to knowledge that is seen as intangible and public as opposed to a new product based on new materials, like the micro PCMs, which is tangible, private, and patented.

That means knowledge products have a short shelf life. After they are on the market for a short time, nimble competitors develop an even better use. That happens constantly in the high-tech industry, where a Motorola microprocessor of the highest speed is outdone by an Intel microprocessor that operates yet a bit faster.

When the economy or large parts of it have products and services of ever shorter life cycles, it leads to a situation where the overall economy may continue to grow but a company's position within the economy is subject to boom-and-bust pressures.

Ubiquity Before Profitability

A certain class of knowledge products fall into the category of universal use and become a standard for the industry. These are cases where technical standardization is more important than technological superiority. Such products follow Brian Arthur's law of increasing returns rather than diminishing returns. Examples are the QWERTY keyboard mentioned earlier and the VHS standard for videotapes, which superseded Betamax. Other cases are telephones, postal delivery, and computer operating systems. In those three cases, the underlying economic principle is "ubiquity before profitability." That is, the service or product has to be universal or ubiquitous first, after which the company can realize profitability. The difference in the three cases is that the relationship between the costs of ubiquity and the potential for profitability are not the same.

Ubiquity was difficult to achieve in an industrial economy because prices were tightly tied to the costs of providing service, and regulated monopoly was a way to break the link. Thus legal monopolies were created for telephones, postal service, and some utilities. American Telephone and Telegraph and Sweden Post were in this category.

In a knowledge economy, the dynamic between ubiquity and profitability changes, because prices become detached from the cost of providing the service. For example, the cost to Sweden Post to deliver its very first letters in Stockholm was high; the subsequent cost to provide ubiquitous service, say north of the Arctic Circle, was even higher.

Microsoft's Windows is different. The cost for the first copy of Windows (or any software) is high, but the cost of subsequent copies is minuscule. That means ubiquity, while difficult to achieve, is easier to maintain. And once ubiquity is present, profitability is assured.

The ubiquity/profitability relationship has to be explored in much greater depth than we have done so far. The Microsoft/Netscape charges of unfair competition are being played out with rules from an industrial era rather than understandings from a mindset of a knowledge economy. Here it is important to advance our understanding sooner rather than later, because the Microsoft case will pale in significance to DNA and cloning cases in a biotechnology future.

Unprecedented Partnering

Whereas industrial companies strive to control as much of their business as possible by doing everything themselves, in the new economy there is no way any one company can have all the knowledge needed under one roof.

Ford Motor Company's River Rouge plant, "The Rouge," became the symbol for the industrial process known as vertical integration. Iron ore taken from barges went into the entrance to the plant at one end and finished cars came out of the plant at the other end. While The Rouge still exists, Ford no longer strives to bring every part of the process in-house. All car companies have extensive partnerships with suppliers and vendors and prefer to operate on just-in-time principles rather than hold inventory, which was part of the in-house system.

Extending one's knowledge through partnering makes sense where the knowledge changes rapidly and where specialization in a particular field of knowledge is seen as necessary. The Massey Ferguson GPS tractor has these characteristics: The tractor comes from Perkins Engines; the computer comes from MF Autotronic Systems; the link to GPS comes from Electronic Linkage Control; and now Massey Ferguson has been acquired by AGCO Corporation.

Questions of who owns which knowledge is a legal issue that is yet to be properly resolved. In professional service firms like KPMG or other consulting companies, the legal restrictions and requirements may be severe. Recent GM cases involving its competitor Volkswagen also point to the limits of taking knowledge and inside information from one company to another. Some cases have shown that even when an employee moves from one firm to a competitor with no intention of revealing critical information, courts have ruled that damages can be awarded to the first company. Such cases are indications that for the knowledge business to thrive, we will have to become much more sophisticated about intellectual property rights, copyright laws, patents, and related issues whose legal, social, and economic rationales were all worked out in industrial times.

Now such issues are changing. How well they can be updated to reflect the concerns that arise in an economy based on knowledge will play a major role in realizing the potential of knowledge communities.

CAN LEGACY COMPANIES
ENTER THE KNOWLEDGE BUSINESS?

With all the media attention devoted to Microsoft, Netscape, and others in the first major antitrust case of the information economy—and with all the books devoted to new companies like Amazon.com—one gets the impression that only "green field" companies that start from scratch are capable of entering the knowledge business. The case of Saturn, which had to be launched in Tennessee separate from GM in Detroit, serves to reinforce that view. However, two-thirds of the examples of emerging knowledge businesses cited in this chapter come from traditional companies, even if they team up with new technology firms to achieve their goals. Legacy firms, to the extent they can be flexible, have the advantages of financial power and market reach that elude many startups. Nonetheless, legacy firms have obstacles to overcome. Most of them are cultures where new ideas and ways of doing business are resisted by the rank-and-file managers.

AT&T provides an important case. Here is a legacy company founded as a legal monopoly more than a hundred years ago that is partly industrial based (stringing and maintaining telephone lines; occasional flareups with its union, the Communication Workers of America; a company culture that is slow to change) and partly knowledge-based (wireless and Internet protocol offerings, smart services like language translation, a rich tradition of research and innovation left from Bell Labs-turned-Lucent). To develop its knowledge business, AT&T has spent several years building and developing six to eight knowledge communities in the division that serves the company's top 2,600 global corporate clients. We turn now to a closer look at knowledge communities.

Chapter Four

Knowledge Communities as Entrepreneurial Ventures

*A honeybee colony
resembles a big corporation that goes after the big markets.
In contrast, a bumblebee colony
relies on entrepreneurial initiative.*

—Adapted from *Bumblebee Economics,* Bernd Heinrich, Harvard University Press

Never underestimate
the power
of a small but committed
group of people to change the world.
Indeed, it is the only thing that ever has.

—Margaret Mead

KNOWLEDGE COMMUNITIES IN ACTION

The Sunday morning at 6:10 A.M. when the joint venture with British Telecom[1] was announced, six AT&T knowledge communities swung into action. They engaged three thousand executives, mostly from sales and marketing. They started with a conference call to corporate leaders and subject matter experts on open microphones plus fax and e-mail connections through the IKE website so that everyone could get questions addressed. The call was repeated three times—first for Asia Pacific, then for Europe, finally for the Americas. By the end of the week, with daily conference calls and constant contact with IKE—which an infrastructure team was updating every two hours around the clock—AT&T community members were fully prepared to make sales calls and submit proposals for new business worldwide. The coordination, speed, and accuracy of the sales brigade were comparable with the hundred-hour rush to victory of the Allies in Desert Storm.

In addition to the Client Business Managers Community (the largest knowledge community with 750 people), members of the Data Community, Corporate Networks, Wireless, Call Centers, and International Communities pulled with them eleven thousand more AT&T managers working in other areas of AT&T. They discovered that IKE was a better source of information and knowledge than the best newswire services and it was 100 percent devoted to the biggest business move their company had made in a decade, with information critical for their own individual roles and success.

In the past an operation of that magnitude would have consumed months or even years of study, preparation, and training. The information and knowledge would have filled endless three-ring binders from headquarters which would have been delivered by armies of postal workers to repositories in each AT&T sales branch office. For example, it took up to six months for a sales branch office to complete its training to start selling wireless services.

Each knowledge community was involved in the action on the joint venture with British Telecom in a way tailored to its job. The 550 members of the Data Community had to roll out global Internet Protocol services. The 120 members of the International Community had a new assignment to ensure the integrity of cross-border corporate communications across EC national borders.[2] The 300-plus members of the Corporate Networks Community had to ensure all the voice networks of major U.S.-based multinationals now worked reliably though the British system, which, as any American who has called to or lived in England knows, is significantly different from the United States.

What lay behind that impressive performance? What did Pat Traynor, the vice president of marketing and the architect of the knowledge communities, have to put into place to make them work? "We were screening for specialists in our fifty sales branch offices as part of a Sales Transformation program I had initiated and my colleague John Wood operationalized. As he identified specialists for the six technical areas, they became members of Knowledge Communities. It may sound odd, but I built the infrastructure starting with membership lists.

"So for example, one hundred sales executives in the Phoenix office had to align into a knowledge community and became specialists. It took a whole year to transform all fifty branch offices across the country. Each individual went from selling all products to specializing in a single one."

The IKE system is the anchor of the knowledge communities. It requires a full-time editor for each community who interacts with subject matter experts and distills, posts, and publishes high-value information, which is the knowledge base of community members. "I originally underestimated this knowledge management function," Pat says. "If we provide out-of-date information just once, the Knowledge Community gets a black eye. If we do it twice, we lose that community member possibly for good."

Sami AlBanna, Chief Architect of the Corporate Knowledge Program for Computer Sciences Corporation, agrees with Pat Traynor. In a challenge coming to be known as the AlBanna test for knowledge management, Sami says that if only 10 percent—two out of twenty hits—is out of date or otherwise obsolete, managers will not use the system.

Updating and evaluating information are not easy. In the AT&T/BT example, such information started with the announcements from CEO Mike Armstrong. It then included official press releases, Q&A sessions (downloadable in written, oral, or video form), sample scripts to be used with customers, a competitive analysis of BT, a letter from Armstrong/Zeglis to all employees, a letter from Armstrong/Vallance[3] to the biggest of the 2,600 best clients, lists of who had received the letter, and when, including a cross-reference to the Client Business Manager in charge of the account, financial reactions from analysts and market and media reactions from the *Wall Street Journal, Washington Post, New York Times,* London *Financial Times,* CNNfn, and other network media providers. All that was updated every two hours, twenty-four hours a day, until ten days after the original Sunday announcement, when things returned to their normal pace: updates when needed and a conference call each week.

The display opposite, printed with permission, is the Hot Zone section of IKE that shows what members of all knowledge communities could receive by Day Three of the AT&T/BT announcement. By Day Ten, each specific knowledge community could get analyses, presentations, and proposals specific to its interests. The Data Community, for example, could learn BT's offerings in high-speed packet-switching networks for intra–data center communication among a client's multiple data and backup centers.

Most community members log onto the IKE system every morning and again at the end of every afternoon. Their total is about an hour a day on IKE, depending on what they are working on. IKE was designed for three thousand community members. Now fourteen thousand use it—that's 11,000 users plus the 3,000 community members. The day after the AT&T/BT announcement, IKE got 134,944 hits. The average is 100,000 hits a day.

In the early conference calls shortly after its founding, the Client Business Managers Community had almost all 750 members on the calls every other week. Now participation has dropped to about half that number, unless an important issue like compensation or new offers is being discussed. Pat Traynor sees this participation rate as normal for such a large community.

Q&A is an important part of the community system. Subject matter experts used to answer all the questions submitted. Now about 30 percent are answered by other community members, attesting to the power of group learning and teaching. In the past field sales people used to say, "All headquarters marketing does is send me mountains of information whether I need it or not. When I call them to ask for something I need, they don't return my calls quickly. If I send THEM some valuable information, I never know where it goes or what they do with it." But now: "With the knowledge communities, everyone knows what the questions and answers are. Today I get answers when I need them through multiple sources and only to the questions that I'm interested in."

In addition to the editing function, each knowledge community has a

Hot Zone
INFORMATION & KNOWLEDGE EXCHANGE

SiteMap | **Search** | To Communities ▼ | **Help** | **Feedback**

AT&T/BT Joint Venture

AT&T announced on July 26, 1998 @6:10 am ET,
our plans to create a new Global Venture with BT

Support Materials and Updates	Customer Materials

• **Sales Advisory** (7/26)
• **Recommended Action Plans**
  - **GM**
  - **CBM**
	• **Customer Contact Call Flow**
	• **Customer Basic Presentation** (ppt)
	
	• **Technology Presentation** (ppt)
	• **Technical White Paper** (doc)
	
	• Letters
	  Mike Armstrong to CEOs
	  - **View Online**
	  - **Download** (doc)
	  - **CEO Recipient List** (xls)
	  AT&T Officers to CIOs
	  - **View Online**
	  - **Download** (doc)
	  Armstrong to other contacts
	  (for Account Team use)
	  - **View Online**
	  - **Download** (doc)
	
	• **Officer Customer Contact List**

AT&T Global Home Page "Your resource for information and knowledge about AT&T's global business"	

Q&A
 	
• **Customer/Account Team Q&A** (7/27)
• **Talking Points and General Q&A** (7/27)
 	
• **Follow-up Q&A** (7/28-8/6)
  - **Search by Date**
  - **Search by Category**
 	
• **Submit Questions and Feedback**
  - **Email**
  - **Fax**
	Market and Media Reactions
	• **Wall Street Journal** (7/27)
	• **Washington Post** (7/27)
	• **New York Times** (7/27)
	• **CNNfn** (7/27)
	• **Other Reactions** (AT&T Today - 7/27)
	• **Broadband Networkg News** (8/4)
	• **Network World (1)** (8/5)
	• **Network World (2)** (8/5)

Initial Announcements • **Press Release** (7/26) • **Armstrong Audix Message** (7/27) (wav*) • **Press Conference Replay** (wav) • **Armstrong/Zeglis Employee Letter** • **All-Employee Broadcast** (7/27) • **Armstrong/Vallance Interview** (7/26) • **Follow-up Broadcasts/Q&A Sessions** (*Click here to download **RealPlayer 5.0**)	**Supplemental Information** • **BT home page** • **Concert home page** • **Joint Venture home page**

full time leader or facilitator. Originally, they were people who were part of Pat's marketing team. She reoriented them into community facilitation. That takes a new set of skills, "especially leadership, listening, and reaching out," Traynor says.

What is the result of all this? Posted in the first column of the web-site under "Results" is revenue growth. "We have double-digit revenue growth for Global Services by the end of our second year. This is up from 4 to 6 percent over the past. This is equal to or higher than all competitors in this area. While not all the growth is due to knowledge communities, sales people will tell you it was a critical enabler," according to Pat.

How did she start? "I just did it. It's a difficult concept to describe tactically early in its development because nobody gets it until you do it. So with continuous communication about our progress, we continued." She had good business reasons for doing it: Technology was changing faster than anyone could keep up with; clients were demanding that AT&T salespeople know both their business and how new technology applied to it; and traditional training methods were failing. "We had to have a better way to serve our clients. Knowledge communities provide just that. When Peter Senge suggested we start the development of Knowledge Communities at the grass-roots level, I listened. It proved to be a sound way to let success build upon success."

Looking over a several-year period, executives at AT&T depict in the accompanying chart their journey toward self-sustaining communities, which they envision as a multiyear journey requiring a vision with consistent leadership.[4]

Without the vision and long-term strategy for building real knowledge communities, it would have been easy to create "information communities" where groups would have been able to share information predominantly from headquarters to field. While that would have been a vast improvement from traditional e-mail systems, it is still a far cry from true knowledge communities, which are capable of rapid responses to changing market conditions and able to contribute to increased sales and greater customer responsiveness.

"Our vision at AT&T called for a major shift from Headquarters running these communities, defining their agenda, answering questions, and solving their problems to a 'Self-sustaining Community.' This self-sustaining community is uniquely defined by peer-to-peer support—people rapidly answering one another's questions, freely sharing best practices and helping one another rapidly solve customer problems."

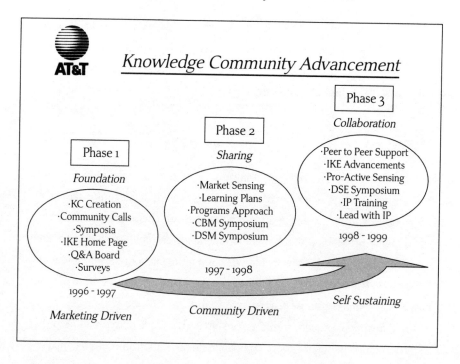

LESSONS LEARNED

The AT&T case illustrates one model of building and managing knowledge communities that is rooted in the business demands of their field. Others—for example at the World Bank or for KPMG's Tax community—are different. One thing they have in common: A community of people is the best way to handle complex and fast-changing dynamics in any field of the knowledge business. And once you're in the knowledge business, you find you need knowledge communities to run them.

If knowledge can be embedded in just about any traditional product or service, then every company in the world should be pondering the possibilities of entering the knowledge business. But don't stop there. Don't just start a division to launch a product with a chip in it. That would be the old way of starting a new industrial product line. Instead, build a knowledge community.

Another lesson from the AT&T example is that its communities are organized like a portfolio of entrepreneurial ventures. They don't require someone from the hierarchy to tell them what to do. They don't need to wait for instructions. Instead, they need to understand a new opportunity and new challenge (like the BT joint venture) and take it from there. I believe that a basic principle and guideline for building knowledge communities is to organize them by the laws of entrepreneurship.

THE SMALL BUSINESS IN A BIG ORGANIZATION

Organize your knowledge communities as an entrepreneur would—as Pat Traynor did. Doing so will give your company what it needs most—radical innovation—and will result in communities that are exciting, entrepreneurial, and highly profitable. Members of a knowledge community should emulate entrepreneurs, acting less like followers and more like founders and builders. When that happens, you will have succeeded in getting the best of both worlds: the small business in a big organization.

Many people equate entrepreneurship with a single person and his or her startup company. But like rivers, companies do not start in any one place, except to people with a need to simplify. The old simple view of singlehanded startups doesn't square with the facts, certainly not in today's complex world, if it ever did earlier. Ask any entrepreneur. All but the most insanely egotistical will tell you whose and how much support was needed to accomplish their dreams.

As MIT's Jim Utterback puts it: "Successful innovators have able collaborators. George Eastman had chemist Henry Reichenbach; Edison had mechanic Charles Batchelor; and Henry Ford relied on the engineering management know-how of Charles Sorenson." Revolutions can be led by a single general, but none are won without an army of soldiers.

Like being on the island of Saturn in the sea of General Motors, belonging to defenders of the future can be an inspiring and motivating experience. It can unlock the potential trapped in the byways of the hierarchies of traditional companies. When you're wondering how to start with knowledge communities, think first of entrepreneurial startups. When you're pondering how to organize knowledge communities, think what an entrepreneur would do. When you're stumped on how to overcome barriers that crop up, ask yourself what George Eastman, Thomas Edison, or Henry Ford would have done. They would not have hesitated to start a new venture. Rather than ask permission, they would ask forgiveness if challenged. On topics of crucial importance to their business, they would act, as CSC Chief Knowledge Architect Sami AlBanna puts it, like "thought leaders, not like 'knowledge functionaries.'"

To get started in building knowledge communities, we return to our old friends from Chapter 1: innovation theory and the four steps to community.

FOUR STAGES IN ORGANIZING AROUND KNOWLEDGE

We can identify four stages organizations go through to get to knowledge communities. They start with (1) the status quo—stovepipes—and then move to (2) sharing information, (3) cooperation, and finally (4) community. (See graphic on page 88.)

1. Most older companies are plagued by "stovepipes," or lack of vision beyond one's own function. Firms in the stovepipe state have a culture of "every man for himself." This mode of operation works so well in industrial settings that companies wanting to dismantle their stovepipes now find them nearly indestructible.

2. At the second stage companies form task forces with a mandate to work together and share ideas on what needs to be done to share information better. Unfortunately, the culture doesn't change much. It remains a problem, and task force members are discouraged. Most corporate employees are still obsessed with how to get more pieces from a shrinking pie. Worse, task forces are often limited in time and scope—underpowered for the job. Many companies are still sharing-challenged by this basic step into simple sharing.

3. At stage three, companies form teams with directives for cooperation. However, cooperation is something not possible to force. It's easier to form teams with a focus on the customer than it is to have teams focus on internal processes. But for all their shortcomings, teams are a giant step up from lone individuals in the stovepipes of the first stage.

4. At stage four, companies explore organizing into knowledge communities. They start with specialization, as AT&T did, or by identifying communities of practice. Those exist informally in just about every company, as the work

from IRL indicates. Peter Henschel, executive director of IRL, says they are "those highly informal groups of people that develop a shared way of working together to accomplish some activity." Further, the IRL work shows that learning takes place in communities of practice, while failure to learn often comes from being excluded from a community of practice, and knowledge depends on engagement in a community, which contributes strongly to our identities. Identifying your communities of practice and giving them the support they need is the best way to nurture and grow knowledge communities. Pat Traynor, for example, gave them full-time editors, a community facilitator, and the IKE knowledge management system.

Companies in the fourth stage embrace a vision of knowledge communities more than just a next step beyond teams or task forces. They speak to people's desire to belong, to grow, and to identify with something larger than themselves and something more than a company's brand name. While appealing to our warmth and passion, this vision is also subject to the cold business fact that any change that does not prove its value is short-lived. Communities organized around the principles of entrepreneurship have the best chance at success. In the AT&T example, if the knowledge communities fail to sustain their high revenue growth and are perceived as just "feel good" exercises, the CEO would cut them out.

The four stages of stovepipe, sharing, cooperation, and community ap-

FOUR STAGES OF ORGANIZATIONAL DEVELOPMENT

Stages	(1) Stovepipe	(2) Sharing	(3) Cooperation	(4) Community
Technology	Desktop PCs	Internal e-mail	One-to-one customer connections	Interconnected to customers and suppliers
Connectivity	Unconnected	Departmentally connected	Cross-functionally connected	Enterprise-wide connected
Culture	Every man for himself	Get more of the pie	Sell the pie externally	Grow a bigger pie for all
Organization	Individual	Task force	Team	Knowledge community

pear at the top of the accompanying table. The typical characteristics described above are summarized at each stage in terms of organization, culture, connectivity, and technology. Stovepipes are organized by individual functions, their culture is every man for himself, and they are essentially unconnected to one another, even if they are outfitted with desktop PCs. That is true for nearly all industrial manufacturing and service organizations in the two decades after WWII and still describes far too many companies functioning alongside the knowledge economy today.

Companies at the next stage have just begun sharing—probably not yet knowledge, but at least they share important information and results of their analyses. Managers serve on task forces. Departmentally, employees are connected with one another. They have internal e-mail. The culture, however, is still focused on getting more from a finite pie, a value that works against deeper sharing.

Companies at the cooperation stage have usually experienced cross-functional teams enough to be able to manage their own affairs. In sports, team members are on the same side. In companies, however, teams that disagree with one another are so common that, "in maintaining the appearance of cohesion," as Peter Senge puts it, they can be "incredibly proficient at keeping themselves from learning."

The fourth stage of organizing around knowledge is the knowledge community. In order to get them well connected and culturally supportive, you've got to think like an entrepreneur, talk like an entrepreneur, and act like an entrepreneur. The next table shows some of the attributes of innovation and entrepreneurship one looks for at each of the stages.

INNOVATION IN LARGE COMPANIES?

As we saw in the first chapter, when new technologies threaten the stability of established markets, most large firms redouble their efforts to make the old technology more efficient. Faced with the competition from new methods of refrigeration, the Tudor Ice Company continued to invest in better saws, sleds, and ships for nearly twenty-five years, until its demise.

Of the five big typewriter producers before World War II—Remington,

ENTREPRENEURIAL ATTRIBUTES AT THE FOUR STAGES

Stages	(1) Stovepipe	(2) Sharing	(3) Cooperation	(4) Community
Business purpose	Produce traditional product, provide usual services	Short-term improvements to traditional products	Customer solutions	Creation of new markets and new enterprise; Co-create future business together
Metrics	Material & time costs; People = cost	Cutting costs, improving efficiencies	Increasing revenue, business, improving effectiveness	Building new business, adding new value; People = investment
Process of innovation	Solo "Garage shop"	Incremental changes	External spinoffs	Radical innovation Internal venturing
Behavior of manager as entrepreneur	"Skunk works" Secretive Hide knowledge	More research Gather better information	Create new knowledge for promoting own group	Create whole new enterprises

Royal, Smith, Underwood, and IBM—only IBM was able to survive the shift first to electric typewriters and then to word processors, which were the death knell for the other four traditional typewriter companies. That is what leads Jim Utterback to the conclusion that failure to innovate is a prime source of business failure.[5]

BEST OF BOTH WORLDS—
SMALL BUSINESS IN LARGE ORGANIZATIONS

As the case of IBM in the above example shows, not all legacy companies are destined to fail. A few large corporations are considered entrepreneurial and have been able to achieve the attributes outlined above. 3M, Corning, General Electric, Kodak, and Volvo are examples of large companies that have been able to incorporate purposeful innovation into their work. They do so by organizing into groups that are small, fast, and innovative—three of the six "laws" of entrepreneurship. When they succeed, they get the best of both worlds, which is many small businesses in one big organization.

Sweden Post, the country's second largest organization after Volvo, is reorganizing itself through an exercise called "The Workplace of the Twenty-first Century." By itself, that is neither new nor noteworthy. Many large firms have had future visions tied to the change of the century.[6] What is different at Sweden Post is the aspiration to organize into 1,500 small autonomous units under the rubric of "the small business in a big organization." The goal is continuous innovation from the small group combined with the inherent power of the large organization. This process is described further by Gösta Hägglund, an executive with Sweden Post, in his article contributed to *Smart Business*.

Skandia Insurance has a similar process, which in-house analyst Scott Hawkins describes as "mitosis," referring to the biological process by which cells continually split. Where there was one Skandia organization there are now five, and more are on the way. Such mitosis gives Skandia the financial benefits of organizational integration with the speed and responsiveness of entrepreneurial autonomy.

Getting a winning combination of small and large was difficult to achieve in the past. Usually, such arrangements broke down over disagreements about money and ownership. But in the knowledge age, alliances and partnerships have become more common. While questions of money and ownership are as important as ever, those who create new knowledge and develop new ideas are in a relatively stronger position. With knowledge as the chief factor of production, combining the powerful ideas of entrepreneurs with the extensive marketing of global corporations makes a strong business case.

Properly done, this is a win-win solution for the members of a knowledge community, as well as for the corporation of which they are an integral part. The laws of entrepreneurship give us some clues how.

THE LAWS OF ENTREPRENEURSHIP

There are six main principles, or "laws," of entrepreneurship, whose attributes are innovative, fast, and partnered (reliance on alliances), and small, opportunistic, and specialized.

Once when I was leading a seminar on innovation and entrepreneurship, I had forgotten my notes. I experienced one of those "senior moments" when my mind simply refused to recall something that was familiar to me. After an excruciating pause, I recovered enough to restart my mind. I vowed I would create a moniker to remember them correctly. Now when I have a senior moment, my mind recites "IFP–SOS."

> **"I"** for Innovative and the *Inc.* 500 (*Inc.* magazine's annual listing of the most successful small companies)
>
> **"F"** for Fast and *FAST* company magazine (*FAST* has monthly stories on successful firms both small and large, including Fortune 500s)
>
> **"P"** for Partnering between the *Inc.* 500 and the Fortune 500, which is a strategy to improve the fortunes of both.

So the IFP part refers to Innovative, Fast, and Partnering between the two. The second part is

> **"S"** for Small
> **"O"** for Opportunistic
> **"S"** for Specialized

The second trio of principles form SOS, the international call for help. The SOS is the signal that should go out when IFP knowledge communities get too large, too dull, and too bland, which can result from bureaucratic obstacles entrepreneurs fear from traditional managers.

STORYTELLING THAT ENHANCES ENTREPRENEURSHIP

All people have creation myths. For Hopi Indians, the story is of the First Tribe's emergence through a small hole in the earth known as the "sipapu," which was part of every Indian knowledge community or "kiva." For Christians, the creation myth is the Adam and Eve story in the Garden of Eden.

Creation myths have their counterparts in business. They are the stories of entrepreneurs, the founders whose innovations and idiosyncrasies are amplified in the telling and retelling of the stories. The story of how Hewlett and Packard started HP in a garage was so inspiring and powerful that when Steve Jobs started Apple with no garage for his motorcycle, he had to have a new story—his visit to Xerox PARC. For Bill Gates, the story pits small against big. College dropout Bill produces the MS-DOS operating system, which he offers to sell to Big Blue, who turns him down. Not once, but three times IBM had the chance to buy Microsoft and declined the opportunity, or so the story goes. With time, surely this story too will be amplified.

It is not important whether the creation stories are factually accurate, whether IBM had one chance or three chances to acquire MS-DOS, for example. Good storytellers often exaggerate or even recreate certain parts of the story to convey a basic principle—that Hewlett and Packard started from scratch, that Jobs was more agile than Xerox, or that Gates was more perceptive than IBM. What is important is that creation myths give people an identity. People want to know where they came from, what they themselves are made of, how they too can benefit by belonging to a group started by a hero or heroine. Thus what these stories also tell us is that entrepreneurs—people who can innovate and create something new—play a role in these stories equivalent to the tradition that goes back all the way to the gods and goddesses of ancient Greece and Rome.

The American economy is strongly entrepreneurial: More new jobs are added by the *Inc.* 500 than by Fortune 500 companies. As Peter Drucker puts it, America has gone from a "managerial to an entrepreneurial" economy. But an increasing number of other countries and cultures have economies that are entrepreneurial and stories that celebrate their entrepreneurs. Japan, too long stereotyped as an economy of copycats, has stories like the Buddhist monk of the sixteenth century who started the business of making religious dolls that grew into one of the country's largest clothing manufacturers today. Likewise, the Chinese are known as entrepreneurs, particularly the overseas Chinese who run the small shops in many countries abroad. Germans, the founders of SAP, for example—the mega successful, enterprise-wide software company—also have their creation stories in business.

Just like people in midlife crisis, legacy companies have forgotten their life songs. For all practical purposes, they have forgotten their startup stories and the basic principles on which they were founded. They could benefit by recalling that there was a time when Ford was entrepreneurial, when Prudential was not so prudent, when Xerox revolutionized the future rather than fumbled it. A former Shell executive, Ari de Geus, recounts in his book *The Living Company* the life histories of those special companies more than two centuries old that have survived to the present day. Recalling their creation stories gives current managers the inspiration to recreate again.[7]

> **THE HUMBLE-BEE**
>
> **Wiser far than human seer,**
> **Yellow-breeched philosopher!**
> **Seeing only what is fair,**
> **Sipping only what is sweet,**
> **Thou dost mock at fate and care,**
> **Leave the chaff, and take the wheat.**
>
> —Ralph Waldo Emerson

Knowledge communities—groups seeking to apply new knowledge to their work—are a natural home for entrepreneurship. The new knowledge they create contains the seeds for change; the community they represent embraces the urge to belong. Properly organized and self-managed, knowledge communities can be the basis for the entrepreneurship and renewal that legacy companies urgently need.

THE PORTFOLIO OF ENTREPRENEURSHIP

3M, Corning, Kodak, and Volvo all have "portfolios" of small entrepreneurial companies in which they have investments. Some enterprises, like the specialty chemical firm Perstorp in Sweden and the high-tech electronics firm Dynatech in the United States, have successfully built whole companies on an integrated collection of entrepreneurial startups. The new firms benefit from the synergy and experience of the older firms and from the market power that the total firm can provide.

For example, Volvo invested in a small firm that had invented a new way to weld together huge petroleum pipelines. The process, however, was dangerous. On its own, the new firm could not get commercial insurance. As a member of the portfolio, however, insurance with Volvo guarantees resolved the matter.

The vision of knowledge communities is thus more than urging each community to be entrepreneurial. The ultimate goal is to organize your company as a portfolio of knowledge communities that act and behave as small companies—innovative, fast, and partnered with the mother corporation and with each other. Here are some steps you can take to make your knowledge communities entrepreneurial.

THE BUILDER'S GUIDE TO
ENTREPRENEURIAL KNOWLEDGE COMMUNITIES

Building knowledge communities is the new work of every leader, not just the CEO but people at any level in the organization who aspire to build. Gary Hamel, in proposing ways to transform the strategic planning process to make it revolutionary and truly strategic, suggests to start by focusing on the following people:

> The young, because they have greatest interest in the future
> Newcomers, because they have fresh ideas
> Those farthest from headquarters, because they have less of the old
> orthodoxy in them

Those same suggestions can apply to the process of starting knowledge communities. To them can be added the following guidelines:

Identify your communities of practice. Find out which communities of practice already exist. They are the groups that embed within themselves how work gets done. They are the process knowledge groups that work together to accomplish a task. In airlines, they are the check-in people, the flight attendants, the pilots, and baggage crew. At hotels, they are the "housekeepers, food servers, certified nursing assistants, engineers, front desk clerks," as Helena Light Hadley describes them for Marriott (see Appendix). In the AT&T example, they are neither horizontal nor vertical slices of the company, but rather virtual networks.

Put motivated networkers in charge. Communities are held together by relationships. Find people who are good at managing people relationships. Often they are networkers, people who know lots of people in the company. IRL's Susan Stucky refers to them as "knowledge brokers." Their job is essentially to be world-class facilitators. They have to be able to enroll people into a new way of working.

Sometimes people think a community implies "of the people, for the people, by the people." Sounds great. It doesn't work, especially at the beginning. It's an ideal toward which a community can aspire. At the beginning, a community needs a community organizer. Otherwise, the urgent drives out the important, and nothing ever seems to get done. As Gary High from Saturn quotes from a famous coach: "When all is said and done, more is often said than done."

The type of networker needed often comes from the people who populate positions like "director of business opportunities" or "director of strategic development." They are people with any title (or none in companies that don't use them) who are always looking, visiting, listening, and learning. One of Prudential's job descriptions says: "Reputation for positive, constructive working relationships with people outside his/her immediate work unit (trust, confidence, pursuit of win-win solutions)."

Start simple with a clear mandate for innovation. Communities need an identity, a mission, and goals just as a corporation does. The simpler and more readily understandable those are, the better. Start simple and build to more complex interconnections. Simplicity in purpose and goals is critical for another reason. The community always knows who's in and who's not. That's part of community life. In cases where this comes into question, the group will want to look at its most basic purposes as a way of reflecting what it wants to happen.

The mandate for innovation means "send out scouts to welcome discontinuity." Communities are naturals for designating good explorers to go check out what's coming in from another field that may represent a discontinuity in the community's work. Ask the scouts to welcome discontinuity. A time-tested practice of ancient native wisdom is to go through a process of severance, transition, and reincorporation. Let the scouts go out from the community (severance), learn the new ways (transition), and come back bearing gifts for their people.

Emphasize the partnership mentality. There's a difference between calling a group a community and acting like one. Community partners look first to the relationship and only later to the particular transaction. For people accustomed to operating in a supplier–buyer or vendor–client mode, the emphasis on relationship selling as opposed to dealmaking comes hard. To make relating successful requires taking a long-term view. Maybe this particular transaction is not the way you want it, but over the long run it's worth the temporary sacrifice.

"As much as anything, it's an attitude." Many from successful community experiences voice it that way. Communities develop cultures, ways of doing things together. Wherever possible, the facilitators and leaders need to emphasize over and over again that this is a partnership. Community comes from "cum," the Latin word for "with." Community members are co-conspirators. They need to treat one another not as the same but as equals. To make a community work, members have to see each other as complements in a shared relationship. As much as anything, it's an attitude.

Develop a team of champions outside the community. Every group doing new things needs a champion. A champion is someone who believes in the idea of the community and works to get it accepted, then implemented. Champions explain, clarify, promote, and when necessary defend. They are like spark plugs, they take the heat.

Champions are rare and extremely valuable. They often get promoted beyond a community's purview. Sound advice to communities is to have a team of champions so that when your most effective champion retires, gets moved, or is promoted, the role of champion is still intact. That is a type of re-dundancy that is worth the effort.

Communicate frequently. An attitude of NIH—Not Invented Here—is a pow-erful deterrent to good communities. An attitude of NRTC—Never Return Telephone Calls—can kill community life. The leading cause of death of other-wise healthy communities is lack of communication.

Percy Barnevik, CEO of Asea, Brown, Boveri (ABB) in Europe instituted a management policy that all communications receive a response within 24–48 hours—no matter where, no matter what. The response doesn't have to be the answer. It can be a response saying I understand the issue and I'm working on it.

True partners learn to share bad news as well as good. The operative word is share. What seems like bad news to one is an opportunity to someone else in the community. Business executives often speak about "responsibility," which is always important. "Respond-ability," or one's willingness and persis-tence in responding and communicating, is equally important.

Think long-term, deliver short-term. Getting long-term results or fostering a long-lived community is often best accomplished by delivering short-term re-sults. That may seem counterintuitive at first glance, but it's the stuff of rela-tionships. It's the little things that count. Trust is built on the tangible experience of shared, easy-to-identify results.

Once when dealing with entrepreneurs who were part of Corning's port-folio of small companies, I heard one of their champions say, "You people are out trying to hit home runs for us. Just give me some singles or a bunt. Just put someone on base so I can explain to others how you're contributing." So in-stead of creating a full-blown program, the entrepreneurial group focused on delivering a progress report. The principle: Think long, deliver short. Think years, deliver next week. Deliver business value now, focus on change in the long term.

Value people. This is a story from a Texas preacher about a father who could neither read nor write and his son Willis, who had just received a diploma:

"Goin' to buy a new car, Dad. I don't need you no more." Willis goes to the bank to arrange a car loan with his diploma under his arm. The banker looks at the young man and asks, "What do ya have for collateral?"

"Co-what?" asks Willis. At that moment, his father shuffles in. "That's my son Willis" he says proudly. "I'll sign for the loan."

Willis protests. "But father you can't even write your name. You're illiterate. All you can do is make an 'X'.

The banker smiles and says, "But it's a mighty good X, son."

Chapter Five

Manage Knowledge so Your Chief Knowledge Officer Doesn't Have to Do It for You

Bee apiaries should never be lost ever again.

—Erickson and Buchmann, "Using the Global Positioning System (GPS) to Establish, Find and Relocate Honey Bee Apiaries," USDA-ARS Carl Hayden Bee Research Center

The basic challenge is
to build a critical mass of healthy communities
so that larger systems self-organize and work effectively.

—Esther Dyson, *Release 2.0: A Design for Living in the Digital Age*

KM OR IT?

Led by consulting and computer firms, many legacy companies are spending millions to develop knowledge management ("KM") systems. Most are standalones. As such, they miss the payoff point: Knowledge management is a tool by which knowledge communities are built, maintained, and operated, and the payoff is profit in the knowledge business. IKE, for example, is the backbone of AT&T's knowledge communities, and its payoff is double-digit revenue growth in six knowledge businesses. The closer you can link knowledge management to knowledge communities and the knowledge business, the more your KM efforts will be successful and profitable.

Too many so-called KM systems are Information Technology ("IT") projects in disguise. As such, they are technical successes undermined by cultural shortcomings. Knowledge management without knowledge communities is like personal computers without the people: In pilot tests they work, in practice they go unused.

Let's take a closer look at managing knowledge—the process of capturing, sharing, and leveraging a company's collective expertise.

KNOWLEDGE MANAGEMENT

Oxymorons—two contradictory words combined, like "short-term remedy" or, in the old joke, "government intelligence"—have the ability simultaneously to stimulate and stump us. So it is with "knowledge management." This slippery quality is why nearly every business says it is developing a knowledge management initiative and at the same time denying that it's possible. Let's convert this stumbling block to a stepping stone.

What are certainly manageable are knowledge environments. Incentives for sharing knowledge; buying, selling, leasing, or hiring formal representations of knowledge such as books or patents—those things can be managed. Those artifacts are formal, codified explicit knowledge. Ironically, we can manage the explicit, but it's the tacit where the real value is.

As Larry Prusak says, knowledge runs on a continuum from tacit to explicit. It's easy to manage and measure the explicit but nearly impossible to do the same for tacit. He tells the story of the GM assembly line worker who masterfully fits doors to the chassis but can't articulate how he does it. He does it by feel. His body knows but his head does not. Or, as Michael Polanyi puts it, "We know more than we can say." Managers who rely on intuition—compressed expertise—often find themselves in this situation. They "know" what is right but can't explain why.

Engineers, economists, and accountants believe there's an answer to every question. Many believe there is *one* answer, or at least one best answer. There are situations where that is true, such as domains where there is a lot of explicit codified knowledge—accounting, for example. But the biggest mistake a company can make is to assume that the certainty that engineers develop or that economists profess applies to all fields of human behavior.

An obstacle to learning and knowledge is to see the company as a giant machine where there is no space for the reflection, judgment, passion, and exploration essential to knowledge creation and its eventual "management." As we know from the history of dictators, it's impossible to command and control what's inside someone's head or whether he or she will consent to the action that turns information into knowledge. But many companies try to do just that. That is true especially for technology-oriented firms that mistakenly assume the passion and knowledge they bring to building a quality computer out of components can be used to build a quality organization out of people.

There is no knowledge without people, and there are no people without culture. Whether knowledge management, the knowledge business, or your knowledge communities are sustainable and successful is a question of culture. The number one question about culture is trust. How do we create and maintain trust—the greatest gift to management of all time? A bond of solid trust is worth more than a bunch of signed contracts.

CHIEF KNOWLEDGE OFFICERS

There's an old Zen saying: "When the student is ready, the master appears."

In many companies, a Chief Knowledge Officer has appeared, but not all the employees are ready to take responsibility for mastering their own process of acquiring knowledge. Some have been ready for a long time. These are the new-style knowledge workers—"early adopters" in the innovation model—who can help lead change. Others are old-style workers—"skeptics"—who resist change. A CKO's first job, then, is to convert as many skeptics to learners as possible. Though it may seem like a Zen koan, the CKO's ultimate job is to eliminate the CKO job by enabling all employees to master their own learning.

If you can turn the skeptics around, you can turn the whole organization into one that is not only more conscious about its learning but also more "care-ful" about its knowledge acquisition. Being ready means caring about your learning, caring about making connections and who you care to connect with. It entails being motivated and taking initiative. Mentors can coach you and masters can inspire you, but to manage the knowledge resource successfully takes a lot more than a single person can provide as a chief knowledge officer.

The larger corporate goal, then, is to develop large numbers of people who are self-organizing, self-managing and self-guided in creating their own flow of learning and stock of knowledge. Inaugurating transformation on such a scale will take new leadership, which we'll explore in a chapter of its own. But implementing, growing, and where necessary reinventing self-moti-vated communities requires care-ful or "networked management."

"Networked management" is a style of management new to most compa-nies, especially to legacy firms still wedded to industrial management models. The elements and outlines of networked management can best be understood by examining what's needed to manage knowledge effectively—a process every manager needs to learn and every chief knowledge officer needs to lead. It's essentially a task of managing a network where each node declares not its independence or its inner-dependence but its interdependence.

MANAGING TO RELATE

People are naturally social animals. They yearn to relate to one another and to belong, whether to a company, a community, or, in earlier times, a tribe. But modern "professional management"—the type of management practiced in legacy companies and the type MBAs study—doesn't enable the relating needed to share knowledge or the connecting needed for concerted action. Instead, it spawns company politics, the antithesis of connecting. By examin-ing knowledge and asking how it can be managed better,[1] we can see the be-haviors, conditions and tools for a new style of management that enhances relationships rather than poisons them.

Jan Carendi, CEO of Skandia AFS, has that type of different manage-ment style. When he meets someone whose talents and values fit those of the company, he offers employment even if no job exists. Percy Barnevik, CEO and Chairman of ABB, the large Swedish–Swiss power-generating equipment manufacturer, had a similar style. When he visited one of ABB's 1,200 small businesses within its integrated network, he would ask "What's the cause of the problem? What are you doing about it? How can I help?" Successive Chairmen and CEOs of 3M have exhibited similar behavior in their support of horizontal information transfers across the company's 3,900 profit centers.

Historically, companies have adopted either a centralized or a decentral-ized form of management. Indeed many, like Volvo, over the years have swung back and forth from one to the other like a pendulum. Neither form works particularly well for instilling the relationships and connections needed for managing knowledge or, for that matter, managing knowledge communi-ties or the knowledge business. To be successful, managing knowledge needs a third type of management model, the networked form, where relationship,

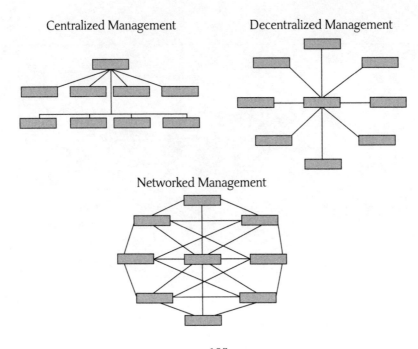

Centralized Management   Decentralized Management

Networked Management

connection, and interdependence are its basic features. Graphically the three forms are shown in the accompanying charts.

Centralized management creates dependence on the center and inhibits innovation and entrepreneurship. A manager's chief role and practice in this model is control. It's frustrating enough to try to control traditional factors like finance (the CFO's job); it's impossible to control the new factor of production, knowledge, as old Soviet leaders of the former Soviet Union found out.

Decentralized management creates independence from the center but often blocks cross–business unit or cross-community learning due to the NIH (not invented here) syndrome. A manager's chief role and practice in this model is coordination. Managers in highly decentralized systems feel frustrated that coordinating seems more like coercing and cajoling.

Networked management creates interdependence among units. A manager's chief role and practice in this model is integration. The main goal is to create new knowledge by converting individual learning to organizational knowledge and to start the cycle of making tacit knowledge explicit and re-integrated as tacit by the whole organization. The transfer and reuse of knowledge within the network require facilitation and resources, and thus

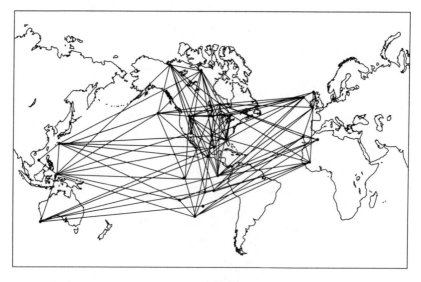

Networked Management Example of Large U.S.-Based Electronics Firm[2]

create a need to optimize the communication costs and process time required.

The example depicted in the map shows the intracompany network relations among the forty-one divisions of a major Fortune 100 electronics company from Morten Hansen's research on knowledge networks at the Harvard Business School. The next diagram is an example from Saturn Corporation, taken from Gary High's article in the Appendix.

In the networked model, there is no "above" and "below." There are only networks nesting within other networks. That is, the entire business can be seen as a giant network where each node in the net is itself a network. When we learn this way of organizing and managing, we can say that an organization is composed of networks, communities, and webs of symbiosis (in nature, the inherent integration of activities among different species) or webs of synchronicity (in business, the inherent integration of relationships among different communities).

Fritjof Capra speaks to this model in *The Web of Life*. He sees knowledge as a network, by which he means that the creation and application of knowledge happen best over a network. In science, the process is articulated by the Hungarian physicist-philosopher Michael Polanyi: "The network is the seat of scientific opinion," Polanyi says, "which is not held by any single human brain,

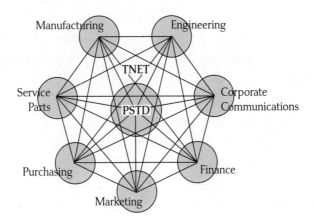

Saturn's network model for learning. "TNET" is the training network. PSTD is "people systems, training and development."

but which, split into thousands of different fragments, is held by a multitude of individuals. . . . The authority of scientific opinion remains *essentially mutual;* it is established *between* scientists, not *above* them."

In business, the same principles apply to knowledge management and its three processes: capturing, sharing, and leveraging a company's collective knowledge. In an agricultural context, they are the three tasks of gathering seeds, sowing them, and then harvesting. In an industrial context, they are the functions of R&D and production; marketing and advertising; and distribution and selling. In the context of a knowledge economy, a manager's main job, then, is to understand and promote the business processes of capture, share, and leverage.

> **Bumblebee colonies have a division of labor. They divide up the foraging from the different flower sources that require different skills. However, this is not based on any plan. Bumblebees simply respond to the work as it is going on. Thus the flower that yields the most net profits will attract the most bees. Even though the bees are free agents, an order ensues out of their combined actions.**
>
> —adapted from Bernd Heinrich, *Bumblebee Economics,* Harvard University Press

CAPTURING KNOWLEDGE

"Capturing" knowledge is a term borrowed from the U.S. Army's After-Action Review process, which is described more fully later. After any specific exercise or action (for example, the policing of Haiti),[3] all troop units debrief the lessons learned in the action (for example, how crowds were handled in demonstrations) so that the troops which follow can be better prepared.

In consulting companies like McKinsey, KPMG, or the Boston-based Forum Corporation, what is captured are proposals to clients that were won or lost so that "AEs" (account executives) who follow can be better prepared. Forum held a "World Cup Capture"—a reference to the World Cup Soccer matches—to encourage its consultants and trainers to make explicit and sharable what they've learned from their latest engagements. As a result, 75 percent of their global workforce captured client solutions.

Capturing involves two closely related processes. One is making tacit knowledge explicit, as illustrated by the consultant example—successful AEs know how to sell a project; now they need to make what they know visible to new AEs by making their tacit knowledge explicit.

Closely related to this is creating new knowledge. The scientists at Los Alamos who explained the earth's magnetic field (referred to in the first chapter) had their methods and results printed in *Nature*. In science, knowledge is not knowledge until it is published and reviewed in a scientific journal—that is, until it is made explicit, visible, and testable. In that sense, capturing knowledge is also creating knowledge.

Creating knowledge is the fundamental process that Ikujiro Nonaka describes in *The Knowledge-Creating Company*.[4] In a masterful description of how Matsushita created a new bread-making machine, Nonaka shows how knowledge that starts as tacit (with the master bread-maker) can be made explicit (by a company researcher who spends a year with the master and shares the "secrets" with her production team) and then back to tacit (as Matsushita employees internalize the knowledge embedded in the new machine), which starts the process all over again (now they know how to create the next new appliance).

Capturing, then, despite its military connotations, is really a creative process. In the Great Earth Teachings of Native Americans, the same idea is expressed in "Look for the teachings." For any significant event in your personal or business world, always look for the lessons learned. Capture them for your own use later on and for the use of others in your community.

The main issue around capturing is our old adversary, the lack of time. Account executives in consulting firms are too busy to take the time capture requires. It took the Matsushita researcher a year to understand the breadmaster's secrets. It probably took another year to prototype the new Bread-Master™ and ready it for production, distribution, and eventual sale. How can we turn this adversary into an ally?

So far, there are two lines of thought. One is to reward the behavior by ensuring that performance reviews make knowledge creation and capture part of the reward system. Another is to embed "create and capture" as a natural and necessary part of the larger business process.

3M regularly builds a "15 percent rule" into its managerial expectations, where 15 percent of a manager's time is for reflection and creativity. But even at 3M, which is more successful than most, that time allocation is always under attack by urgent tasks crowding out the important. Solutions to the time constraint will be a major victory for all managers in the knowledge economy.

Some middle managers already have "create and capture knowledge" in their job descriptions, and more will follow. A job description from Forum Corporation: "Responsible for creating a capability to systematically capture, share, and leverage knowledge throughout our global organization . . . to bring our best thinking, collective knowledge, practical experience, and strategic insight to each client relationship . . . as well as creating a culture that supports and values knowledge sharing." One from Prudential: "Oversight for establishing curriculum standards and measurements across the Learning Community." Or "responsible for the quality of the sales and marketing knowledge repository," from another company's job openings. The fundamentals underlying activities like these are learning and creating new knowledge.

SHARING KNOWLEDGE

The process of sharing knowledge is at the heart of the networked management model and can be summed up in three words: communicate, communicate, communicate. In order to communicate, you have to use three more words: connect, connect, connect. Sharing is all about connecting and communicating.

We've already examined AT&T's knowledge communities in the Global Services Division and their success in connecting and communicating. Another success story is AT&T Solutions, a new venture into the knowledge business which allows client companies to outsource the management and technology of their internal networks—things like Intranets, which form the backbone of knowledge communities. This is not about long-distance (though it may cover a client's global network) but about internal connecting and community sharing. The future of AT&T Solutions (which now looks bright, growing from zero to $2 billion in two years) is a bellwether for the telecommunication giant's future.

All companies have always valued the skill of good communications in their managers, just as they have always valued good leadership skills. What's different in this call for communicating and connecting in the service of knowledge sharing?

What's different is the scale and the scope. It's not only individuals who need to communicate and connect but large groups of people—from ten-person workgroups to hundred-person communities to 100,000-employee companies. And it's not only managers in corporate communications or other functions like marketing where communication is basic to the task, but everywhere. Line managers, whether in production or in finance, need to communicate and connect.

Saturn makes it possible for a car owner to connect with a person on the assembly line who built the car. Skandia makes it possible for a contract owner to have a long-term connection with a person who knows his or her personal situation. Other companies with customer focus are developing similar capabilities. Now this same external skill needs to be applied internally. Internal company culture needs to reflect the external business reality the company's in.

Some companies spend heavily on technology to build a knowledge management system. They get the latest in Intranet servers, software, and systems. Like Arthur Andersen's first failed attempt, they build the system and nobody comes to use it. Why? The issue is not technology, the issue is culture.

Some companies, like Herman Miller (office furniture), have sharing built into their culture (the "Scanlon" process). Others, like Harvard University, are somewhere in between ("every tub on its own bottom"). At the far end are some companies where it's "every man for himself!"

There's an old adage that the route to culture change is through the graveyard or, as E. O. Wilson says in *Consilience*, "old beliefs die hard even when demonstrably false." The problem this poses—and a great challenge for legacy companies saddled with old cultures—is that the birthrate of knowledge workers is exceeding the death rate of industrial management. Young knowledge workers are coming on line faster than their seniors are departing. That is why it's often easier for companies born in the information age to succeed while those founded in industrial times find the transformation daunting. From the previous example, it's not surprising to learn that AT&T Solutions was an internal startup company.

LEVERAGING KNOWLEDGE

Leverage means the power to act effectively, literally to take advantage of the action of a lever. In mainstream legacy companies, there are two basic ways to leverage the internal knowledge of the firm. The first is to increase revenues by developing a new product or service; the second is to cut costs, for example by reducing training time and expense. Radically improving core competencies can sometimes accomplish both.

GM uses knowledge management to support its On-Star service, which is a revenue enhancer. Motorola University uses knowledge management to switch from classroom training to on-the-job learning, which reduces time and cost. KPMG's Washington-based tax unit uses knowledge management to improve its core competencies in tax advice and consulting, which both cuts costs and enhances the services available to clients.

Increasing numbers of legacy companies have launched initiatives to build knowledge management systems. Prominent among them are the oil companies (like Norway's Statoil Faros project or Shell's PRISM project), automotive companies (like GM, Ford and Daimler–Chrysler), and others, which are taking the plunge daily. Many companies have serious doubts that knowledge can be managed or that the results are worth the costs. Whether and how to commit to this new far-reaching process keeps top management awake at night.

The last time management faced such a new challenge was during the movement to embed quality into the manufacturing process and its associated services. At first the belief was that higher quality meant higher costs. Slowly but surely that mindset did a 180° turn: Building in quality meant lower ongoing costs. Companies that built quality into their products gained a competitive advantage. Eventually nearly all companies adopted the new quality approach, which moved from being an advantage to being a necessity.

Knowledge management is following the same course as quality did. Like quality, it affects every part of the company. Like quality, it is thought at first to be expensive, and many people doubt the wisdom of trying to manage something so pervasive. Like quality in its early years, knowledge management initiatives have to be carefully targeted to ensure their business payback is worth the investment in time, people, and money. And finally, like quality, it initially yields a competitive advantage, but as everyone adopts the process, managing knowledge will become a requirement for staying in business.

The critical success factors for leveraging and managing knowledge are a supportive culture, a clear business rationale, multiple champions, and keeping humans, not technology, in the driver's seat. One of the advantages of a good knowledge management system is that it saves time. As Doug Izard, director of KPMG's Tax Knowledge Sharing system says, "You don't have to re-research the issues or reinvent the wheel."

THREE TYPES OF KNOWLEDGE MANAGEMENT

Carla O'Dell and C. Jackson Grayson, President and Chairman respectively of the American Center for Productivity and Quality, identify three approaches to KM shown in the accompanying graphic from a survey of over 300 companies.

Self-service, which is the most common approach, links people to information by putting it on the desktops of knowledge workers. Networks link people to people via communities of practice. Facilitated transfer, the most expensive, duplicates KM in one locale to another. ("It works in Peoria, let's move it to Omaha," explains Carla.)[5]

CONDITIONS FOR KNOWLEDGE MANAGEMENT

Dee Hock, CEO Emeritus of Visa, describes the "chaordic" organization of the future as one that embodies both chaos and order. To be successful, it must

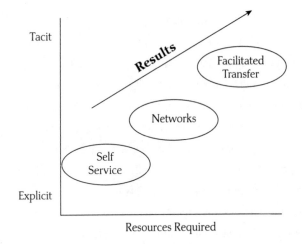

Tacit

Results

Facilitated
Transfer

Networks

Self
Service

Explicit

Resources Required

Three Approaches to Knowledge Management

From Carla O'Dell and C. Jackson Grayson, American Center for Productivity and Quality.

meet certain conditions—equitably owned by participants, power must be distributive, malleable yet durable, embracing diversity and change. Managers contemplating knowledge management would be well advised to listen to Hock because managing knowledge has much in common with chaordic processes. Chief among these conditions for successful knowledge management are the following:

Openness. A fundamental principle for self-organizing systems is that everyone in the company or community has access to all the information on the system. The goal is to let everyone see what everyone else is doing so that everyone knows what else has to be done. Openness is based on confidence in people's ability, in people's trustworthiness, and in the individual's worth. At 3M, it was former chairman William McKnight's "deep, genuine, and unshakable belief in the ability of the individual" that became embedded in the company culture.

There is a famous psychological test where playing cards from a deck are shown one at a time to test subjects who are asked to quickly identify them. What they don't know is that the deck contains a red ace of spades and a black queen of hearts. Most subjects will unconsciously ignore the discrepancies and mentally fill in the color to match their own belief.

What the experiment shows is that the human mind will fill in to fit preexisting beliefs and, in the absence of any information to the contrary, will simply invent what it expects to see. Cigarette advertisers use that phenomenon to evade regulations on marketing to teenagers: A picture of Joe Camel on a billboard without any words at all causes the mind to fill in the blanks, often with regrettable consequences.

The same is true in knowledge management. The human mind always fills an information vacuum, often with thoughts that are exaggerated. But restricting access to sensitive information like cash flow difficulties creates problems more severe than the ones the secrecy was supposed to hide.

Of course, there are situations where openness has its limits. The GPS satellite system, originally installed by the U.S. military, is intentionally inaccurate in order to protect a key defense installation. Commercial users of the GPS, however, have been able to "fill in" the picture by developing their own algorithms to correct the misinformation. Los Alamos National Laboratory, in its transformation from a bomb-designing organization to stewardship of the existing stockpile, has lived all its fifty-plus years with the tension between secrecy (which was its heritage) and openness (which is its future).

Many people in Europe have a deep concern about protecting the privacy of the individual. When I host in Boston executives from FIAT (Italy), Nesté (Finland), and other European firms, they are shocked to see that the salary of top officers of U.S. corporations is public information, and one can get this information easily on the Internet. Most of them feel that America is going too far with disclosing personal information.

As Europe integrates further and the European Commission adopts regulations to protect individual privacy, Americans will feel that their principle of openness is under attack. At the same time, Europeans feel that their rights to privacy are being violated. Balancing rights to privacy with responsibilities for openness will have no easy answers. Most American-based companies and their U.S. managers are woefully unprepared for this contest and run the danger of losing a quality they often take for granted. Worse yet, legacy companies trying to preserve their hierarchical command and control may use the privacy issue as an excuse to hold onto their power.

Friendly competition. The Olympics are the best example of "friendly competition." Managers responsible for managing knowledge should look to the Olympics for inspiration and practical advice on how to assure some competition in the creation and use of knowledge, and how to ensure it remains friendly. Forum's "world cup capture" initiative is a good example.

To some people, the word "community" connotes cooperation where there is no room for "competition." But community without friendly competition loses its edge. Human beings want to excel. They take their learning and use of knowledge most seriously when they sense some competition. IBM didn't take PCs seriously until it saw the competitive Macintosh. The old GM of past decades didn't take Japanese front-wheel-drive cars seriously until Ford started to produce them!

Ikujiro Nonaka, Xerox Distinguished Professor in Knowledge at UC Berkeley's Haas School of Business, calls for "internal competition" as a way to create the best new knowledge. Even at the risk of redundancy, where two internal teams are engaged on the same project, internal competition gives Japanese firms an advantage in product development. While not known for breakthrough inventions, Japanese firms excel at incremental improvements (*kaizen*) and countless variations in their product lines because, according to Nonaka, they follow "the principle of internal competition." One of the things competition does is to bring in alternative and different perspectives. In that sense, a close cousin of friendly competition is valuing diversity.

A new role for R&D. R&D is the most knowledge-intensive function of traditional companies. In the industrial model, R&D was separated off from the rest of the company. That was the case with Xerox PARC, IBM's Watson Lab, and AT&T's Bell Labs. National Laboratories like Los Alamos were for different reasons separated off from the mainstream of life. Now, with the possible exception of "Bill" Labs (Microsoft's new research effort), the pressure is to bring R&D closer to the markets it serves. Use of the Internet and development of Intranets for knowledge management will intensify this trend.

AT&T's Bell Labs, even before it was divested into Lucent Technologies, had built a Consumer Lab to forge a closer connection between customer needs and research results. Now that Bell Labs is the backbone of a separate company it has direct contact with customers. Likewise, Los Alamos National Laboratory has developed an extensive partnership program with industry to make its basic research agenda more relevant to peacetime needs. At 3M, research is decentralized into more than a hundred lines of business. At ABB, over 90 percent of research takes place at the 1,200 operating companies. Does all this herald the end of basic research? Hardly.

Scientific discovery is at an all-time high, especially in brain sciences, in astronomy, and in gene mapping. In those areas more has been discovered in the last ten years than in the previous ten centuries. Much of it is due to the acceleration of research results. Listen further to Polanyi, the Hungarian physicist and philosopher of epistemology, the branch of philosophy that studies the nature of knowledge. He says that advances in science are like a group of workers trying to assemble a giant jigsaw puzzle. Each worker can take several pieces and try to fit them together. But since each piece is dependent on other pieces, that method is likely to fail. Better is to allow each worker to keep track of all other workers so that each time one piece is fitted, new possibilities are immediately evident.

> The way this works in the scientific community is through publications and professional friendships. Alerted by their network of scientific publications and professional friendships—by the complete openness of their communication—scientists rushed to work at just those points where their particular talents would bring them the maximum emotional and intellectual return on their investment of effort and thought.[6]

The slow rate of communication through journals kept each scientist a year behind the times, unless of course they lived next to one another as they did at Los Alamos. Enter the Internet, intranets, and knowledge management. Eliminating the lag time of communicating scientific discovery from years to days not only has accelerated the growth of knowledge but makes that knowledge more accessible to more people. In business, this means beyond the R&D lab to other parts of a company and even to its customers and suppliers.

Knowledge management systems, then, intensify the trend to bring research closer to the market place. At the same time, the industrial model of managing R&D will migrate to a networked model of managing knowledge. CKOs charged with knowledge management can be seen as successors to R&D managers charged with research.

A new role for emotions. Emotions were never part of the industrial models of management. Watch out, they will play a big role in networked management.

"Emotional" means different things to different people. One meaning is "agitated and out of control." That was the accepted meaning in the industrial era and still predominates in most companies today. Industrial machines have no emotions. Instead, the machine metaphor emphasizes rationality, predictability, and responsibility, which are strong values for industrial-strength management.

The other meaning of "emotional" is exciting, engaged, and passionate, which can be seen in phrases such as "an engaged workforce is more productive" or "he has a hard driving passion." "A passion for excellence" speaks of involvement and commitment. As Hegel once said, "Nothing great in the world has been accomplished without passion." Companies seeking to accomplish something great will learn to incorporate emotions into their culture and management style.

Two factors conspire to make room for emotions. One is that the next generation of business leaders are the idealist boomers for whom emotions are positive. The other is that the next generation of Internet technology will have enough power to express them. As bandwidth and multimedia become plentiful, the sounds, colors and full motion video that are the hallmarks of emotion will become practical.

In *Descartes' Error* the neurologist Antonio Damasio recounts the famous case of Phineas Gage, the construction foreman who survived a freak accident in 1848 when a 3-foot iron rod blasted through his skull.[7] His rationality was left intact, but his emotions were disabled. Before the accident "he was looked upon by those who knew him well as a shrewd, smart businessman, very energetic and persistent in executing all his plans of action," according to Dr. Harlow, his physician. During his cure, he "regained his strength, could touch, hear and see, and was not paralyzed of limb or tongue. He walked firmly, used his hands with dexterity, and had no noticeable difficulty with speech." However, several months after his astonishing physical cure, "Gage was no longer Gage. The balance between his intellect and animal propensities had been destroyed." He was "irreverent," "capricious," and "vacillating: devising many plans of future operations, which are no sooner arranged than they are abandoned."

His employers would not take him back. He took jobs first on horse farms, then as a circus attraction. He was featured in Barnum's Museum in New York, quit in a capricious fit, and went to South America, where he became a stagecoach driver. In 1860 he returned to the care of his mother and sister, who was married to D. D. Shattuck, a prosperous San Francisco merchant at the time of the Gold Rush. But as Nathanael West put it, he "had come to San Francisco to die." In 1861 he had an epileptic fit and expired: Not in cold blood, but, as Damasio calls it, "in colder blood," because he was not only dead but devoid of any emotions when he died.

The work of Rosalind Picard at the MIT Media Lab on "affective computing" further shows how scientific findings contradict the misguided belief that emotions are a luxury. Rather, she says, emotions play an essential role in basic rational and intelligent behavior.[8] As the case of Phineas Gage shows, the absence of emotion and feeling is a source of irrational behavior and makes wise decision-making impossible.[9] Dan Goleman, in his best-selling *Emotional Intelligence*, argues persuasively that your EQ (emotional intelligence quotient) is more important in business than IQ (intellectual intelligence quotient).[10]

The marketing and advertising functions in business already use emotions in their messages. Companies that adopt the communication-intensive networked management style will want to extend such attention to emotions into all their communications. As a consequence, successful knowledge management systems will be packed with emotional content.[11]

For Chief Knowledge Officers charged with building and operating knowledge management systems, an important guideline is connect, connect,

connect. Go with whatever enhances connection. One of those factors is emotions. Embracing emotions is more important than you probably think.

TOOLS FOR MANAGING KNOWLEDGE

Some managers hear the word "system" in "knowledge management system" and equate knowledge management with their company's computer technology. That view is far too narrow. Business purpose and company culture are the two most critical factors in managing knowledge, not technology. Nonetheless, tools for assisting in the processes of capturing, sharing, and leveraging knowledge are sorely needed to make networked managing a reality. Often such tools take the form of software.

Lotus Notes was one of the first breakthrough software examples that enabled sharing. Before Notes, the conventional wisdom in IT circles was that there should be a single centralized database controlled, updated, and maintained from a single source. Notes stood that idea on its head by keeping multiple copies of the database on the network, one to each node. With every change, the changes were automatically made to every copy at every node. That enhanced the openness of the system and the sharing that is able to take place. While other software now provides similar capability equally or more effectively, the Notes example represents a new way of thinking and managing that is important for the concept of managing knowledge.

Other software tools are being created that, while not as seminal as Notes, bring the rules for knowledge management down to reality. One example are products that collect information from external and internal sources, filter it, and make it available in the form of a personalized newspaper to each member of a company or community. Even in cultures alien to sharing knowledge, such systems find nearly universal acceptance, because they do something each individual needs to do—stay up to date on information critical to performing one's job. Those types of software can overcome cultural barriers, especially if they make a dent in the information overload problem.

Still, much remains to be done. The fundamental guidelines for development of new hardware, new software, and new conceptual tools are those that assist in capturing, sharing and leveraging knowledge. Plus those that enhance openness, friendly competition, and new roles for R&D and emotions.

PROTECTING KNOWLEDGE ASSETS

The patent system, put in place in the nineteenth century to protect knowledge assets and intellectual property, needs some updating. Some industries like pharmaceuticals rely heavily on it. Others like electronics and computers use it sparingly if at all.

In *Paths of Learning,* business historian Alfred Chandler shows that two knowledge-intensive industries—biotech and personal computers—started almost simultaneously in the early 1980s. The PC industry avoided patents, gave away its "secrets," and prospered. Sales are in the billions, profits in the hundreds of millions, and the one PC company, Apple, that kept its Macintosh code secret lost out.

In contrast, the biotech companies were all bought up by the pharmaceutical firms, where patents are pervasive. Biotech companies pursue patents vigorously, keep their genetic engineering techniques secret, and have yet to show a profit. Sales are only in the millions and profits are nil in all but two of the top genetics firms.

While one example does not make a rule, this particular one substantiates that the best way to protect knowledge assets from competitors and predators is not through the legal system but through continuous learning. Like quality before it, learning is not covered by patents. Rather, learning-based management and knowledge management systems can provide a powerful barrier to entry because they evolve and grow too quickly to copy. The more widely an organization's learning takes place, the more of a protective shield it provides to preserve excellence.

Part of the leaders' new work is to create the conditions and articulate the changes that all companies need to break through their past or current success and move on to the challenge of realizing the potential of new knowledge in their industries.

Chapter Six

Learning to Lead the Knowledge Revolution

Remember
you can't see inside
of a beehive because it is dark.

—Bee Stories from Mrs. Clark's Fourth Grade Classroom

For a learning organization,
"adaptive" learning must be joined by
"generative" learning that enhances our capacity to create.
—Peter M. Senge

WHY LEARNING IS THE CORNERSTONE OF THE KNOWLEDGE BUSINESS

E. O. Wilson, in his book *Consilience and the Unity of Knowledge*, writes: "Scientists as a rule do not discover in order to know but rather, as the philosopher Alfred North Whitehead observed, they know in order to discover. They learn only what they need to know, often remaining poorly informed about the rest of the world."[1]

Discovery, new knowledge, and learning are inextricably entwined in a process we value highly: creativity in the sciences and arts, entrepreneurship in economics, and innovation in business. Of course, imagination, originality, fantasy, and similar qualities are also necessary. They are god-given, inborn, and, for most of us, mysterious. But all who have explored the creative process agree that learning plays an important role in its development.

Developing a knowledge business is just such a creative discovery process. Learning that creates new knowledge is central to the knowledge business. Indeed, the learning that creates new knowledge is the cornerstone of the knowledge business. What type of learning is it?

Many business people think you have to be "adaptive" to innovate. But General Gordon Sullivan, former Army Chief of Staff, believes otherwise. He says: "You cannot build a winning organization by simply adapting, trying to accommodate what is going on around you. To win, you have to get out in front."[2]

You cannot lead a knowledge revolution by adapting to it. If you try to adapt to it, you'll spend all your days, as the Los Alamos rapporteurs said earlier, "drowning in data, thirsting for knowledge." The type of learning that's needed for the future, for creating, for innovating, for discovery is what Peter Senge calls "generative" learning and what the Club of Rome report *No Limits to Learning*[3] termed "innovative" learning, which instead of adaptation emphasizes anticipation.

HOW THE URGENT CROWDS OUT THE IMPORTANT

To busy business people, generative or anticipatory learning sounds academic. Managers are so busy responding to the demands of customers and bosses that they don't have time to think about any learning at all. There's a game many companies unconsciously play called "Rushin' Roulette." If you do *ready, fire, aim* too often, eventually, as in the actual Russian Roulette, you draw the real bullet rather than the empty chamber. If you're too busy to reflect on what you're doing, you'll eventually shoot yourself in the foot. That is the consequence of letting the urgent crowd out the important.

A frustrated employee sighs: "At AT&T, our people are rushing, rushing, rushing so fast to try to sell, service the customer, and gain new ones that the emphasis is on doing, not learning." Another manager says: "This is Prudential's hyperactivity problem. No time for reflection." Another: "We're all in perpetual motion at RR Donnelley. It's impossible to find time for learning."

That is what General Sullivan calls the "paradox of action": Working harder and faster without strategic direction will merely drive you deeper into a hole. "Caught in the paradox of action, doing the wrong things better and better, an organization will fail." We've heard words to that effect before from innovation experts, "the disturbing regularity with which industrial leaders follow their core technologies into obsolescence and obscurity."[4]

Honeywell's Kate O'Keefe has a novel idea: "Part of our knowledge management system would build in sacred learning and reflection time—four hours every fourth Friday." At CSC, Dave Bogan created a 15:4 rule. "Did you take fifteen minutes to think about what you were doing before you started to do it? Invariably, people will say, 'I don't have time to do *that*.' But if they'd spent the fifteen minutes, they'd have saved four hours later on." At GM, Wendy Coles describes an alternative approach she calls "learning observers." When senior executives request help, learning observers are assigned to their teams to capture the issues and insights for busy members. GM has made learning observers inherent to their Knowledge Network.

THE FOUR GREAT DILEMMAS OF LEARNING

Despite all the spending in recent years on learning, education, and training—and despite efforts by some companies to become learning organizations—the enterprise of learning still faces four serious dilemmas. They are the dilemmas of space, time, scope, and scale. Until we figure out how to balance the competing demands across those four dimensions, even our best efforts toward learning and transformation will continue to frustrate us.

THE FOUR GREAT DILEMMAS OF LEARNING

Time: Immediate/Future	Space: Local/Global
Scale: Few/Many	Scope: Individual/Group

THE DILEMMAS OF TIME AND SPACE

We've already referred to the first dilemma, the dilemma of time. The immediate and urgent get first attention and priority. Before the introduction of electronics into car engines, the average auto mechanic could fix just about any car by referring to a 500-page manual. That same mechanic today would have to absorb 500,000 pages of manuals, the equivalent of 300 books each as thick as the Manhattan yellow pages. That is why GM developed CAMS, profiled in an earlier chapter.

Saturn Corporation employees spend more than 130 hours a year in official training exercises, making Saturn one of the most education-intensive companies in the country. Demands to keep up with rapidly changing technologies and processes are just as urgent in other industries as well. If the training arms of GE, AT&T, or IBM were spun off as public universities, their revenues would exceed the budgets of Big Ten powerhouses like Ohio State, Michigan, and Purdue.[5]

School-age children diagnosed as hyperactive are provided with Ritalin, administered by their teachers. Eager-beaver reengineering types high on hyperactivity might benefit from similar treatment in corporations where time means more stress than money.

Attention, time, and imagination are the scarcest resources in business today. Reengineering and its headcount reduction is the worst offender in the stealing of time, closely followed by information overload. The more information becomes an infinite resource, the more attention, time, and imagination become the scarce resource.

The graph on this page depicts the time–space dilemmas. Most business people are clustered in the lower left. Those toward the upper right are so few as to be invisible. Business managers are often criticized as shortsighted. We operate in terms of today and tomorrow, next week, next quarter, and the fiscal year, but seldom longer. We seldom think about next year, the span of our career, whole lifetimes, or our children's lifetimes. We can think of this picture as our "business time line." The human brain operates in milliseconds. It takes about twenty-five milliseconds to retrieve an image from long-term memory via neurons and synapses. We can think of this as "biochemical time." Computers, which operate in nanoseconds, can help compress our business time line—which is mostly what we use them for—to do things quicker. This is the ultimate folly. Why would we use high-speed technology to make us shortsighted faster?

Nature takes years to grow a tree, decades to replenish the atmosphere,

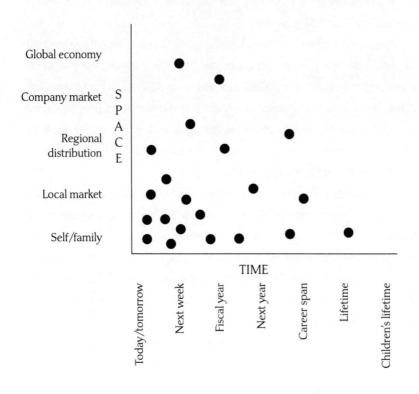

127

and centuries to restore depleted resources. We can think of this as "ecological time." Computers, which can simulate ecological time, could help us expand our business time line, but they're seldom used that way. This is ultra-shortsighted. Creative and innovative business strategy of the type that revolutionizes industry plays out over a company's lifetime, but we never see the whole movie—until, as for the Tudor Ice Company—it's too late.

The failure of business to embrace a *both-and* process encompassing both short- and long-term perspectives is serious. Myopia is the leading cause of death in the corporate world; resolving the both-and learning time dilemma is its most promising cure.

The dilemma of space, shown on the same graph, is similar. Most people orient themselves on what they can see, which is usually themselves, their family, and co-workers in their immediate geographic surroundings. Salespeople think of their efforts in their local market or the marketplace in their job description. That perspective is natural. Nature built the human brain for survival primarily (instinctive behavior) and only incidentally for broader understanding (learned behavior).

Some people, however, have learned to see farther. To continue the analogy with sales, they see the global market first, then the company's market, regional distribution, the local market, and so on down the chain to the individual. If we draw a time-space graph and plot the number of people who fall into each category, we get a graph like the one above, where more people are clustered at the self and today quadrant in the lower left than in the global and long-term quadrant in the upper right.

As business people, we think we are observant. We think we can see everything right in front of us, but of course we can't. Light visible to the human eye is only that sliver of the electromagnetic spectrum from 400 to 700 nanometers. Bees see light outside that range. They use ultraviolet light for navigation and infrared waves to identify flowers and food sources. With technologies such as night vision goggles or electron microscopes, we too can learn to see things not visible to the naked eye.

The impacts of a local or regional economy gone sour are likewise visible to anyone who can see. Unemployment lines, idle factories, and disillusioned youth are some of the signs we recognize. Economic impacts of a global economy in distant lands are more difficult to see without traveling widely or watching news reports closely. The uneven distribution of economic resources is nonetheless real, but it seldom crosses the threshold to our consciousness. To be able to allow it in is not instinctive behavior but has to be learned.

THE DILEMMAS OF SCOPE AND SCALE

The dilemmas of scope and scale are similar to those of time and space but with some differences of special importance to business. The dilemma of scope refers to whether one sees learning as an individual activity (the usual case) or a group activity (the rare case). Its cousin the dilemma of scale refers to who is doing the learning—those who already have the knowledge (the

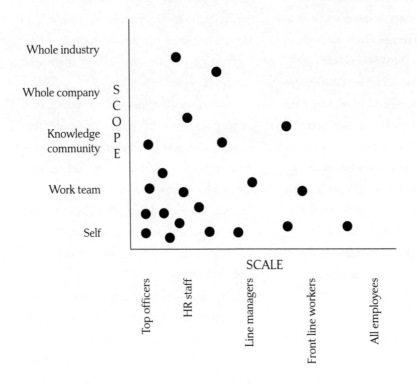

usual case) or those who need the knowledge (the rare case). This has special importance to business, because we need to make more usual the two rare cases: organizational learning for line managers and front line workers. The two dilemmas are shown in our nearby graph.

The dilemma of scope is relatively new. In the past people thought of learning solely in individual terms. That too is natural. Nature wired the human brain directly to an individual soul. Unless we are Siamese twins, we do not directly share neurophysiological connections. Since we believe what we can see, and since we don't see direct brain connections to one another, many managers remain skeptical about group learning. That is an unfortunate misperception. Work on learning organizations has gone far to dispel the myth and to restore corporate learning to its rightful place, but we still have far to go. There are a lot of managers out there who "just don't get it."

In terms of our innovation model, they are skeptics about the relatively new idea that organizations and communities learn, even if some of them understand they belong to a community of practice. But the numbers of skeptics are dwindling. Compared to other nonbusiness professions like education, business is actually ahead of the curve in its faith in group learning.

General Motors University, AT&T's School of Business, and Skandia Insurance Company all base their learning initiatives on group learning—teams, communities, and partnerships respectively. But like the rest of traditional companies, they have a long way to go. Wherever learning is an explicit component of your salary,

---

In the case of honeybees, nature has integrated thousands of insects into a higher-order entity, one whose abilities far transcend those of the individual bee.

The study of bees teaches us how lower-level entities work together to form the higher-level colony. A honeybee colony operates as a thoroughly integrated unit in gathering its food. It monitors the flower patches in the countryside, it distributes foraging activity among these patches so that nectar is collected efficiently, and it properly apportions the food between present consumption and storage for future needs.

—From Thomas D. Seeley, *Wisdom of the Hive: Social Physiology of Honey Bee Colonies*

---

as it is in firms like KPMG, you are still rewarded on what you as an individual learn or fail to learn. Saturn is one of the few companies where learning is done in teams of three and a bonus paid only if all three meet their learning objectives. In good years the bonus can be as much as 10 percent of salary. In poor years it's correspondingly less.

The dilemma of scale is that those with knowledge are the first to explore learning opportunities, whereas those who most need to know too often are left out or opt out. As shown in the graph, top officers have lots of opportunities to learn in the form of retreats or conferences, limited only by their hectic schedules. Only 10 percent of training funds are spent on programs for front line workers; the lion's share goes to top management and middle managers. But the dilemma goes far deeper than money.

Learning environments and training classes are usually created by human resources professionals. Most have never worked on an assembly line or serviced their company's products. In many companies such staff personnel have little credibility with line workers, who from their perspective don't see the need for knowledge they fear will be too theoretical and not practical—just as it was in school. Given a chance, many of the most action-oriented line managers will opt out of formal learning activities. They say they don't have time. What they mean is they don't see the practical value of staff-designed learning. The best way to handle this dilemma is to include line managers in the learning enterprise, draw on them for teaching where possible, and listen to their views on what they want to learn and how.

Chief Learning Officers (CLOs) play a valuable role in supporting and nurturing a company's learning environment. At the same time, like the Chief Knowledge Officers in the previous chapter, the best CLOs try to work themselves out of a job by making each individual or each community responsible for its own learning.

WHAT KIND OF LEARNING?

In the years when I was living in Schloss Leopoldskron, the Austrian castle made famous by the movie *The Sound of Music* and the site of my employer the Salzburg Seminar, I had the chance to meet the president of the Club of

Rome, Aurelio Peccei, who later became the most important mentor of my life. We were both intrigued with the concept of societal learning. In particular, he was upset that learning was absent from the MIT models in the *Limits to Growth* report to the Club of Rome, which acquired an undeserved reputation as a prophet of doom.

I accosted Aurelio, thirty years my senior, at the first seminar break. "Your predictions will never come true," I said. "Your models don't account for creativity and learning!"

"Very interesting, young man. The question is not *whether* human learning will intervene. The question is *what kind* of learning. And when."

With this exchange began a life journey that spanned five years, fifty countries, and five hundred world figures, each with different perspectives on learning. The result was a report to the Club of Rome entitled *No Limits to Learning,*[6] which I wrote with Mircea Malitza and Mahdi Elmandrja.

The first message in *No Limits* is that there are no physical limits to learning. We don't use all the brain cells Nature gives us. New technologies like the PET[7] brain scanning device are becoming more sophisticated. Scientists who study the brain have learned that children by age two lose nearly 50 percent of their brain cells to insufficient stimulation. By age twelve, 50 percent of what are left lie dormant. By the time we are adults, we typically use less than 10 percent of our original brain capacity. Science has further shown that brain cells unused lose their connections to other brain cells and eventually die. That means the brain is the ultimate use-it-or-lose-it part of humans.[8]

Not all of this is waste. In fact, it can be seen as a gift. Nature guarantees survival by providing overcapacity of brain processing power to ensure adequate adaptation in widely different environments. She wasn't thinking of radically changing business environments, but why should we question her wisdom? We've got the equipment, let's develop it rather than take it for granted.

If the limits are not physical, what are they? Most limits to learning are administrative. In some political systems, for example, dictators forbid certain types of information and prohibit sharing knowledge they consider threatening. During the writing of *No Limits* I tried to quote Jefferson to the effect that education is necessary for all people in a democracy. Mircea, my co-author from the then Communist Romania, said, "If you quote one of your country's founding fathers, I'll need to quote one of mine." When I learned it was the tyrant Nicolae Ceauşescu, who was later executed by some of his own ambassadors, I dropped the reference to Jefferson.

Corporate limitations are, of course, nowhere near so severe as Communist ones were. Nonetheless, learning is too often limited by culture and controls. For example, AT&T, KPMG, and CSC all have leadership development programs. All have strategies for doing more business globally. But for a manager to get approval to participate in a global leadership development program held outside the United States is unnecessarily difficult.

Most U.S.-based companies require special permission to travel internationally. Mainly this is a cost-containment measure, but it is often cultural as well. American managers in New York, for example, will opt for a global leadership program in Chicago even if the same session in Mexico comes at half the cost for travel and lodging. French managers from Paris are no different in this regard. They consider going to events outside Paris a faux pas.

A second message of *No Limits* is that learning varies by social culture. In the Muslim world, for example, learning is linked to the study of the Koran. Even in top Middle Eastern universities like Morocco's Université Mohammed V, rote memorization of Koranic texts is highly prized. Respecting the Islamic prohibition against usury, Middle Eastern management schools avoid teaching about interest rates in finance class.

In the Communist world before the fall of the Berlin Wall, learning for the political elite (*nomenklatura*) took place in specialized cadre schools such as the Stefan Gheorghiu Institute outside of Bucharest. That is where Romanian party members were trained for leadership and where I was housed while co-authoring with Mircea.

Just as Islamic schools ignore interest rates, Communist industrial enterprises omitted concepts of profit and loss, wreaking havoc with standard accounting procedures. When General Electric tried to acquire Tungsram in Hungary, for example, Coopers & Lybrand had to be engaged for a year to ascertain the assets of the Budapest-based lighting company, because it had never been done.

In the United States interactive learning processes are valued. Americans put in a cross-cultural context are frustrated when told they can't question the speaker who is the known authority in his or her field. Likewise, European managers at American training events resist hands-on exercises like operating a computer to search the Internet. As learning gradually becomes more global, those differences begin to blur.

DISTINGUISHING MAINTENANCE FROM INNOVATIVE LEARNING

Most companies have adopted a pattern of continuous *maintenance learning* interrupted by short periods of innovation stimulated largely by the shock of external events. An example is the shock of a competitor in the Chutes and Ladders case earlier. Maintenance learning is the acquisition of fixed outlooks, methods, and rules for dealing with known and recurring situations. It enhances our problem-solving ability for problems that are given. It is the type of learning designed to maintain a company's status quo or market share. Maintenance learning is indispensable to the stability of a corporation. Professor Chris Argyris at the Harvard Business School calls this "single loop learning." Peter Senge calls it "adaptive learning"—important for surviving but not for thriving.

For thriving in turbulent times of change and discontinuity, another type of learning is essential—*innovative learning,* which brings renewal, problem reformulation, and transformation. Innovative learning is the process of preparing groups of people to act together in new, possibly unprecedented, situations. Argyris calls it "double loop learning" and Senge calls it "generative learning"—enhancing our capacity to create.

The conventional formula used to stimulate innovative learning has been to rely on the shock of external events. Sudden adversity and competition interrupt the flow of maintenance learning and act painfully but effectively as ultimate teachers. Even up to the present, senior managers continue to wait for events and crises to catalyze or impose this primitive *learning by shock.*

Many companies, unable or unwilling to wait, will create a "burning platform," an artificial emergency whose purpose is to convey urgency and through fear to stimulate change. The challenge is "to recognize and react to environmental change before the pain of a crisis," as Arie de Geus, the legendary planner from Shell, explains. It requires successfully revolutionizing a successful organization.

Maintenance learning in business is all about training. It is about mastering data and analyzing information. It is the activity General Motors engages in for its auto technicians to prepare them to repair electronics-intensive car engines. It is the activity KPMG uses to train its CPAs in tax law changes. Maintenance learning is indispensable for doing your job today and incrementally improving it tomorrow.

Innovative learning in business is rare. If it were more frequent and more successful, the ice kings, textile barons, and computer gremlins would still be with us and leading the revolution into the next economy, just as they once led an earlier transformation that brought harvested ice to market, the first textile mills to America, and an end to the dominance of the mainframe.

Is your company learning as fast as the world is changing? Maybe you're spending 5 percent of revenue on training, as Arthur Andersen does. Maybe you've committed to 130 hours a year per person, like Saturn. Maybe you've just started a new research laboratory for natural language processing. So what else is new? Remember that when the Tudor Ice Company went down, it had just gotten patents on nearly fifty new ways to harvest pond ice.

Practically every individual in your company, whether schooled or not, experiences the process of learning, and probably none of us is learning at the depth, intensity, and speed needed to cope with the dilemmas we face. Organizations are not keeping up with even their best individuals. The problem with maintenance learning is that when the rules change and the outcomes are unexpected, shock follows; then people finally stand up to look for the lightning that has already struck. Shock learning follows maintenance learning the way thunder follows lightning. Companies rumble in panic to catch up with what they should have learned earlier.

Saturn's failure to develop a larger, more powerful version of its original design, a decision blocked by its parent GM, left it vulnerable to a downturn in the small car market, intensified when VW introduced its newly re-designed bug, cutting further into diminishing small car sales. KPMG's slug-gishness to develop knowledge management capabilities left it behind Ernst & Young. When it tried to merge with E&Y—catch-up by merger—it proved too late to get enough partners to agree on the union.

Until we learn how to embrace radical innovation, tap the potential of knowledge communities, and lead the knowledge revolution so we can grow from it, we shall lag behind events, be subjected to the whims of crisis, and let magnificent opportunities to flourish and grow go by.

> Knowing nothing shuts the iron gates;
> the new love and learning opens them.
>
> The sound of the gates opening
> wakes the dormant community sleeping.
>
> Kabir says: Fantastic! Don't let a chance like this go by![9]

BUILDING BLOCKS OF INNOVATIVE LEARNING

Anticipatory learning. A primary feature of innovative learning is *anticipation*, which is best understood by contrasting it to adaptation. Whereas adaptation suggests reactive adjustment to external pressure, anticipation implies proac-tive preparation for possible contingencies and long-range alternatives. Antici-patory learning prepares an entire workforce of knowledge workers in techniques such as scenario planning and simulations. It encourages them to consider trends, to evaluate future consequences and possible side effects of present decisions, and to recognize the global impact of local, national, and re-gional actions. Its aim is to shield an organization from the trauma and reactive nature of learning by shock. It emphasizes the future tense, not just the past. It uses both "eyes"—intuition and imagination—but is based on hard fact.

When the gradual deterioration of the competitive environment does not move those who should be alarmed, then anticipation either is not present or is not given sufficient priority. The essence of anticipation lies in identifying desirable events and working toward them; in averting unwanted or potentially catastrophic events; and in creating new alternatives. Through anticipatory learning, the future may enter our lives as a friend, not as a mugger.

Many people, unaware of the distinctions between anticipatory learning and adaptation, equate all learning with problem-solving. When the Xerox technician comes to fix your copier, he or she goes through a problem-solving sequence to identify the cause of the breakdown, seek replacement remedies, and put together the solution. Many challenges are of this fix-it nature, and they reach all the way up to top levels of management, such as issues of pricing or production scheduling.

Another way to look at learning is to anticipate problems so as to avoid having to fix them. Otis has technology built into its elevators that detects a problem before it occurs and places a call to a technician before the elevator breaks. This is smart service. The advantage is that early replacement can bypass a whole series of more costly failures, some of which, in the case of elevators, could be life-threatening. Xerox's opportunity to recharacterize itself as "the knowledge company" instead of "the document company" is another case where anticipatory learning, coupled with participatory learning, should be at work.

Participatory learning. Another feature of innovative learning is *participation*. One of the most significant trends of our time in business and in society as a whole is the near-universal demand for participation. Groups of every description are asserting themselves and rejecting a subordinate status in hierarchies. In many companies in automotive or other traditional manufacturing industries (GM, UPS, AT&T), the issue continues to be workers seeking participation in management decision-making. At the same time the issue is rights of women and minorities to share in important decisions, and that applies not only to employees, who are increasingly knowledge workers, but to customers and vendors as well.

For participation to be effective, it is essential that those who hold power do not block innovative learning. Participation is more than the formal sharing of decisions; it is an attitude characterized by cooperation, dialogue, and empathy. It means not only keeping communications open but also constantly testing one's operating rules and values, retaining those that are relevant and discarding those that have become obsolete. Both Saturn and Volvo have made great strides in this direction, the former with its union–management partnering processes and the latter with its codetermination policies. I recall attending a panel discussion in Gothenburg at Volvo headquarters. The panel was composed of finance and factory personnel. When asked who were union members, they answered "we all are."

It is vital that anticipation be tied to participation and vice versa. It is not enough that only the CEO and Chairman are anticipatory when the resolution of companywide issues depends on broad-based support from a critical mass of employees. Besides, participation without anticipation can be counterproductive or misguided, leading to paralysis or to an unintended outcome with negative consequences.

Global consciousness. General Motors requires that its top officers have experience outside the United States; the current CEO headed European operations before taking over the top headquarters spot. European firms like Volvo and Skandia require not only foreign experience but other languages as well. With English as the language of business, even some internal dialogues in Volvo are conducted in English rather than Swedish.

American executives who speak only English have the advantage that their mother tongue is an international standard. At the same time, they have a disadvantage that they are limited in their understanding of events and cultures expressed in other languages. The situation is not exclusive to the United States; it happens in many countries with large geographic areas (like Brazil) or with an historical internal focus (like Russia).

Until 1984, AT&T was almost exclusively a domestic monopoly and had little, if any, need to operate globally except to the extent that it was party to international agreements such as the International Telecommunications Union (ITU). After divestiture, it instituted large-scale operations in Europe, and now nearly half its business comes from overseas. Prudential Insurance is in a similar situation. Today most of its business is restricted to the United

States and Canada. With deregulation of finance laws in the United States, its future business is likely to have a sizable overseas component.

Instilling a global awareness is no easy task for organizations made up of mostly one nationality, but it's an essential element for innovative learning. Partly it is just the ability to operate in more than one culture, but equally it's the attitude that comes from knowing a second way of living that underlies an attitude of more tolerance and cooperation.

Systems thinking. In industrial times learning meant breaking large, complex problems into their component parts and analyzing each part. Herb Simon, in his classic parable of the two watchmakers, shows the value of that approach.[10] Tempus and Hora both build watches and receive frequent phone orders. Every time Tempus receives a call, he drops his assembly and after the call has to start over and resumes from scratch. Hora, however, builds subassemblies, so that each time she receives a phone call, she can take up where she left off. Breaking the watch assembly process into its component parts works well in her case.

> **Bumblebees can see where others can't. They are able to use the polarized light of the sky for navigation. They have three "ocelli" or small simple eyes located on the top of their head between the two large main pair of complex eyes. The ocelli enable bumblebees to begin foraging sooner and cease later. With ocelli intact, workers can spiral to get their bearings from the sky and make a beeline for the nest even when landmarks are no longer visible. They have been known to fly in snowstorms, wind, and rain. Bumblebees regularly fly over open ocean in Maine to forage on the offshore islands.**
>
> —adapted from Bernd Heinrich, *Bumblebee Economics*

In the 1960s Asian watchmakers introduced electronics to watchmaking, and the Swiss watch industry was shocked, stunned, and nearly decimated. Nothing in the experience of Tempus or Hora prepared them for a change in rules of that magnitude. They had learned the rules of the game of watchmaking for the industrial age but could not adjust to a radical technology change. Decades later the Swiss watch industry rebounded, but the lessons were clear. Like Tempus and Hora, many managers fail to see the forest for the trees.

This is not an either/or problem. The trick is to see *both* the forest *and* the trees. Systems thinking is a methodology for doing both simultaneously. It's more than a methodology, it's like learning a new language and takes nearly as long as learning a foreign language to achieve fluency. The human mind is notoriously poor at predicting the performance characteristics of multivariable systems. Systems thinking, aided by computer software like Ithink or Ventana, can help. What you can train your mind to do, however, is to look for counterintuitive leverage points and to construct scenarios where results beyond the obvious are possible.

ARROGANCE IS LEARNING'S ENEMY NUMBER ONE

Compared with learning by failure, it might seem easier to learn from success. That is not the case. The problem of success is that it leads to arrogance. And arrogance is enemy number one of learning. The reason is that companies successful over sustained periods of time believe that their own competencies and ways of doing business are superior to those of competitors. General Sullivan calls this the trap of "Doing Things Too Well." When everything is going great is the precisely the time when learning is most needed.

IBM exemplified this behavior when its success in mainframes put it behind in personal computers. That caused major trauma when conditions changed and its stock price fell to less than a quarter of its high. General Motors, long considered the model of industrial organization, nearly lost it: "Size and success led to complacency, myopia, and, ultimately decline," says Jack Smith, brought in as CEO to stop GM's North American Operations from hemorrhaging $500 million a month.

Successful companies either fail to benchmark or refuse to take seriously benchmark results that do not support their position. Motorola, cited for years as the top corporate university in America (not only by many others but by me too) has fallen from grace. "Too smug," *Business Week* reported.[11] CEO Chris Galvin's task: "Renew the business again, just as Motorola has renewed itself in its history." Alvin Toffler, the futurist, says, "The illiterates of the future are not those who cannot read and write, but those who cannot learn, unlearn, and relearn."

Believing in their home base, successful companies fail to take seriously "global competition," a coin whose flip side is ethnocentrism. Take Boeing. Despite important customers from Asia, Europe, and Latin America, Boeing was stunned when United switched its orders to the European Airbus.[12] The moral for an overconfident company? Arrogance is not only learning's enemy number one but the number one enemy of your future.

WHAT'S A CHIEF LEARNING OFFICER TO DO?

You're the Chief Learning Officer of a major corporation.

Maybe your company's in telecommunications where competitors are offering major enticements chipping away at your dominant market share, and each day brings new rulings from regulatory commissions. There's talk of a new chairman taking over.

Or maybe your company's in the office equipment market where your products are once again under Asian competitive threats strengthened by currency fluctuations that make their goods cheaper in your marketplace. There's talk of a new CEO coming on board.

Or your company's in the printing business. New technologies are changing the way printed material can be created and distributed, but the timing and cost factors seem to produce more uncertainty than opportunity. Your company's reorganizing yet again, and middle managers, first to feel the squeeze, are getting restless. They want a better understanding of what's happening, or what will happen to them if they don't do something to change the situation.

What's a Chief Learning Officer to do?

First, put away the usual training procedures. They are well known to professionals in the business, the directors of training, VPs of corporate education, heads of corporate universities, multimedia specialists, curriculum developers, and conference coordinators. You may find some allies among them, but while there's pressure for more on-the-job training and just-in-time learning, most of them continue to follow a corporate classroom model that works for standard training. But to create and sustain innovative learning—to make any headway at all on resolving your company's greatest learning dilemmas— you'll need to develop a new set of rules.

Select a specific knowledge community with strategic importance to the company and identify a learning event as a kickoff—maybe it's the annual three-day off-site retreat for reflecting on future developments in your industry. Resist the urge to think of the individual personalities, and think first about what the community needs. Is the challenge globalization? Is it technology? Is it the art of the long view?

Think of leadership in learning. Every knowledge community needs good leadership. It cannot be overemphasized that innovative learning without leadership quickly reverts to the more familiar maintenance learning patterns of sitting back to listen to experts (highly effective for information transfer, highly toxic for knowledge acquisition). Identify a facilitator as Community Learning Officer to be your sibling "CLO."

The community needs to go through a four-step process. The details will vary depending on your industry, company, and challenges, but the "corporate rules for innovative learning" stay constant.

1. *The community has to determine what it wants to learn.* It's your job to figure out how. Invent if necessary, but find a process that allows the community to participate in determining what it's going to learn and how it's going to learn it.

In many corporate settings, most Chief Learning Officers find this opener a show-stopper. It seems to challenge their expertise and experience as learning chief. Why risk letting a group set the agenda—especially a broadranging and challenging one—rather than a leader versed in the subject?

Trainers tell trainees which information is important. That's natural. Knowledge acquisition, however, is not business as usual or normal, it's paranormal. It requires action. It requires active participation. There is no "answer" to what you're hoping the community will learn. Instinctively, they know that. If you're going to enroll their commitment, you'll have to engage their trust. Inviting the community to formulate their own questions is an important trust builder.

Omit this important first step and your knowledge community will eventually fail. Follow it, and even in the worst case, where your specific session falls short of your hopes, your community will have learned by failure—which it must do in order to survive and will do because members own the basic decision of what they aspire to learn. Follow it, and in the best case your specific session will create alternatives and actions you never thought possible in your wildest dreams.

Skeptics like to imagine that this rule is based on well-researched premises of adult learning. It is rare, and for understandable reasons. Schools, whether urban, suburban, or rural classrooms, need more structure. They've never dared let students set the agenda. Business, however, is different. Do not let your personal experience with schooling interfere with your learning experience as a business executive.

2. *Prepare the learning environment as a safe space.* Have everyone in the room introduce himself or herself. Stand strong against timekeepers who say this will take too long.

In a meeting held at the prestigious Aspen Institute, a chairperson opened the session by saying, "We don't have time for introductions, we have to get right down to work." My own reaction was, "I don't work until I know with whom I'm working." Maybe in politics there are good reasons why a chairperson wants to forgo introductions, but in business, group work depends on having group members know who else is in the room.

Taking the time for introductions is a critical trust builder. You set an expectation for trust by having the community set the agenda. You create the actual trust by having each learner introduce himself or herself. No exceptions. Every person in the room. If you're in a virtual room, then everyone on the call or online introduces himself. If someone comes in after introductions are over, stop at the first appropriate moment to introduce the newcomer.

Why do this with a "community"? Doesn't a community know its own members? While it does, the nature of any community is that it's always changing. There will always be some new faces in the crowd who were not present the last time the community assembled. A facilitator's rule for leading communities is "when in doubt, always spout." That applies particularly for publicly determining who is in the room and what their relationship to the community is.

The larger the community, the more challenging the introduction process. If the group is twelve, you can let each person take five minutes. If the group is fifty, you can let each person take two minutes. If the group is one hundred, you can still do a minute per person and let some do two minutes. If the group is more than a hundred, you may need to get creative. Take five minutes at the opening to have each person prepare to introduce himself or herself and a neighbor. If the group is too large to perform introductions, your community is probably too big to gain the business benefits of community.

3. Learn it. If the topic is knowledge management, build a prototype KM system. When you can get a top-authority speaker like Tom Davenport,[13] have him make a presentation. Lecturing is currently considered less desirable than interacting, but when you've got great presenters, use them in their most comfortable medium. If the subtopic is how to conduct an After-Action Review for your company, modeled on the U.S. Army's innovative learning system, find a West Point consultant to help you design an action to capture territory ("markets"). Assign authority relationships like commander to footsoldier ("CEO to assembly line worker"), form into platoons ("mini-knowledge communities"), assign recorders with videocameras ("learning observers"), and get a knowledgeable expert like Joe Horvath[14] to debrief your platoons using the same techniques developed by CALL—Center for Army Lessons Learned. High priority in the KM case is translating tacit knowledge to explicit. Engage Brian Helweg-Larsen from London to lead a behavioral simulation of The Knowledge Puzzle.[15] Participants start by learning to manufacture a cube; when they do it successfully, they have to make explicit to new workers the manufacturing steps they know tacitly. Then move to marketing the widget to consumers; assign the marketing team to elicit from consumers what they like, dislike, or want changed in the widget. Explain this fuzzy tacit market feedback to your workforce explicitly enough to induce them to change their manufacturing techniques. Now debrief what the process was, which specific knowledge was valuable versus nice to know, and how you would capture the good stuff in a KM system. Now try to use your new understanding to disseminate the processes and the content you've built into the system to further groups of people who did not participate directly in The Knowledge Puzzle.

Thus, engage in whatever exercises, presentations, small group work, simulations, speeches, question-and-answer periods, role plays, demonstrations, experiential/outdoor exercises, electronic dialogues, or any other activity to accomplish the desired learning outcomes.

Most planners, when they set an agenda, overschedule. They fill every waking hour with an activity. They think it shows that the group is busy, which will look good. I think it shows you fear an unsupportive boss.

To be sure, a lot of important innovative learning happens in formal activities that can be scheduled. On the other hand, a lot of essential learning comes through personal relationships that happen outside the formal program. Mealtimes are important networking times when sharing insights informally can lead to understanding. "Food for thought" is not an idle phrase.

Different individuals have different learning styles. While ethnological research shows that the largest number of people in every culture are auditory/visual learners (that's why every conference center has an "audiovisual" department), a significant portion are kinesthetic (need to experience something bodily) or analytic (need to work through the equations or data). The more you can identify a community's preferred learning styles and use them to learn new knowledge, the more effective your session will be.

Different cultures have different learning practices. I'm sensitive to the issues of learning and culture ever since the *No Limits* book, where my co-authors were from Romania (Latin) and Morocco (Arabic). North Americans value interactivity above all else. U.S. knowledge communities like to question the so-called experts at the outset. Latins in South America or Europe value expertise, which has to be demonstrated before question-and-answer interactivity takes place. French managers have been schooled to establish their own viewpoint first. Asians value group consensus and spend a lot of time to ascertain that all are in agreement. That enables them to proceed swiftly when decisions need to be put into effect—the meaning of the phrase "go slow to go fast." Many of those different cultural characteristics are well documented in Fons Trompenaars *Riding the Waves of Culture.*[16]

When designing learning content, be conscious of the dilemmas cited at the beginning of the chapter. Design a double track: one short-term, the other long-term; one local, the other global; one practical, the other conceptual; and one for individuals, the other for group learning.

4. *Specify the action to be taken to convert the learning to knowledge.* Have participants work in small groups to determine which information can be put to productive use. Focus on a few items that can be implemented as first steps. Then ask each person to report which are the most meaningful to them— what the knowledge takeaways from the meeting are.

Harvesting learning from a several-day meeting is not easy. Converting high-value information into actionable knowledge is a real challenge. It sounds easy, but it's hard to do. The biggest challenge is to take the new knowledge gained from a seminar and bring it back to the company so that the entire organization benefits. Without special efforts, the usual pattern is for individuals to reenter their home corporate environment and find themselves frustrated by resistance to change.

The new knowledge needs to be captured and recorded. In a technologically advanced learning environment, this can be done by having managers engage in electronic dialogue that distills their thoughts as well as captures them. It requires a good facility such as CSC's Washington D.C.-based Executive Briefing Center, which provides a high speed Internet connection for laptops at every seat.

When learning is captured, it permits feedback on its quality, how it was used, and what results ensued. The Knowledge Network at General Motors, for example, seeks to capture and record decision-making processes around future car designs—which models will be built two years from now and why. The purpose is to improve the decision-making process next time around, either with the same executives if they are still there or with new executives who may be making these decisions for the first time. That use of capture and record is reminiscent of "Ariadne's thread," a reference to the Greek character who walked into a labyrinth trailing a thread behind him so he could follow it back out. Following the "red thread" over time yields good results.

Chapter Seven

Cultures That Question Are Cultures That Trust

*The most
thought-provoking feature
of a honey bee colony is
its ability to achieve coordinated activity
among tens of thousands of bees
without a central authority.*

—Thomas D. Seeley, *The Wisdom of the Hive: The Social Physiology of
Honey Bee Colonies*

The first people had questions,
and they were free.

The second people had answers,
and they became enslaved.

—WindEagle and RainbowHawk, *The Earth Wisdom Teachings*

"YOU AIN'T GOT NO CULTURE"

When we speak about "culture" in society, we evoke images of the arts, good
taste, and refinement of intellect, as in "musical culture" or "French or Japan-

ese culture." In such cases "culture" refers to the pattern of human beliefs, behaviors, and knowledge, especially as they are transmitted to succeeding generations. In American TV sitcoms, the expression "you ain't got no culture" means you don't *know* anything.

When we speak about "culture" in agriculture (agri-culture), we evoke images of cultivation and growth. Likewise in biology, "culture" refers to living material that grows in a prepared nutrient medium.

When we speak about "corporate culture," however, in the context of older industrial companies, the image is anything but one of knowledge and growth. As *Business Week* put it, corporate culture—those hard to change values that spell success and failure—evokes images of dinosaurs or other monoliths. The fate of companies with old-fashioned unchanging corporate cultures is first a failure to recognize a competitive threat, then an unwillingness to respond, followed by a refusal to experiment, and finally a long, slow, painful death. It's not "You ain't got no culture." It's "You got the *wrong* culture." In the context of knowledge initiatives, the misalignment between industrial cultures and the new beliefs, behaviors, and values needed for knowledge communities is especially painful. AT&T's Pat Traynor overcame cultural obstacles to her formation of knowledge communities by just doing it rather than debating whether to do it. There were about 10 percent of branch employees who just *couldn't* do it because they were too skeptical that it would work. I think of that 10 percent hard-core bunch as a "skepto-meter," a measure of the skepticism in your culture.

Every corporate culture has skeptics. They can play a valuable role by providing insurance against overconfidence. With a lack of healthy skepticism, you risk arrogance. An overdose of skeptics and you've got paralysis. When your skeptometer shows 10 percent who can't abide by knowledge communities, that is par for the course. Should your skeptometer register 50 percent of your population, this is a red flag signaling a situation that will require special sustained countermeasures.

Consultants have developed change management programs to teach their clients how best to change their cultures. That approach is a must when your skeptometer is at 50 percent or higher.[1] But for companies in the 10 percent range, another approach is less expensive, more effective, and preferable. That approach relies on asking the right questions more than giving the right answers, as outlined below.[2]

CHALLENGES OF CORPORATE CULTURE CHANGE

When Honeywell tried to develop a corporate knowledge strategy, it had all the right stuff: technology, vision, and a mandate from the CEO. What caused headaches, however, was the biggest hidden thing in plain sight: corporate culture. When GM established its Knowledge Network Integration and Development Center, it knew instinctively that to succeed in capturing the value of knowledge in the automotive industry, one of the world's most contentious in management–labor nonrelations, it would have to tackle questions of culture. Saturn, a GM company, succeeded in developing a partnership culture, but then it started from scratch. When KPMG started gearing up for its Tax Knowledge Sharing system, its new director knew he'd have to navigate between a rock and a hard place—between a hundred-year culture of autonomous offices and a recent declaration by the chairman to take a one-firm approach that integrates multiple offices.

Motorola, while it still has farther to go, is on the right track of changing its culture from one that spurned formal training and education to one that takes seriously the value of providing continuous learning to all 150,000 Motorolans. It does so through a worldwide Motorola University that is the gold standard for corporate universities. Similarly, 3M has successfully reinvented itself by changing its culture—another example of how legacy companies can consciously change, in 3M's case from a mining and manufacturing mindset at the end of the industrial era to an innovative and entrepreneurial belief that is at the heart of the modern 3M. Skandia Insurance is another case in point, a traditional firm that has reinvigorated itself through the use of knowledge—in this case, through the concept of "intellectual capital."

Motorola is at the brink of changing its knowledge environment further. The company wants to introduce distance learning with technology connecting regional delivery centers in Beijing and Singapore, London and Paris,

Brazil, South Africa, Australia, and ten more sites. It's also experimenting with extensive technology systems in learning, but as Mark Schleicher, Motorola University's director of knowledge management, attests, the key is culture.

CULTURE TRUMPS TECHNOLOGY

When it comes to knowledge, culture always trumps technology. When the telephone was invented, people thought it would enable direct contact among world leaders and result in world peace. Of course, it didn't. Culture trumped technology, in this case, competing national cultures. When television was invented, people thought TV would elevate the arts and political discourse in America, but again culture trumped technology. With the creation of the Internet and corporate intranets, some people still focus on technology as the tool that will make people share knowledge. But it's not technology that makes or breaks a company's knowledge strategy. It's culture.

Steve Denning, director of knowledge management at the World Bank, considers overcoming cultural barriers the bank's main challenge. Kate O'Keefe, director of executive education and a knowledge leader at Honeywell, despairs that the first request for funding that the knowledge strategy committee proposed was to buy more bandwidth.

CSC, whose main business is technology consulting, has to keep its guard up not to make Arthur Andersen's initial mistake: build a technology marvel that no one uses. IBM tried to partner with a major client to build a learning system but wound up putting the total frame of learning into an IT box. Any knowledge management system that spends more than a third of its budget on technology is not a KM initiative but an IT project—"dead metal," as Larry Prusak calls it.

Systems don't count where people don't. The challenge is to integrate the technology with the people systems. In looking at a corporate knowledge management plan, Motorola put the corporate IT officer on a team with the senior OD officer, a senior strategy person, and the head of training and education. That was expected to generate more "ask-oriented" conversations, as 3M's Bruce Moorhouse puts it.

HOW CAN CULTURES CHANGE?

In *The Stirring of the Soul in the Workplace,* Alan Briskin speaks of "the shadow of the collective." The "shadow" is C. J. Jung's name for the dark side in all of us that is the opposite of good and represents the specter of confusion, errors, defeat, and all that is evil. The shadow is usually repressed and ignored—"tacit knowledge" in our terms—and is seldom illuminated or acknowledged. "The shadow of the collective" is another term for the negative attributes of corporate culture, the ones everyone wants to change but feels powerless to affect. The reason is that culture, and especially its negative side, is not only tacit but taboo.

CEOs of many companies try to change their organization's culture by mandating that employees be more customer-focused or more open to new ideas. But culture doesn't change by command. Joe Weber recounts how, as a member of the management committee of one of the largest pharmaceutical companies, he watched its CEO try to order culture change to make the company more service-oriented. But mandating a culture change, by itself, is not very effective. Instead, culture change must become an organic process that comes about, in most cases, by changing personnel at or near the top.

When taking over, a new president brings in people he or she has confidence in and feels comfortable with. That explains why so many companies continue to look like their presidents. What is needed is management with new ideas, new experiences, and a willingness to change. Then real culture change will come not from the top but from a series of micro-actions from within the organization. Peter Senge says, "What's important is that the actions be in alignment."

New knowledge strategies offer us the possibility of aligning our organizations around a common theme. The central focus of the strategy is to make the knowledge visible. What does it mean, "to make knowledge visible"?

When Art Fry developed Post-It Notes at 3M, the company had a grand-scale celebration. Fry received an award for innovation from the chairman and was feted at company events and his name became known to 3Mers as an example of someone who had tried more than forty different approaches to the innovation that later became the familiar Post-It Notes. As Art put it: "I kissed a lot of frogs until I got a prince." Stories like that make the knowledge visible.

Of the six thousand "technical tax" submissions KPMG's Tax Knowledge Sharing system receives, its subject matter experts accept six hundred for inclusion in the system's repository. When users access the repository and find one of the six hundred nuggets, they also learn the person's name who submitted the high-value information. That is making knowledge visible two ways, one technological and one social.

In science, knowledge is not knowledge until it appears in a scientific journal. In business, knowledge is not knowledge until you speak it, as Larry Prusak says, or until it is written down (tacit becomes explicit) and embodied in the way work is done (is passed on from knowledge creators to knowledge users). Embedding knowledge into work routines is the stuff of culture change.

By itself, making knowledge visible is not enough to induce culture change. Strong leadership from the top is essential. The role of the 3M chairman in making Art Fry's Post-It Notes visible was not incidental. He created and retold the story of Art's Post-It Notes on every possible occasion.

In the KPMG case, the Chairman issued a policy on knowledge sharing. When I first heard of the move, I thought to myself, "That's never going to work. Issuing a policy statement to four thousand professionals in one hundred offices. How absurd!" It turns out that in the world of professional tax advisers, it's not absurd at all. Tax professionals are used to getting important IRS rulings and other policies in such a form. "It is hereby now from henceforth (with apologies for the parody of legal terminology) the policy of this firm to share technical tax memoranda, letters that go to clients, as well as any proposals where we propose services to clients, and any speeches or articles or other things of expertise." This resonates with people who speak tax-talk.

At Motorola, Bob Galvin, son of the founder, took an active role in making knowledge and learning visible in the culture. When the first proposal for a training and education center was brought to the board—where one member said Motorola would put a man on the moon before it would ever build a training center—it was voted down 11 to 1. However, the one was Bob Galvin, and the Motorola Training and Education Center was established shortly thereafter.

Leadership around knowledge, as we'll see more fully later, has to be driven by the business and a vision of where you want to go in your business. If you don't know where you're going, you'll never get there. If you don't care where you're going, anywhere will do. But if you want to align your culture with your business future, you'd better know where you want to be in ten years. As Mark Schleicher, director of knowledge management for Motorola University, puts it, knowledge management is not a mechanism to fix a screwed-up business. It can only optimize the business strategy you've selected.

Leadership entails nurturing a common mindset and language that people can use around the business vision for practical day-to-day applications, so that the vision is interpreted by the line operator and senior VPs in the same way. It also entails having a main set of core values that are consistent with what you're asking from people.

WHAT CORE VALUES AND NORMS PROMOTE KNOWLEDGE, LEARNING, AND INNOVATION IN YOUR INDUSTRY?

Companies that have knowledge-friendly cultures—Saturn, Skandia, 3M—have several traits in common. They share certain cultural characteristics that are embedded in the stories they tell and in the work routines they use. Of course, not all such companies have all the following attributes, nor any one of them all of the time. But in seeking to develop cultures that maximize knowledge as a business resource, legacy companies would do well to consider the following principles.

View Failure as a Learning Opportunity

Professor Chris Argyris of the Harvard Business School says that one definition for learning is detecting and correcting errors. Most managers, however, are quick to point the finger when they detect an error. Then they play the "blame game." But blaming breaks the learning loop. It closes minds rather than opens them to learn from mistakes. How can we get our organizations to view failure as a learning opportunity rather than a blaming exercise?

• At 3M, over 50 percent of the ideas for new products fail. The legendary former Chairman William McKnight tells the story of his turning down requests for funding a new thin insulating material. He thought it was an idea without merit. The 3M inventor, however, persisted. McKnight finally relented and gave his blessing (and funding) to Thinsulate™, which went on to earn many times its development costs. What McKnight learned from his failure to recognize and support this development—and what became embedded into 3M culture with this story—is that worthy innovators will persist even in the face of top management's failure to understand them.

• At Saturn, the company itself was the outcome of the failure of all American manufacturers to build a successful small car. The "Group of 99"—the task force that Gary High highlights in his article in the Appendix—"created a vision for a 'new way' that involved sweeping changes on both the union and management sides of the house. The vision itself was only possible as the result of an intensive learning process based on the research and shared knowledge of the 99." The creation of the Group of 99 and its vision that created Saturn is a rare and refreshing case where a major corporation learned from its failures.

• At a company to remain anonymous, John really screwed up. His company had just adopted a new quality initiative where getting it right the first time was the catchword of the day. It was the first time anyone had asked him to design a new corporate knowledge strategy—and it was the CEO who'd asked! Rather than seek help, which he thought would be a sign of weakness, he plowed ahead and put together a technology-heavy proposal that, when presented, drew heavy fire from members of the executive committee. John was labeled a failure and taken off the assignment. Rather than learn from the experience, John became defensive and blamed his subordinates for their lack of insight. The company too lost an opportunity. The executive committee tabled plans for a knowledge initiative, leaving itself open to competition from competitors.

The consequence of failing to learn from failure is that only the successful get promoted. Left unchecked, the company winds up with a group of experts who have never experienced failure, much less learned from it. That reinforces the tendency to suppress rather than explore what went wrong. This dynamic leads to the paradox that smart people can make lousy learners, which was the subject of an award-winning article by Professor Argyris.[3] Organizations heavy with PhDs can fall victim to this paralyzing situation, especially those which, like Los Alamos and the World Bank, have to answer to governmental oversight or public scrutiny, which treat failure with ridicule instead of reason.

BAKING IN BEIJING

Before joining AT&T's School of Business as its dean and vice president for education and training, Albert Siu was stationed in China to develop business for Hewlett Packard. His story is about living in Beijing and really missing good chocolate-chip cookies.

"I remember we'd go to Hong Kong and buy the Hershey's unsweetened chocolate chips, and we were very excited. We went back to our apartment in Beijing which had a Whirlpool oven. All of us were eagerly awaiting the cookies coming out. Guess what? They didn't turn out.

"We assumed the flour that we got in Hong Kong is the same as flour in America. But there must be something different. The cookies were so hard you could break your teeth on them. We used the same ingredients, I had a cookbook with a recipe, even the same type of oven with the same temperature on the dial. Everything except one little thing. It didn't work. It was a very vivid experience for me."

The lesson is you can't just apply a cookbook recipe. You have to understand the core, which is often buried in the operations.

Value Diversity

When I lived in New Mexico and traveled to the east coast, I saw what Navajo tribal police officers Jim Chee and Joe Leaphorn see in Tony Hillerman's novels when they visit the FBI buildings in Washington, D.C. All the men wear "uniforms." They consist of white shirts, ties, and umbrellas. To Native Americans from the Southwest, everyone in Washington looks the same.

Like Chee and Leaphorn, I was invited to lunch in an executive dining room, not at FBI headquarters but at GM. That was many years ago, when what was most striking was the uniformity of those in the dining room: not a female to be seen besides the waitress, nor a single person of color. In later years the dining room was shut down and more minorities were hired. Yet like most companies, the Big Three American auto manufacturers have a long way to go in implementing and valuing diversity among their management ranks.

- In the United States and Scandinavia, diversity means including people of all races and minorities as well as hiring, promoting, and paying women equal to their male counterparts.

- In some parts of Europe, diversity means bringing union members into management decisions in a process known as codetermination. In some cases, diversity also connotes bringing scientific and other professionals into the management process to get a wider view of alternative courses of action.

- In Mexico the pulp and paper giant PIPSA uses teams comprising those close to retirement, those active in management, and those just entering the firm. Those PIPSA communities are "sticky learning cells," where the learning from past, present, and future "sticks" to make employees agile and flexible. As René Villarreal explains in his article in the Appendix, PIPSA is spearheading an effort to change the mindset that thinks of Mexico as a source of cheap labor to one that sees productive knowledge workers.

- In Sweden, Skandia uses a process similar to PIPSA's. When the company developed its Futures Center, its director, Leif Edvinsson, put together teams representing three populations: the "in power" generation, the potential generation, and "generation next." Jonas Kjellstrand, who manages the Center, points out that the ground floor was designed by forty-somethings, the first floor by thirty-somethings, and the top floor by twenty-somethings. Whatever happened to us elder-somethings?

In the agricultural economy, the chief factor of production was land, which was owned and controlled by one class of society. In the industrial economy, the factors of production were capital, largely controlled by the same landed-gentry social class, and labor, which, while more diverse, still put minority groups at the bottom of the pecking order. We still have a long way to go in the knowledge economy, which, as of this writing, is stratified into those who know and those who do not. What will it take to build a future where diversity is truly valued rather than one where the educated elite take on the role of the landed gentry?

"Hard on Ideas, Soft on People"

Senior vice president Michèle Darling of Prudential Insurance brought this norm into the InterClass community when she was still at CIBC, the Canadian Imperial Bank of Commerce. What she observed was that in community situations where everyone knows everyone else, a culture develops unconsciously as people are either too polite or too contentious with one another. Her formulation of how business conversation should take place separates the ideas from their initiators. The ideas need to be scrutinized and subjected to debate, while the spokespeople need to be valued and validated for the role they play. Her formulation is "Hard on ideas, soft on people."

Go too hard on people, and only those with the thickest skin will volunteer new knowledge. Go too soft on ideas, and only feel-good group-think survives. Get the balance right, and you've got an effective "conversation model for creating new knowledge," as Honeywell's Kate O'Keefe calls it.

- Lawyers are taught to demolish other people's arguments. The "advocacy" method is still thought to lead to "the truth." Yet when high-profile trials are televised, one is justified to wonder if it leads to the truth or to theatrics. That style of engagement should never be encouraged in a boardroom and would be anathema in a knowledge community.
- Scientists both build on one another's work and tear it down. Carl Jung practiced hard on ideas, soft on colleagues in his early years with Freud; in his later years, however, Jung rejected both Freud and his theories. Generally speaking, science is a good model for corporate culture, though scientists have been known to engage in some fairly petty feuds from time to time.

Many managers in Western countries behave more like lawyers than like scientists. They've been taught to "slash and burn" their way to the top rather than "build and earn" the respect needed to hold communities of practice together. Many Japanese managers, on the other hand, are known for seeking consensus before acting. They practice the concept of "nemawashi," which means preparing the roots of a tree before transplanting it. In the United States, this translates into "go slow to go fast." Take enough time to get everyone's buy-in as a way to implement quickly when the time for action comes.

Having personally participated in hundreds of seminars with thousands of international speakers at the Salzburg Seminars, the Club of Rome, and the InterClass sessions, I've had a chance to observe and explore many different styles of interaction. I've been held captive by protesting Buddhists in Japan, threatened by Lyndon Larouche followers in Mexico, and stymied by Red Army Faction members in Berlin, who made off with the meeting microphone. Soft on people does not work in all circumstances.

I've also witnessed business meetings chaired by senior executives who have espoused ideas that were patently ridiculous, but no one in the room had enough courage to be hard on their half-baked thoughts, as Albert Siu was on his baking in Beijing. What is the right balance of "hard on ideas, soft on people" may be the single most important question for new knowledge communities to ask over and over again.

Promoting Consensus, Not Voting

Management of knowledge communities is an art. On the one hand, communities need to be able to make joint decisions that affect all members so they can move forward. On the other hand, if the decision-making process alienates a portion of the group, the community will be set back. Most Americans assume that a community will be democratic and thus adopt a political model of management. Another option is the scientific model, which is more meritocracy than democracy. A third option, more readily associated with Japanese companies, is consensus-style management. Each has its advantages and disadvantages.

IRL, the Institute for Research on Learning in Menlo Park, California, is one of the premier centers devoted to understanding the learning process. One of its chief contributions has been the notion of communities of practice. They are first cousins to knowledge communities, sharing many of the same dynamics but operating without formal leadership or management, which is what many members prefer.

IRL recently reorganized its own internal decision-making processes. Its fifty to sixty full-time researchers are formed into teams, which follow the scientific model. Best proposals based on superior knowledge carry the day. Tough calls where it's not clear which decision to take may be referred to the executive director or associate director, who intervene as little as possible. One thing is clear: IRL doesn't vote.

In the consensus case, how do you know when you've got agreement? Wayne Townsend, a thirty-year GM veteran at General Motors University, developed the 70–100 rule. "Consensus is when you feel 70 percent agreement but commit to 100 percent support. Disharmony is when you just can't live with the decision under consideration."

One of the issues a facilitator of knowledge communities faces is that the membership changes over time. New individuals come into the group, long-time members retire from the group, old standbys are absent when a key decision is made. That is a problem associations like InterClass or SOL[4] face frequently. Each community needs to find its own solution to the issue. One that works is that all prior decisions made by members then present are accepted by the whole group unless and until the next group agrees by consensus to reopen and review a past decision.

THE ANSWERS ARE DIFFERENT THIS YEAR

Albert Einstein, while he was at Princeton, once proctored a graduate exam in high-energy physics. A research assistant came to him in distress saying that this year's exam had the same questions as last year's. "That's all right," said Einstein undisturbed. "The answers are different this year."

Role of Confidentiality and Competition

All knowledge communities have to develop practices around confidentiality and norms around competition, which can work in strained and wonderful ways. The strain comes from the fear of abuse of sharing by competitors. The wonder is to maximize the depth of shared understanding achievable with confidentiality assured. Too much competition or too little confidentiality, and the community's work falls below its potential, because the sharing process is superficial. The goal is to maximize deep understanding in every learning opportunity and every business conversation. For example, when a Motorola executive starts his presentation with, "Here's what we tell the public," he is testing the waters and his own internal comfort level around confidentiality and competition. When he continues with, "Here are the issues we actually face," then you know he perceives high levels of confidentiality and low levels of competition. It is difficult to get this balance right in knowledge communities that cross company boundaries or strategic alliances among formerly competitive companies, because the competitive scene is constantly changing in unexpected ways. For example:

- Chevrolet felt more competition internally with Saturn (both GM-owned) than externally with Volvo (partners in trucks).
- Kinko's is Xerox's chief customer and chief competitor at the same time.
- Motorola used to compete directly with AT&T; now it competes directly with Lucent Technologies.
- RR Donnelley's main competitor is not a company but a technology—Internet publishing instead of paper.
- Prudential Insurance doesn't compete with Skandia Insurance, but both are poised to compete with banks and brokers.

When I was at business school, I thought I knew who competed with whom. Now, on meeting employees from any company, I always ask," Who are your competitors?" As Einstein said of last year's exam compared with this year's, the questions are the same but the answers are different every year. When building a knowledge community—especially one comprising several different external companies or internal divisions—look early on to develop a set of shared practices and norms around competition policy. Don't leave it to chance or fail to articulate what your community's policy is. It can be very restrictive ("We never invite competitors to our meetings") or it can be very open ("We can learn a lot from our competitors"). What's important is that all community members understand the policy, share in its beliefs, and abide by their shared understandings.

Ultimately It All Comes Down to Trust

Trees that take years to grow can be chopped down in minutes. Trust doesn't take that long to develop but can be breached in an instant.

Narrowly construed, trust is anticipated reciprocity. More broadly speaking, trust is our reliance on the integrity, ability, or character of another. The opposite of trust is skepticism, doubt, and legal contracts. As Esther Dyson puts it, the basic value of a community is trust among its members.

An abundance of legal precedents are activated when trust is breached concerning tangible resources like land, labor, and capital, and antitrust legislation becomes conspicuous when the public trust or private market power is abused. While lawyers are working on intellectual property, the legal foundations for abuse of intangible resources like knowledge and learning is only at the fledgling stage.

- Knowledge without a trusted source is like a check that's "in the mail"—you can't base your actions on either.
- The antitrust suit against Microsoft is because we don't trust any one company to become our sole source of information.
- It's as hard to get tax information into KPMG's Tax Knowledge Sharing system as it is to get an applicant into an Ivy League college; only one out of ten requests is accepted. Acceptance confers a high level of trust that the information in the KPMG system is valid and valuable in the same way that an applicant's acceptance by an Ivy League school confers a social perception that the person must be studious and smart. The key is the selectivity of the screen: The more Pat Traynor's editors can be selective as to which information goes into IKE, the more its users will trust the system.

The more Doug Izard's editorial team discards data and information not directly relevant to the users of the KPMG Tax Knowledge sharing system, the more the trust in his system and the KPMG community will grow. Remember the Sami AlBanna test for knowledge management referred to in an earlier chapter: If only 10 percent—two out of twenty hits—is out of date or otherwise obsolete, managers will not use the system.

When aroused, guard bees are on the alert at the entrance of the hive. They examine the incoming bees, letting pass their own foragers, but checking the drifters suspiciously. A suspicious few, they fight to the floor and kill, but most are allowed through unharmed. Returning foragers loaded with nectar are usually welcome no matter what colony they are from. As to stragglers who are meek, guard bees grudgingly accept them.

−adapted from Sue Hubbell, *A Book of Bees*

Hidden agendas are the antithesis of trust. Management meetings where people feel they are being manipulated can at best produce compliance but never commitment. Senior management seeking commitment from employees to undertake a new course of action or to practice new behaviors need to take an honest trust test, an exam that too many executives in too many different industries would flunk cold.

The presence of trust can best be detected when learning from failure is practiced. It takes an enormous amount of trust to admit, lay open for scrutiny, and draw lessons from failure. But knowledge built on prior failure is far more powerful than knowledge built on complacent success. In that sense, trust is the bedrock on which effective knowledge communities are built.

CULTURES THAT QUESTION?

Questions are an invitation to open a conversation, answers are a prelude to shutting it down. More "ask-oriented" conversations lead to a greater amount of open communication; the greater the openness, the greater the trust. That simple metric is what lies behind the observation that cultures that question are cultures that trust. Of course, something as complex as trust is much more than raising questions. But it's a good place to start.

Note your own behavior around this theme. Are you considered "an answer man or woman"? Do you have such fixed views that others suppress information they think may just elicit the same old answer? If your response to an experiment is, "We already tried that and it didn't work," you might want to consider your role in your organization's culture. Remember, culture is nothing more than the sum of our collective behaviors over time that become embedded in our work routines. Remember that nothing is more important than modeling the behavior you think will help your organization develop a positive culture that is knowledge-friendly rather than knowledge-averse.

Chapter Eight

Leadership Is Building Your Community's Future

Certain bee colonies,
sometimes feel impossibly crowded.
This is why they swarm to split a parent colony into two
and fly off with the old queen to take up new quarters.

—Sue Hubbell, *A Book of Bees*

Leadership
is creating a future
for your organization.

—General Gordon Sullivan, former Army Chief of Staff

EAST BERLIN, WALLING UP

Lauris Norstad, former Supreme Allied Commander of NATO and Comman-
der-in-Chief, U.S. Forces in Europe, was in his tank in Berlin in 1961 when the

East German Communists began building the Berlin Wall. In a frantic call to the White House, he said, "Mr. President, they're putting up cement blocks, shall I open fire?" Kennedy didn't hesitate: "Let them wall themselves in; we'll build a bigger future."

I'd met General Norstad at the Salzburg Seminar,[1] where I was responsible for recruiting Fellows in Eastern Europe. On hearing his story, I vowed to be a part of that bigger future by bringing the first East German through the Wall to participate as a Fellow in the Salzburg Seminar in the West. Ultimately I was successful, but not without trial and tribulation.

The trial happened when, exiting East Berlin through Checkpoint Charlie, my then wife was detained for interrogation. Imagine my anguish: I on the Western side, she held back in the Eastern sector! At the time, I wished Norstad *had* opened fire. After an agonizing hour she was released with no explanation, typical for authoritarian regimes.

The tribulation came later, when I finally understood the wisdom of Kennedy's words. Leadership is about building the future—for your community, your country, and the world. That applies not to just the President or the CEO but to leaders at every level, whether in political or business life. Leaders are people who aspire to be builders, and responsibility for building the future is the main task of current leaders. In this sense, we are all leaders. Willingly or not, wittingly or not, we all take life's class on leadership development.

Perhaps it was always so. Great American leaders like Martin Luther King and George Washington were all about building the future. The same is true for Mahatma Gandhi and Nelson Mandela, as well as great business leaders like Henry Ford and Thomas Watson. But most of us think of other characteristics first: "I have a dream"; Father of the Country; nonviolence; overcoming apartheid; leading the automobile revolution; capitalizing on the computer revolution. Focusing on the specific rather than the general loses sight of the ways in which we are all leaders. In business, leadership is building a future for your organization, especially in times like today, when the present seems so different from the past and success in creating a viable future so uncertain.

WEST BERLIN, TEARING DOWN

A generation after Norstad, General Gordon Sullivan, former Army Chief of Staff, cites the fall of the Cold War's most potent symbol as an incredible surprise coming at the midpoint of the transformation of the U.S. Army after Vietnam. It was so momentous it was nearly incomprehensible. "It was as if we were IBM contemplating the first Apple Computer, or General Motors the first Volkswagen or Toyota," he writes. "Our task was to transform a successful organization, to take the best army in the world and make it the best army in a different world—a world moving into the Information Age."[2]

Business can learn a lot from the military, and not in the simple-minded examples of Attila the Hun (a recent popular book) or in quotes from the nineteenth-century Prussian military writer Clausewitz (another recently touted book). But to transform the U.S. military into "the best army in a different world," its leaders had to rethink the basic purposes, operations, and readiness of the military, just as many legacy companies need to rethink how to take their best business leaders in the world and make them the best business leaders in a different world. To do so requires that we ask some fundamental questions about how we view leadership:

Are the old models of a dominant lone leader really dead?
Are there powerful models of team leadership that really inspire?
What role do listening, learning, and linking play in the leader's new work?
How do you lead a knowledge community?

There are no easy answers to those questions. The Center for Creative Leadership (CCL) in Greensboro, North Carolina, is one of the world's premiere institutions for teaching leadership to managers and for articulating new and changing roles of leaders in business. CCL hosted a meeting of Inter-Class companies on "the leader's new work," which underscored the issue: No one, not even the best of the experts, has "the answer" to what constitutes world-class leadership in a knowledge economy. We know that the present model doesn't work, and just as the Army has had to do, we have to explore, discover, and eventually incorporate into our own organizations the leadership traits that will prove successful in the future.

WHERE HAVE ALL THE LEADERS GONE?

In ancient times, when we were hunters and gatherers, leadership meant dominance. It referred to tribal organization, pecking order, and hierarchy. Whoever controlled the most territory or accumulated the most wealth was the de facto leader. That model of leadership operated in Ancient Rome and persisted throughout much of the history of warfare.

Dominance is strength leading to compliance. Its underlying process is the creation of feelings of fear and protection that shape behavior, causing clustering around a dominant individual. That is what happens in primate groups. It also still happens in some companies, where leaders are referred to as "moguls" or "czars."

In the Bolshevik revolution, Lenin sought control over factory machines. In the former Soviet Union, Gorbachev lost control over fax machines. The old guard of the U.S.S.R. had learned to control the means of production, but when it lost control over the means of disseminating information, it lost its dominance over empire. That sounded a death-knell for leadership by dominance and illustrates the difference between the old factors of production and the new knowledge/information factor.

Why haven't more corporate leaders gone beyond the dominance model? Our companies are still all too often filled with Lenin types and Soviet-style leaders. Why don't we have corporate leaders attuned to tomorrow? Is it too much to ask for leaders who command our respect, engage our passion, and win our commitment?

After Vietnam, the U.S. Army faced similar questions. It did three things, which have transformed the military and have special relevance for companies, especially those struggling like the Army did to enter the information age. They are After Action Reviews (AARs), Center for Army Lessons Learned (CALL), and requirements for making the future real.

After Action Reviews

After every real or simulated action, deployment, or training exercise, the Army conducts an After Action Review. The purpose of an AAR is to learn, improve, and do better the next time. The AAR was instituted as part of the "Louisiana Maneuvers," which George Marshall had used to change the army fifty years earlier, and was now recast after the fiasco of the Vietnam War to transform the army yet again. This time the "Louisiana Maneuvers," as described by General Sullivan, were used to facilitate high-speed exchange of information, plus coordinated access to knowledge in real time on the battlefield.

"Harnessing the microprocessor, the tiny computer in the hands of individual soldiers and embedded in their equipment or uniforms, represents the most important technological advance in land warfare in at least fifty years, maybe since the dawn of the industrial age," is the way Sullivan puts it. This new technology coincided with new missions. The Army was being asked not only to fight and win the nation's wars, but to provide humanitarian assistance in Africa; hurricane relief in Florida; peacekeeping in former Yugoslavia; riot control in Los Angeles, and fighting forest fires and environmental disasters in a host of national and multinational operations.

The After Action Review became the mechanism for stimulating the organizational learning around the two challenges of new tech-

It is a misconception to think bees have leaders. Except in the case of swarming, bees don't have leaders and even in this case, it's not entirely clear whether the leader is the queen or the scouts who search out the location for a new hive.

Another misconception is the popular notion that bees are busy. "Busy as a bee" is an English expression that doesn't stand the test of science. In the 1950s, the entomologist Martin Lindauer observed that one typical bee, during 170 observation hours, did absolutely nothing for 70 of them and "patrolled" the nest as though looking for work for 50. Thus, during roughly two-thirds of her time she was performing no productive work.

Professor C. F. Hodge marked bees and watched them from daylight to dark. His report: "No single bee that I watched ever worked more than three and one-half hours a day."

—adapted from Sue Hubbell,
A Book of Bees

nology and new missions, and also the process by which the distilled learnings were captured.

The Paradox of "ship or talk." At the loading dock, an HR manager charged with process improvement was interviewing a line foreman responsible for shipping. Exacerbated, the foreman said, "Look, I can either ship product or talk about it. Which do you want me to do?" Equally frustrated, the manager replied, "Both," thus voicing one of the great paradoxes facing leaders today. In recounting this story, Sullivan says, "It took a decade for the AAR process to become respected in the Army, for us to learn that you can do both—ship product and talk—and that carefully structured talking leads to more effective shipping. It is an investment that no one can afford not to make."

AARs involve all participants, including soldiers, commanders, and a facilitator, who in the Army is called an "observer-controller." General Motors uses a similar process where it assigns a "learning observer" to an action team. Whatever the name, their purpose is to conduct a dialogue and capture the learning. In an AAR such dialogue may last two to three hours or all afternoon if necessary. About 25 percent of the time is spent reviewing "ground truth," or what actually happened during the event being reviewed. Another 25 percent is employed evaluating why it happened as it did and how that was what was expected or, more often, different from expected. The final 50 percent is spent with each participant speaking from his or her different perspective on what to do to improve the outcome.

Few companies engage in AARs; many would benefit if they did. Sullivan says the return on investment, measured by improved performance, is "very high." Why don't more companies do this? Lots of reasons, but none that can't be overcome. An AAR requires a discrete event, identifiable players, and a nonthreatening environment—a tall order for some companies. To derive a return on the time invested, it requires a willingness to take personal risks in order for the players and their teams to learn and grow. Not a lot of companies have cultures yet that support such personal risk-taking. And then there's that nasty time dilemma again.

WHY NO ONE WENT NUTS IN LEESBURG

Xerox CEO David Kearns led the company through its first brush with disaster when it was nearly bankrupted by Japanese competition in copiers. To do so, he had to engage many Xerox people in a process similar to the AAR. In his book *Prophets in the Dark,* Kearns recalls an early two-and-a-half-day meeting at the Xerox Training Center in Leesburg, Virginia. But not all were in favor of taking the time to be there. "Why do we need this?" he remembers some asking. "We'll go nuts spending two and a half days in Leesburg." Nuts or not, the deep dialogues were fundamental to bringing Xerox back from the brink.

Establishing an AAR or some similar process is an act of leadership that represents a first step in creating a future for your organization. At its core it says our present actions need a performance upgrade to survive; none of us alone can create that future; and a community's organizational learning is the process that can get us there.

Let's be clear. The leader's job is not to predict the future, which is an impossible task. If you don't believe it, look at some of the most famous mispredictions in the following list.

LEADERS WHO TRIED TO PREDICT THE FUTURE AND FAILED[3]

"Everything that can be invented has been invented."

—Charles H. Duell,
Director, U.S. Patent Office, 1899

"Who the hell wants to hear actors talk?"

—Harry M. Warner,
Warner Brothers Pictures, ca. 1927

"Sensible and responsible women do not want to vote."

—Grover Cleveland, 1905

"There is no likelihood man can ever tap the power of the atom."

—Robert Millikan
Nobel Prize in Physics, 1923

"Heavier than air flying machines are impossible."
—Lord Kelvin
President, Royal Society, ca. 1895

"Ruth made a big mistake when he gave up pitching."
—Tris Speaker, 1921

"It'll never work, Tom. You'd have to string wires clear across the country."
—Thomas Edison's mother

"It'll take 100 generations to settle the west." (It took five.)
—Thomas Jefferson

The leader's new work is to engage his or her community of interest in the process of co-creating its own future. It has to be done jointly or else the people involved won't play their part when the desired outcome eventuates. When the process is done jointly as a community, the participants feel they "own" the results and feel responsible for their success or failure. The best leadership is "when the people say we did it ourselves."

The leader doesn't make decisions so much as make meaning. Leaders make sense out of chaos. To do so is not solely an individual act. Leaders today set the conditions, processes, and environments for the people to say, "We did it ourselves." That is very close to what Peter Senge means when he says leaders are designers, or the architect-builder of the ship is more the leader than is the captain of the ship.

CALL—CENTER FOR THE ARMY'S LESSONS LEARNED

A second initiative that helped transform the Army was its Center for Army Lessons Learned (CALL). Organizational learning can occur only when the group is communicating and has a mechanism for sharing. Most corporate trainers recognize that problem when individuals return home from a conference but have no effective way to share what they've learned with the larger organization. CALL is the mechanism for sharing developed by the Army to solve this diffusion problem.

CALL was established in army training headquarters at Fort Leavenworth, Kansas, where some thirty people disseminate the learning of half a million soldiers. Sullivan writes that the policing of Haitian presidential elections is a good example of the way CALL works. When the assignment was given to the 10th Mountain Division, CALL went to its home base at Fort Drum, New York, and equipped the soldiers with digital video cameras, life-finder sensors to sense body heat in dark alleys, and laptop computers to downlink all available intelligence. With those capturing technologies in place, CALL personnel could then deliver "knowledge packages" to the next division to rotate in behind the first. New soldiers were able to review the videos of crowd control, house-to-house searches, and nighttime alley patrol much as Monday morning quarterbacks are able to review their next week's opponents in football.

Such knowledge is useful only if it can be identified and disseminated in time to contribute immediate value. Sullivan provides important lessons for any company building such a knowledge network:

- Use both a *pull* and a *push* strategy. The pull is having the information widely available on an electronic network so individual soldiers can analyze the parts of greatest interest to themselves. The push is having CALL personnel appear in person to drill home the lessons learned.
- Short-term applications are essential to long-term implications. Quick fixes for failed planning assumptions, or unanticipated problems, and on-the-spot fixes for unanticipated obstacles are critical feedback for basic policies, organizational concepts, and formulation of long-range plans.
- Develop competent data collection teams. Such teams need competence in the lessons-learned capturing process as well as expertise in the subject matter. Neither of those alone is sufficient. Isolate the team from hierarchies that want to filter out bad news. Bad news—failure—is the most valuable information on which usable knowledge is built. It is also what bureaucrats want to sanitize. "Sanity" is not what leadership and learning are about.
- Protect the messenger. Nothing substitutes for high-level sponsorship.
- Exploit technology. Paper-and-pencil systems don't work.
- Select activities you do repetitively. Examples are sales calls to large buy-

ers; repair operations to equipment you service; strategy sessions for long-range planning.

- Keep it simple. Sullivan writes, "Developing a simple system, particularly in the early stages, keeps expectations within bounds and facilitates early success—both of which are important to long-term success."

REQUIREMENTS FOR MAKING THE FUTURE REAL

One of the most difficult challenges for leaders in times of change is making the future real. Leaders need to create a discovery process that makes tomorrow's challenges palpable for rank-and-file employees. And the process has to give people a view of the organization as a whole, not just the individual parts. Here are some suggestions.

Small-scale experiments. The Army started a series of small-scale experiments in sharing battlefield information. First it shared horizontally. In the Army that meant, for example, sharing information among tanks in a tank platoon. In business, examples are sharing information among assembly line workers in Saturn's Spring Hill plant or among print operators at two or more of RR Donnelley's forty-five printing plants.

Then try sharing across systems. In the Army this meant between tank platoons and artillery units. In business it means sharing stories between manufacturing and engineering or between engineering and design. Or it would be between consultants specializing in the financial industry and others in the retail business. The point is to bring people from separate stovepipes together. As a result, Army commanders could create a common perception of the battlefield, and all the available information was in the hands of everyone who could use it. At an auto assembly line, this would mean that when a line operator pulled the cord that stops the line, everyone immediately knows why and can take steps to correct his or her part of the problem.

In the case of the military, it is hard to overestimate the value of such instant information sharing. When Napoleon invaded Russia, it would have taken years for him to be successful (not to mention more men and better supplies than he had). When British and American troops landed at Normandy, it took weeks to coordinate a successful outcome. When Desert Storm ground troops hit the Iraqi deserts, it took a matter of hours.

When the military was slow to outfit each soldier with a GPS satellite positioning device in a Caribbean campaign, many infantrymen before leaving home called on their cell phones to order one by credit card from Radio Shack to be delivered by Fedex, so as not to risk getting lost.

The final step—which is not a small-scale experiment—is for information sharing among Army, Navy, Air Force, and Marines. For General Motors this means sharing lessons learned from the Toyota–GM partnership NUMMI plant in California with the Oshawa Chevy plant in Canada; or the Saturn plant in Spring Hill with the Corvette plant in Bowling Green.

Thin threads/red threads. The Army uses a concept Sullivan calls "thin threads" to connect the present with the future. InterClass companies use a concept we call "red threads" to connect the common features of different learning agendas. The important point is that leaders make the connections. For the military, creating a digital task force or digital battlefield simulation was an important mechanism for a thin thread that could be used to test assumptions and clarify understandings.

In developing red threads, InterClass companies began by selecting observers, people whose assignment was to track commonalties through a series of meetings to be used as feedback into subsequent meetings. For example, learning sessions on innovation often touched on the leadership role in promoting innovation; another session on workforce development would also touch on leadership roles—but in the former case, the leader's role was promoting something new, while in the latter it was reinstilling old values and norms in a next-generation workforce. It was the job of the red-thread observer to articulate and track common questions, such as, Are we demanding too much from our leaders?

Eventually, these higher-level overarching issues were seen as important learnings for not just the red thread observers but the entire community. In the military, large-scale training exercises, with structured feedback and careful learning processes built in, are expensive but extremely valuable. In business, large-scale learning exercises are more and more common. What most often is neglected is the structured feedback that can span several exercises. Identifying those red threads is an essential part of the job of leaders responsible for learning, whether Chief Learning Officers or Chief Knowledge Officers.

What is not happening? In his Sherlock Holmes story "The Hound of the Baskervilles," Arthur Conan Doyle includes this dialogue:

> *"Is there any other point to which you wish to draw my attention?"*
>
> "Yes, to the curious incident of the dog in the nighttime."
>
> *"The dog did nothing in the nighttime."*
>
> "That was the curious incident," remarked Sherlock Holmes.

Military commanders are trained to ask:

What is happening?
What is *not* happening?
What can I do to influence the action?

Michael Dell, when he saw that customers were *not* connecting directly to manufacturers, built a system to connect user and maker directly, thereby dispensing with inventory. Jim Barkley saw that computer users were *not* taking advantage of the Internet and built an easy-to-use browser to fill the gap. Steve Jobs saw that "the rest of us" could *not* make sense of DOS and arcane computer commands and launched the Macintosh. Like Holmes's curious incident in the night, it is often what is *not* happening that is the key opportunity. A leader's ability to detect what is not happening is crucial to making meaning out of chaos.

LEADERSHIP TRAITS

How do you lead a knowledge community? What is different about knowledge in contrast to capital, or about community in contrast to teams, that influences what traits are needed to lead a knowledge community? The three Ls stand out: Leader as Listener, Learner, and Linker.

Leader as listener. Jan Lapidoth, founder of the Customer Focus Institute in Stockholm, spends a lot of time advising his clients to listen to their customers. He cites the lessons from *Moments of Truth:* You have 10–15 seconds to hear a customer in distress and win his or her confidence that you want to help. "Many people have their ears open, but few know how to listen to hear clearly what others are saying, especially when it's negative. You've got precious few moments to win them over psychologically so that they feel you're on their side."

Listening, an important life skill anywhere, is doubly important in knowledge communities, because you're constantly dealing with new subject matter and with often conflicting views from multiple members. It's the skill we wish more political leaders exhibited; it's the trait we value most highly in good doctors when they check symptoms. Good leaders spend a lot of time listening, especially listening to negative feedback, strong resistance, and doubt as well as genuine disagreement.

Leader as learner. Gary High oversees learning at Saturn. Recently, his assignment was extended to education and training for all small car employees of GM North America. He makes a distinction between "knowing leaders" and "learning leaders." In the past, automobile executives came across as knowing leaders. They always had an answer for everything. Not having an answer was seen as a sign of weakness.

"At Saturn, we wanted to develop learning leaders rather than knowing leaders. That is, leaders who can learn how to operate in a new environment rather than leaders who project yesterday's rules of the game into tomorrow's completely different game."

It is not an easy trait to develop. It represents a major personal transition to many current high-level executives. Someone who has thought a lot about how to guide this transition is Mark Schleicher, director of knowledge management for Motorola University. Mark distinguishes among three groups: first-time line managers and other new hires; experienced middle managers; and expert senior managers. The first require "basic architecture" training courses. The second require "interactive coaching" supported by knowledge banks. The third need a "knowledge nugget" focus with peers. His goal is to develop leaders as learners.

Leader as linker. Community is an exercise in networking. To start building knowledge communities, put a first-rate networker in charge. Forging alliances, building partnerships, creating working groups, connecting visionaries with pragmatists and conservatives with early adopters. Those are traits of the knowledge community leader. As Sullivan puts it, "Leadership is a team sport."

Sometimes people mistakenly think that successful communities are those that avoid conflict. On the contrary. Successful communities are those that can use conflict as a learning opportunity. Science didn't advance by avoiding the clash of ideas; new paradigms destroy old ones almost like capitalism's creative destruction. Nature builds new growth by burning down old forest. Humans try to fight and extinguish such fires, but they are a natural phenomenon as basic as life itself to the creative process. Successful communities welcome conflict as learning but preserve the passion of the dissenter. Hard on ideas, soft on people.

Leader as lighter. There is a fourth L for leaders, first suggested to me by Karin Bartow from the Forum Corporation's Experience Center: leader as "lighter" or illuminator.

Good leaders of knowledge communities illuminate which are the problem or opportunity areas to which the group should turn its attention. That trait takes its cue from science, where researchers constantly ask themselves—subconsciously if not consciously—which are the areas or domains where we should concentrate our attention? Which are the contributions that will advance our knowledge, which are the directions that will have value to peers, to science, and to the advancement of knowledge in the world?

KNOWLEDGE MAPS AS LEADERSHIP GUIDES

Leaders of industrial companies are often known for their skill in one or more of the important factors of production. Roger Smith, when he was CEO of General Motors, for example, was known as a finance man. He knew how to manage capital and its returns. Robert McNamara, when he was head of Ford, was known as a numbers man, which drew President Kennedy's attention to make him Secretary of Defense in 1961. Per Gyllenhammer, when he was CEO of Volvo, was known for his labor skills; he initiated the Kalmar plant, where workers assembled a car in its entirety rather than piece by piece. Skip Lefauve, former CEO of Saturn, and Mike Bennett, his UAW counterpart, were known for their union–management partnership in an industry plagued with labor disputes and strikes.

As business acquires more experience with knowledge as a corporate resource, we shall begin to modify our views as to what makes a good leader and how we assess what makes a good company. Leaders of the knowledge business will become known for the traits of knowledge advancement and leverage. We'll say so-and-so excelled as a learner and listener; they were exceptionally good at building alliances and mediating disputes.

As companies gain experience in capturing, sharing, and leveraging their collective expertise, they will begin to formulate "knowledge maps"—the sum total of what a company and its communities know collectively. To the extent that we can articulate and measure what we know, such knowledge maps can provide a guide to the future potential of companies, rather than a testimony to former competencies and present accumulations, which is what our current accounting systems measure.

The more a firm knows and can articulate, the stronger its knowledge map. Like a normal roadmap, a knowledge map also can tell you where you're going. It contains the seeds and growth processes by which the firm is likely to develop. It is the corporate genome, the DNA map, that at once outlines a company's past and its likely futures. Most of all, a good knowledge map will be the legacy of great leaders—not just the CEO, but leaders at all levels who aspire to build the future.

The military has such a map. It's called "doctrine" and is described by General Sullivan as the "engine of change" for the Army. He writes that "doctrine is the Army's collective understanding of how it will fight and conduct other operations. It guides how the Army organizes, trains, and modernizes. It has no precise equivalent in business. It may be a level of thinking lacking in the business world."

Doctrine sounds close to the process of capturing, sharing, and leveraging a company's collective expertise—the process of managing knowledge. The more companies develop their knowledge management, business, and communities, the more robust their corporate knowledge map can become, and the closer they will be to having a base from which to evaluate the present and set a course for the future.

Chapter Nine

"Not for Tangible Business Purposes" and Other Pitfalls

*It is thought that
the so-called "killer" bee,
introduced from Africa into South America,
will not invade the northern regions of North America.*

—adapted from Bernd Heinrich, *Bumblebee Economics*

But we need to keep "guards out" in case they do.
Knowledge programs,
with no specific business objectives,
have little business impact, and fail.

—Charles Lucier and Janet Torsilieri, "Why Knowledge Programs Fail"

GUARDS OUT

Bad news is the most valuable information on which usable knowledge is built. Failure, the source of bad news, is the best possible feedback you can get, because if you listen to it without filtering out your own role in the mishap, you can grow older and wiser in time to try again.[1] Seasoned entrepreneurs know this well. Their rule of thumb is that less than half of new business ideas come to fruition and less than half those make money. The biggest failure in making mistakes is failing to capture the lessons they hold and neglecting to understand how to transform them into successful outcomes.

To learn how to convert stumbling blocks to stepping stones, you have to be alert, or "guards out," as it's expressed in the Earth Wisdom Teachings of the ancients. Capture the teachings, gather the lessons, and seek the wisdom they contain. Like all innovations, knowledge in business calls for guards out as we move forward. Many things can go wrong along the way, as the pitfalls in the following examples demonstrate.

NO TANGIBLE BUSINESS PURPOSE

Situation: In their article "Why Knowledge Programs Fail," Charles Lucier and Janet Torsilieri report on their study of more than 70 programs in knowledge management and learning organizations.[2] They estimate that only "about one-sixth of these programs achieve very significant impact within the first two years; half achieve small but important benefits; and the remaining third—the failures—have little business impact." CEOs under pressure for short-term results decide in a disturbing proportion of cases to cut long-term knowledge programs initiated with great fanfare only two to three years earlier. Their shortsighted conclusion: "Knowledge is an additional cost that does not generate significant business value."

Symptoms: Individuals in a knowledge management team, participants in a learning organization, or the members of a knowledge community are enamored of the process. Cooperation makes them feel good. They begin to resemble a church group of professional educators I once addressed who were described to me this way: "They like to hold hands and pray." Their problem is that they fail to recognize unpleasant realities like competition, in the church group case, from fundamentalists. The question in business cases is how to get people who love process to value profits also. Such groups need to go beyond aspirations like "stimulate cooperation" to include "generate new business" as well.

Diagnosis: No Tangible Business Purpose

Solution: Get top management actively involved in the life of a knowledge community or knowledge management system. The Booz • Allen authors Charles Lucier and Janet Torsilieri write further that sponsorship without active, ongoing involvement is one of the main correctable problems. It's not that top management is disinterested. The issue is, many older executives recognize that knowledge and learning require different management practices, which make them uncertain and unwilling to participate actively.

Motorola, for example, when it started its management training and education center, had to overcome the resistance of ten of its executive board members, but it got the active and ongoing participation of the eleventh, Chris Galvin, the next-in-line CEO. Motorola University is now considered one of the top corporate universities, precisely because of its business results. In fact, Motorola became so successful with its business leverage—each dollar invested in their workforce training led to thirty dollars of return—that the company became arrogant and subsequently failed to listen to customer feedback.

SWEEP OUT THE OLD

Situation: It took AT&T several years to establish its knowledge communities in the Global Services division. Then-president Bob Allen was an active supporter. When the communities held their annual face-to-face meetings at headquarters in Basking Ridge, the president would attend and address the group. The CEO's attendance at an annual meeting made a particular community's members feel that they were doing something new and important. It made them feel special. But then, not long after his participation in the annual meeting of several communities, Bob Allen retired after fifteen years as CEO.

Symptoms: The Chinese word for crisis (*wei ji*) is the two ideograms that represent danger and opportunity. Winston Churchill once said that optimists see opportunity in every danger and pessimists see danger in every opportunity. Whenever a new CEO takes over, both optimists and pessimists start to make their predictions. Pat Traynor, an optimist, sees further opportunity to expand the knowledge communities she initiated. Pessimists, on the other hand, see the danger that a new CEO will curtail an innovation he did not initiate. Some newly appointed CEOs eliminate *all* their predecessors' pet programs, sweeping away not only the deadwood but the good as well.

Diagnosis: This is the Sweep Out the Old syndrome.

Solution: Allen's successor, Mike Armstrong, initiated his tenure as AT&T's CEO not only with the joint venture with British Telecom, which strengthened the company's international business, but also with the acquisition of TCG (Teleport Communications Group), which put AT&T into the $21 billion business local service market. Pat Traynor is not only strengthening the International Knowledge Community but, with the help of other senior VPs, has established a new Local Community. As she did from the outset, she's just doing it with the conviction she's doing the right thing. The way to deal with a "sweep out the old" leader is to convince him or her that expanded knowledge is new—never old.

SMART PEOPLE MAKE LOUSY LEARNERS

Situation: In a famous and influential article "Teaching Smart People How to Learn," Harvard Business School's Professor Chris Argyris argues that smart people make poor learners. Managers too smart to fail never have an opportunity to learn from failure. Further, if they are perceived as experts, they are always expected to have the right answers, even when there are none. The World Bank, which is staffed by hiring experts from all the countries it serves, is a case in point. When the Bank tried to implement President Jim Wolfensohn's strategy to become a knowledge bank, part of which included building a knowledge management system (KM), it encountered considerable opposition from the middle-management level.

Symptoms: There was lots of verbal support for KM but lots of hidden resistance as well. KM builders found it very difficult to get people to ask questions, which would be admitting that there was something they didn't know. That ran counter to a culture that expects everyone to know everything.

Diagnosis: The "Smart people make lousy learners" bug.

Solution: A change in values and attitudes toward the role of smart individuals has to come about. For the World Bank, that took many forms coming from different places at the same time: the natural process of renewal of older managers; new evaluation systems for assessing managers and staff; even new spatial arrangements to support community work—open space. The Bank seeks to change its hiring practices so that, for example, PhDs in economics can be productive in client developing country situations, where 70 percent of the job is process-oriented and 30 percent is economic expertise.

The Bank has started by organizing knowledge communities across four sectors (like agriculture or environment) and six geographic regions (like Africa or Latin America) by identifying sixteen communities of practice. It's too early to declare victory; some Bank staff think it may take as long as ten years to fulfill the vision of a knowledge bank.

INCAPACITATED BY EXPERTS

Situation: Ann was eight months pregnant, Jane was 80 pounds overweight, and the rest of the gringo group of business executives were beginning to feel the heat of the Mexican sun. An InterClass group was headed toward the ancient Aztec ruins of Xochicalco as part of a management seminar taking place near Cuernavaca. The assignment of "Business 21—Leadership Now" was to explore emerging business paradigms for the years ahead by examining those of the past: What lessons for today's successful companies can be drawn from the failure of ancient Indian civilizations, which were at their peak of power when their worldview failed to explain the appearance of the Conquistadors?

The facilitators knew trouble was in store when, unannounced, the archeological director of the site came to lead the tour. "No, no," she said. "I'm the director here and I know the best way." Rather than move toward a gently sloping pathway, the group of sixty veered toward the steep staircase where one hundred knee-high stone steps led straight up. Halfway up, a manager from Otis Elevator joked, "I think I see a business opportunity." At that point, Jane swooned. She was probably the highest in rank, but at that moment the lowest, as she lay stretched out sweating profusely beneath the sun.

Symptoms: A community far from its familiar surroundings encounters a bend in the road where an expert appears to assure the group she knows the best way to go. She speaks so confidently her words appear to make sense. No one at the time catches the telltale sign: "No, no. I know the way."

Diagnosis: Incapacitated by experts sickness (The opposite to the smart people make lousy learner's bug, but with the same debilitating effects)

Solution: While the particulars of this case are unique, we've all been in situations where our intuition has told us something is wrong but we didn't trust it enough to act. Ever since that incident, I personally keep my "guards out" to trust my intuition, check out the path less traveled, and question vigorously the so-called experts. As in this case, you may find out that they don't know the context of why there were good reasons to take the longer but less strenuous path. Or you may find out that they are not really experts at all but pseudoexperts.

COMMUNITY WALLS

Situation: In *Communities of Practice,* Etienne Wenger shows how communities unconsciously develop a culture. Members tend to dress alike, use idiomatic language, and learn what to expect from one another. Such codes of conduct can form invisible barriers to noncommunity members. The Institute for Research on Learning, where Wenger and others developed the communities of practice concept, uses this pitfall to explain why many communities encounter problems learning from one another unless specific countermeasures are taken.[3]

That is what happened when the Center for Creative Leadership—a leadership training organization in Greensboro, North Carolina[4]—invited the InterClass community to join it in articulating new models of leadership to supersede the old industrial model. The two communities dialogued for two days and, while some significant points emerged, they were unable to articulate a shared understanding robust enough to be incorporated into CCL's new simulation focused on change and chaos as the leadership norm rather than stasis and control.

Symptoms: CCL uses a technique common in many types of training where observers can view participants through one-way mirrors. Indeed, CCL facilities are filled with such glass partitions where people on one side can see what's happening, but those being observed cannot see the observers on the other side. In the bustle of the opening meeting, the CCL director neglected to explain this practice. When the guests learned they were being observed through one-way mirrors, they were upset.

Diagnosis: Community Walls Disease

Solution: The obvious solution in this case is to get agreement on ground rules at the outset. However, both communities learned something more significant as a result of the experience: Communities are always constructing invisible walls that define who is "in" and who is "out." When two communities meet for the first time, each feels like an outsider to the other, until they get enough common experience and understanding to trust working together. There are many ways to develop such trust, like the "Trust Walk"[5] that Saturn uses or by asking each person to tell how he or she became members of their community. The challenge is to do it consciously and purposefully until it becomes embedded in the group's norms and practices.

There are some cases where a community may want to protect its knowledge from hostile competitors; here a community should be strengthening its barriers against outsiders. There are other cases, however, where a community needs to open itself to the fresh thinking that outsiders provide; here a community should be conscious of its walls and devise ways to overcome them. The most successful communities learn how to incorporate building walls and removing walls as required into their community practices.

ELDERS ABSENT, YOUTH EXCLUDED, DIVERSITY DRIED UP

Situation: Many knowledge communities are homogeneous in age and outlook. Except in special cases, they seldom cross generational lines. Boomers tend to belong to boomer communities, Generation-Next to Gen-X communities, and so on. Where that is the case, it is an opportunity lost. Diversity in age means access to the fresh ideas that the young bring with them and the seasoned perspectives that elders carry.[6]

Gary Hamel tells the story of the young representative of a strategy-creation team invited to present its findings to the management committee. He writes that the twelve-member executive management committee with more than twenty years of seniority was sitting in an enormous boardroom when the invited young representative appeared. He "never stood a chance. Less than five minutes into the four-hour talk, he was being pelted with disbelief and skepticism." Rather than demonstrate enlightened self-interest, the management committee demonstrated its capacity for intimidation.[7]

Symptoms: At face-to-face meetings, you notice that all the members of the knowledge community are about the same age. In the Japanese fashion where the nail that sticks out is quickly hammered down, no one in the community sticks out with radical ideas or time-honored memories. In severe cases, members are all the same color and gender.

Diagnosis: The Common Cold: Elders Absent, Youth Excluded, Diversity Dried Up

Solution: It's a mere palliative to echo empty phrases like "value diversity." Rather, you have to pay attention to process. In Gary Hamel's story, facilitators at the next management committee meeting turned the tables: The meeting was held offsite on neutral territory. All twenty-five members of the strategy-creation team were present, thus outnumbering the executives. Also, the management committee sat in a semicircle with no table to hide behind. Finally, each member of the management committee was assigned two members of the team for a four-hour discussion on how the team had arrived at its conclusions.

PIPSA does it by consciously creating tri-generational knowledge communities. Skandia does it by forming teams of the "in power" generation, the potential generation, and "generation next." Those two processes are excellent for curing the common cold where elders are absent, youth excluded, and diversity dried up.

PITFALLS IN THE STUDY OF BEES

People have lots of misconceptions about bees. One of them is that bees have leaders. They don't, except in the one case I cited in the chapter on leadership: When they swarm, they are led by the old queen, who then sends out scouts to find a location for the new hive while she, like old generals on battlefields of yore, sits and waits until reports come back on whether the scouts have been successful. That is not a very inspiring role of leadership; rather, the lesson from bees is that large numbers of workers can be mobilized without any apparent leadership, making them quite different from human populations.

Another misconception is the popular notion that bees are busy. "Busy as a bee" is an expression that doesn't stand the test of science. In the 1800s Professor C. F. Hodge marked bees and watched them from daylight to dark. His report: "No single bee I watched ever worked more than three and one-half hours a day." In the 1950s the entomologist Martin Lindauer observed that one typical bee, during 170 observation hours, did absolutely nothing for 70 of them and "patrolled" the nest as though looking for work for 50. Thus, during roughly two-thirds of her time she was performing no productive work. In this sense, bees share some of the traits of humans: They can be as lazy as we are.[8]

Knowledge communities and the knowledge business generally are just as demanding as traditional business and then some. Knowledge is not a panacea that will make life easy. Soon, all businesses will be based on knowledge, and they'll be competing as fiercely as ever. The pitfalls discussed above are perhaps not surprising, but it cannot be overemphasized that bad things happen to good people. Both organizing for the knowledge future, and keeping "guards out" against slip-ups, will be essential to survival.

Chapter Ten

A Smart Business Engages the Knowledge Revolution and Grows from It

*These are
traditional Chinese
characters read as "Da Fong."
They represent our name—literally,
large bees. However, they also sound like
large wind or large harvest.*

—Bumble Bee Laboratories, Singapore.

If you plan for a year, plant a seed.
If for ten years, plant a tree.
If for a hundred, teach the people.
When you sow a seed once, you reap a single harvest.
If you teach the people, you reap a hundred harvests.

—K'uan-tzu, 47 B.C.

MAKING, MEASURING, AND MANAGING
KNOWLEDGE COMMUNITIES

Many companies, contemplating knowledge communities, ask how to get started. There is both a quick answer and a comprehensive quiver of answers. Like an arrow, the quick answer gives you a single shot: If it hits home, declare victory. But when there's more than one objective, a quiver of arrows will serve you better.

The quick answer is to identify your communities of practice, make them visible and accountable, and give them all the support they need to thrive and flourish. I call this the "communities of practice approach." Referring to the aphorism cited at the head of this chapter, that method yields, "When you sow a seed once, you reap a single harvest." There are many cases in business where all you need is a single harvest, and in such cases I recommend the communities of practice approach.

The quiver of answers starts with more questions, asking what knowledge business you're intending to grow, what base for your knowledge communities will best suit the business, and how you intend to manage the new organization and business. This alternative approach can be visualized as a 3 × 3 matrix, where one side is the "3Ks" (knowledge business, knowledge communities, and knowledge management), and the other is the "3Ms" (making, measuring, and managing). I call this the "nine questions approach" which, while more complex, is the more comprehensive of the two: "if you teach the people, you reap a hundred harvests."

THE COMMUNITIES OF PRACTICE APPROACH

Communities of practice don't appear on the organization chart, because they are invisible, informal, and largely unaccountable as a group for what they do. Transforming them into knowledge communities is a process of making them visible, formal, and accountable.

The original concept of communities of practice (CoP), as developed by the Institute for Research on Learning, enunciated by Etienne Wenger in his book *Communities of Practice*, and reviewed by Peter Henschel in his article in the Appendix, has a small but strong group of believers. Many of them appreciate that CoPs are informal. Their value, they argue, is in research on how learning takes place and a better understanding of how work actually gets done. As such, they argue further, they are better left informal.[1]

However, if your goal is to transform your organization, the quickest route is to build on what's already in place. The first step is to identify your communities of practice and make them visible. That may not be as easy as it sounds. It is likely you will need to engage the skills that business anthropologists possess. That entails having one or more persons "live" in your company to record on paper or videotape how real work actually is accomplished.[2] Those are similar to the methods used by Margaret Mead, the social anthropologist famous for her work in Samoa, but applied to business.[3]

Your company is likely to have more than just one CoP. It may have many—dozens or even thousands, if you're the size of Chevrolet or Xerox, which has done significant work in identifying its CoPs in several of its business units. So which CoPs are we talking about here? Answer: the most significant ones in the product or service area where you wish to transform the organization. KPMG, for example, has three principal professional services: tax, audit, and consulting. It started its knowledge community with tax professionals by establishing the Tax Knowledge Sharing system headed by Doug Izard. The firm also has five different lines of business that each of the three serve. To hone its knowledge strategy, its next step is to identify the CoPs in each of those five lines of business in the tax area.

Traditionally, companies have had to balance organizing by product, markets, function, or geography. Matrix management is a method to cross any two of those categories: Doug Izard, for example, reports functionally to KPMG's Vice Chairman for Tax and operationally to the Chief Knowledge Officer. Organizing into knowledge communities by the communities of practice approach largely bypasses that balancing act because it looks first at how the work is actually done as it has evolved over time. That approach has the advantage that it is based on reality. Its disadvantage is that it is based on a past reality you may be seeking to update.

After you identify a key community of practice, make it visible. At first, this means membership lists. They may take the form of paper-and-pencil lists or, more likely, electronic lists. If the business area has legal confidentiality requirements (as tax does) or client-imposed confidentiality guidelines (as most consulting has), then the electronic membership list requires passwords to computerized knowledge bases. Later, making visible means talking up, citing, and praising the community in the company newsletter, at award ceremonies, or on every appropriate occasion.

The act of making a CoP visible is the first act of formalizing it. Formalizing may evoke a whole raft of management issues. Those include, among others, whether a particular community member, redundant or unsuitable in an invisible community of practice, needs to be transferred or let go in a formal and thus visible knowledge community.

Making the CoP formally accountable is a matter of matching the compensation and reward systems congruent with community performance. Saturn, for example, has a bonus system as much as 10 percent of base salary, but the bonus is given based on the whole community's performance.

THE NINE QUESTIONS APPROACH

Visualize the challenge as nine questions, as displayed in the accompanying tables.

Making the Knowledge Business

When considering how to make, build, and launch the 3Ks of a comprehensive knowledge strategy, I purposely start with the knowledge business as the main driver. Too many companies launch into other aspects of knowledge with too little thought to the business it is designed to serve. Chapter 3, "What's the Knowledge Business in Your Business?" covers that subject. Refer back to it if you need a refresher on what is meant by the knowledge business and how you can find it in your industry.

Making Knowledge Communities

To build one or more knowledge communities from scratch, you have to decide what to base them on. Your choices are usually product/service; mar-

THE NINE QUESTIONS APPROACH

Knowledge Business (KB)

Make What's the knowledge business in your business?

Manage What are the measures for a knowledge business, especially metrics that differ from those in traditional business?

Measure How does the Networked Model of management play in your industry?

Knowledge Community (KC)

Make What's the most critical element in the KB around which to base your knowledge communities?

Manage How do you know if your knowledge community is excelling, just existing, or about to exit the scene?

Measure What are the new management roles, norms, and practices needed for your KC to excel?

Knowledge Management (KM)

Make What are the critical success factors for building a capability to maximize your community's knowledge creation and sharing?

Manage How do you measure the value of a knowledge management system, or how would you discern whether a competing KM is better or worse than yours?

Measure Who "owns" the KM system and to whom does he, she, or they report? Who takes action when the knowledge management system goes down?

---

kets/clients; function; or geography. Those are the same basic choices that years ago led to matrix management. In the AT&T case, Pat Traynor had to choose whether to organize the communities by product or by market. She chose product/services, and thus ended up with the Data Community, the Wireless Community, and so on. The alternatives would have been the Banking Community, which would have sold all products just to that one market; the Hong Kong Community, which would have sold all products to all clients in Hong Kong; or the HR Community, which would have provided HR internal services to all other groups within the Business Markets Division.[4]

The reason why AT&T ultimately made the product/service choice is that it is the one most closely aligned to its knowledge business and has the fastest rate of technological change. An equally valid argument could have been made to organize by markets/clients. However, that was how Traynor's organization had been oriented earlier, and it wasn't working.

KPMG made a similar choice when it chose tax services because that's how the professional services industry is organized. As for AT&T, an argument could be made that the knowledge community should start with a line of business—for example, the health care industry—and the community should be able to provide all tax, auditing, and consulting services. That's not the way the U.S.-based professional service firms are moving. Arthur Andersen's consulting arm, for example, is a separate business. But that doesn't mean a competitor couldn't take the road less traveled.

The KPMG Tax Knowledge Sharing system also made the implicit choice to be a community on U.S. tax law. Because each country's tax laws are so specific to the country, that seems to be an obvious choice. When a global corporation needs tax advice that crosses multiple national boundaries and involves tax codes from many countries, this can be handled by one nationally based community communicating with one or more other communities. Or, if the business warrants it, KPMG could establish a global tax knowledge center composed of specialists with expertise in multiple national tax codes.

Ultimately, your choice should be based on your business. If the bulk of your business is U.S.-based tax advice, organize a U.S.-based tax knowledge center. If it's global tax advice, organize the Multinational Tax Knowledge Community.

Making Knowledge Management Systems

A knowledge management system without a community is like an orphan without a home. It's left to chance whether it gets the TLC it needs to thrive. The more knowledge management systems are linked to a specific community of users linked to a specific business, the more synergy the whole system gains.

IKE[5] is the knowledge management system for AT&T's knowledge communities. KPMG's Tax Knowledge Sharing system is what anchors its community of tax advisers. The World Bank's knowledge management system is the backbone of the communities that make up the Knowledge Bank concept. Community members come to depend on the system to perform their everyday work. Thus they have a direct interest in how accurate, timely, and selective the information is.

It is possible, of course, to have knowledge management systems independent from the knowledge business or knowledge communities. Statoil has Faros, which serves a very large traditional oil company. Forum has Foresite, which serves a small, conventionally organized training company. Both are impressive and effective systems. The more tightly they could be linked to their firms' knowledge strategies for business and organization, the more effective they would grow.

The role of technology versus culture is so important that it bears reiterating. When Pat Traynor says IKE is the anchor of AT&T's knowledge communities, she is putting the accent *not* on technology but rather on the capacity to enhance the daily sharing of information and knowledge. "The choice of which technology is not the point," she explains. "It's the capabilities to support the culture and behaviors that determine its success." The system includes not just IT but also editors, facilitators, conference calls with open microphones, fax machines, and other non-IT items.

Measuring the Knowledge Business

Sometimes we forget that, like traditional business, the knowledge business is measured in sales revenues, margins, and net profits or losses. That is obvious for older knowledge businesses like consulting or computer hardware and software companies. In that regard, Microsoft is the most successful knowledge company yet seen and proven. Dell and Gateway are close behind. But when conventional business moves into the knowledge industry, as Amazon and Barnes & Noble are doing, we get mixed signals: Amazon, which has yet to show a profit, has a stock price higher than B&N, which is profitable by virtue of its conventional bookselling channels.

Thus stock price or a company's "market cap" are not really reliable measures of a particular knowledge business. What they measure is the market's current thinking about the KB's future prospects. That type of measure worked well in a slower-paced industrial economy, where there was a firm connection between profits and stock price. In the knowledge economy, that connection has been weakened if not completely severed, because the knowledge economy is driven by boom-and-bust dynamics to a far greater degree than the older industrial or agricultural economies were.

The concept of intellectual capital (IC), developed by Leif Edvinsson at Skandia and Tom Stewart at Fortune,[6] holds the promise of a measurement system geared to the knowledge business that provides an alternative to traditional accounting. Intellectual capital seeks to measure human, customer, and structural capital as the main components of a company's assets and its growth potential. Accepting IC as a future standard for measuring KB would represent a great conceptual and legal leap forward.

Measuring Knowledge Communities

Knowledge communities are ultimately measured by their results in whatever knowledge business they are formed to conduct. But it is in many cases difficult to establish a direct causal relationship. This difficulty is similar to those in quality programs, education and training initiatives, or any reorganization program, because most of those focus on enhancing internal capabilities that are more difficult to measure. But, like quality, there are plenty of other indicators that specify how well or poorly a KC is performing.

The first indicator is active participation. Passivity is the kiss of death for a knowledge community. While there is not yet enough experience with KCs to give time-tested guidelines, a rule of thumb I use is that participation rates of 75 percent or higher indicate a lively, healthy community, whereas lower than 50 percent is a cause for concern. But 50 or 75 percent of what? On a conference call, what percentage of the total membership is participating? In face-to-face meetings, what percentage of the total community shows up for the whole time or part of the time? What percentage take part in annual policy review meetings to set expectations, operating practices, and future agendas?

A second indicator is backlog. How many additional people or potential members want to join the community? Is it actually growing if the community desires to grow? Is it actually consolidating if the community sets that goal as its priority? Is it financially solvent—budget allocations in the case of an internal community, membership fees in the case of an external one?

Participation and backlog are quantitative measures. What about qualitative ones? How smart or skilled is a knowledge community? To answer questions of this kind, it helps to look at the university world, where people have been asking the same questions for a long time. How good is Stanford? How good is U.C. Berkeley? How good is Worcester Polytechnic Institute (Massachusetts) versus Rensselaer Polytechnic Institute (New York)? The same can be asked about research institutes. How good is Los Alamos National Laboratory versus Lawrence Livermore? How good is Xerox PARC versus Bill Labs at Microsoft?

Answers on the quality of institutes or communities rely on rankings, which in turn rely on informed judgment. The faculty at one institute rank the faculty departments in another. A whole industry of ranking business schools or research labs grows up. Informally, the same is happening with corporate universities, but these have the advantage over traditional universities that they belong to a particular company that is judged by profit-and-loss statements. Research labs are judged by their funders and regulators: Congress, DOE, and the regents of the University of California in the Los Alamos case.

Knowledge communities will follow that same pattern of informed judgment when it comes to qualitative measures. Members of other knowledge communities can sometimes provide such judgment. Knowledge brokers or learning observers who travel between and among knowledge communities may provide a source of informed opinion. Working with measurement concepts like intellectual capital, professional associations of knowledge community facilitators may emerge—similar to the American Productivity and Quality Center for the quality movement—that will take on this challenge of qualitative indicators.

Measuring Knowledge Management Systems

Measuring knowledge management systems is particularly challenging, because there is a whole body of literature and consulting practice on measuring management information systems or IT—which resemble KM systems—but no similar understanding of how to measure knowledge has yet developed.

For example, IT professionals measure the age of their hardware and software systems, budgets allocated to IT over multiyear time periods, and what those figures indicate for the stage of development the IT function of a company is in. Numbers of users are tracked, end-user opinions are sought on user satisfaction surveys, and management judgments are recorded on how strategic the IT department is to the overall business strategy.

Those types of measurements—especially how well or how poorly the KM system is linked to the corporate business strategy—are essential to gauging KM effectiveness. Is the head of your KM system part of the strategic business planning process? Is he or she considered a main contributor to the company's business plan? Those are indications of how tightly or loosely a KM system is coupled to the firm's knowledge strategy. However, it's important to note, as Mark Schleicher, head of Motorola University's KM does, that "knowledge management is not a mechanism to fix screwed-up business; it can only optimize the business strategy that you've selected."

Other measures that look beyond traditional IT and more toward knowledge are some of the following: KPMG's Doug Izard tracks the number of captures accepted by his center and published on the system versus the much larger number of submissions. AT&T's Pat Traynor records the number of hits and number of unique users represented by the hits over time and related to key events. When her KC membership is 3,000 and unique users of IKE number 14,000, she speaks of this as a vote of confidence in the KM system. However, both Doug and Pat are quick to acknowledge that those are not very satisfactory yardsticks, because the numbers don't tell you what the users did with the information or knowledge they received.

Tom Davenport of Andersen Consulting and Boston University has collected what he calls "Knowledge Results."[7] In R&D knowledge management systems, these include $40 million a year at Dow in patent and license management and six months faster to FDA approval at Roche. In sales, both Genentech and Astra-Merck credit their KM for doubling their face-to-face customer time, and Sequent says it enables 10 percent higher sales for new sales reps after six months.

In manufacturing and production, BPX (British Petroleum Exploration) claims two days less downtime per incident is attributable to its knowledge management, while National Semiconductor believes it gets faster production curves. In customer support, Rank Xerox has achieved a 15 percent reduction in dispatches, while HP claims as much as a 50 percent reduction in cost per call.

Consulting companies in the knowledge business can measure the impact of their KM on their business: the number of new projects gained as a result of KM, the amount of time saved in creating new proposals for potential clients by using captured and catalogued former proposals. Not having to reinvent the wheel saved Motorola an estimated quarter-hour per employee per quarter: But in so doing, "are we creating the time for our businesspeople to be creative for a customer?" Motorola's Mark Schleicher asks.

Managing the Knowledge Business

If you're in the knowledge business, are you still caught in the old pendulum swings from decentralized to centralized back to decentralized management models? What experiences have you had or prototypes have you consciously undertaken to test the networked management model? If you're considering launching a knowledge business, are you prepared for the new management styles it will pressure you to adopt?

The GM Star service, which provides directions and other services to new owners of certain makes and models, is organized on the network model. Car owners can use their cell phone to call the Star Center operators, who in turn know where the car is from the satellite-based GPS locator. That same database also gives them access to what drivers want to know: the location of the nearest gas station, restaurant, or theater they can't find. Star operators are networked to one another and to the GPS system, as well as to the caller. Their organization stands in stark contrast to the older model, which is still subject to labor unrest.

No management model can guarantee good labor relations, especially in the knowledge business. It is wishful thinking to say that new management models will avoid all the pitfalls of the older centralized/decentralized models: The biggest labor unions in the United States—where there are now fewer union members than temps—exist in the knowledge-intensive world of education.[8] Whether networked management styles will lead to better labor relations will depend on the extent of rollercoaster economics driven by sometimes gargantuan egos. Managing a university, whose sole product is knowledge, is often more challenging than managing a company, whose next products will be knowledge-based.

Managing Knowledge Communities

Successful management of knowledge communities calls for new management practices and roles. The new roles include full-time leaders-facilitators, a team of full-time editors (AT&T and KPMG both have five or more), and web masters. Other new roles include knowledge brokers or "ambassadors," who perform intercommunity communication, and a "red-threads" team, who articulate common principles learned from one assignment to the next, much like the U.S. Army's CALL function (Center for Army Lessons Learned). Such an overview function can help in the critical process of developing and articulating community beliefs, norms, practices, and expectation of community members.

Collaborative principles may include confidentiality, consensus decision-making, truthful and thoughtful feedback, and, in the case of external knowledge communities, policies, practices, and protection from competitors. Knowledge communities also have to develop procedures for bringing in new members, acclimating them, and deactivating retiring members. Many of those issues are covered in Chapters 4 and 7.

Managing Knowledge Management

Managing knowledge management is one of the main responsibilities of a Chief Knowledge Officer or a Chief Learning Officer (more or less the same thing), and not, barring special circumstances, the Chief Information Officer or Chief Technology Officer.

KPMG has a Chief Knowledge Officer who oversees the firm's knowledge strategy: business, organization, and KM. Doug Izard, Director of the Tax Knowledge Sharing system, reports to the Partner in Charge of Tax Knowledge Management, who in turn reports functionally to the Vice Chairman for Tax and operationally to the CKO. Like the Vice Chairman for Tax, the firm's first CKO was at the vice chairman level. At Motorola, KM director Mark Schleicher reports to Senior VP and Motorola University Director Bill Wiggenhorn. The point is that in companies that take KM most seriously, managers of such systems report to very senior levels in the organization.

The reason it is less appropriate to rely on CIOs or CTOs for KM is that those positions are often too focused on technology. For successful KM, knowledge and user relationships should be the major focus; technology, though important, is the minor subject. The exception may be in a company (CSC is an example) that thinks of itself as primarily a technology business with a culture of technologists.

QUESTIONS IN CONCLUSION

How does a smart business engage the knowledge revolution and grow from it? I believe it takes wisdom, a quality in short supply in our fast-moving world of business people who often long to live their ideals but don't feel empowered to do so.

In the film *The Milagro Beanfield War,* set in a village near Santa Fe, New Mexico,[9] there is a scene where the old sage Amarante Córdova is faced with the challenge of developers overrunning his rustic community. He calls on his ancestors for advice. "It's going to take a big sacrifice," the spirits say. Amarante gets himself shot and wounded, which galvanizes the community, exposes the plots, and thwarts the plans of the dispossessing developers. Both Amarante and community members celebrate their newfound life.

Leading or engaging the knowledge revolution is going to take some big sacrifices. But as we've seen and learned from the bees, new life from near death can be a blessing.

The Economics of Knowledge

Eric E. Vogt,
Chief Learning Officer,
Omega Performance

If you are a line manager in business today, you can ignore the ideas in this book. But if you do, you might as well bend over and kiss your corporate assets goodbye. Your business is already being driven by the new economics of knowledge and knowledge communities. You are simply operating with blinders. And, depending upon your industry, you have between six and thirty-six months to figure out how to shift your mindset and your skill set toward a knowledge community orientation. Failure to do so will lead to missed opportunities, misuse of intellectual assets, and perhaps an unwelcome early retirement.

Why do I make these claims? Simply stated, knowledge is the fuel of the future. And knowledge communities are the factories of the future. *Smart Business* provides a blueprint for the design of those future factories. The downside of ignoring the messages of this book is that you will attempt to navigate the knowledge economy without a map or a compass. You can conceivably travel this treacherous territory relying upon your past experience. But your past experience is misguided. Almost by definition, your experience was formed in the bygone industrial and information economies. Your internal gyroscope will send you blithely in the wrong direction because, unfortunately, the economics of knowledge bears little resemblance to the economics you and I grew up with. The economics of knowledge and knowledge communities are governed by a less familiar set of laws. I will attempt to describe the new economics of knowledge and knowledge communities through a set of principles.

KNOWLEDGE IS A PERSPECTIVE

We unconsciously operate as if knowledge is solid. We speak of the body of scientific knowledge, medical knowledge, or software knowledge as tangible. Our libraries, databases, and web sites serve to support that view. We accept that the amount of knowledge is growing exponentially, and that new knowledge replaces old. We spend millions on electronic knowledge management systems. However, hidden in our language and the metaphors we use to describe knowledge is an assumption of knowledge as solid, tangible, measurable, and factual. That unconscious assumption will prevent you from saving yourself.

A better definition of knowledge, for the purpose of understanding the economics of knowledge, is to say that knowledge is a perspective shared by a community which allows for some effective action. This definition begins to provide the keys to creating productive knowledge. It opens different questions, such as, "How do we create new perspectives?" or "How does a community rapidly share new perspectives?" or "What is the perspective that inhibits our effectiveness today?" Those questions are more important to your success in the knowledge economy than your investment in knowledge management software.

IDEAS ARE THE RAW MATERIAL—
GIVE THEM AWAY AND THEY GAIN VALUE

Comparative advantage, supply and demand, dominant market share, information is power. Almost all of the basic economic concepts and metaphors that inform our common view of economics derive from a bygone era. When raw materials were coal, iron ore, and petroleum, these economic concepts all made sense. Simply lock up the supply and share with no one. Now the critical raw material is human ideas. We know that there is nothing more powerful than an idea whose time has come. But for those ideas to gain value they have to be exchanged with associates and colleagues. Often in the exchange, the idea is improved or amplified. The economics of knowledge and ideas can be simply exemplified by a facsimile transmission. You've noticed that when you send a fax, you still have the original! More importantly, someone else has shared your idea, and the idea often becomes more valuable for two reasons. First, the idea is beginning to influence one more mind, and thus is more valuable. And second, the idea is often improved upon by another reflective mind.

One challenge for the knowledge economy is that we seldom operate naturally in an environment of open idea exchange. Fear of criticism and ridicule or concerns about proprietary information often prevent us from tapping into the full value of our idea creation and exchange. Knowledge communities can achieve this value.

PRODUCTIVE CAPACITY IS A COMMUNITY PHENOMENON

Since the value of ideas is enhanced through exchange in a community, creating productive capacity in the knowledge economy requires more the skills of an anthropologist than those of an engineer. You cannot simply hire the right individual and hope for performance. It is the design of the community that produces above-average results. We all have worked in knowledge-worker environments that were conducive to creativity and those that were not. I am willing to wager that the difference in productivity between the extremely good knowledge-worker environment and the extremely poor knowledge-worker environment was easily a factor of ten. Estimates of the percentage of the U.S. economy that currently operates under the rules of a knowledge economy range from 40 to 60 percent. Imagine the impact on our standard of living stemming from a tenfold difference in productivity for half of the economy!

We must pay more attention to the design of knowledge communities and their culture. As specialists in industrial design, engineers helped us design productive factories in the industrial economy. As specialists in culture, anthropologists may help us find some of the keys to designing productive knowledge communities.

TRUST IS THE ESSENTIAL CATALYST

Ironically, one essential ingredient is available worldwide but often hard to find. Trust nurtures knowledge creation. Simply put, baby ideas, if born, will not flourish in an environment of distrust. Conversely, communities with trust breed creative ideas at a high rate and encourage everyone to participate willingly in their growth to mature, innovative concepts. It takes a village to raise a child. It takes a trusting community to grow new knowledge. So simple, so fundamental, and so amazing that most of our organizations today do not have the essential catalyst for knowledge creation.

And yet, upon reflection we recognize that one of the principles of work organization since the dawn of the industrial economy has been *mistrust.* Time clocks, management hierarchy, labor unions, and efficiency experts were all invented to address an underlying assumption of mistrust. Assembly lines personify the illness, knowledge communities represent the antidote. If we were somehow to measure the level of trust in a GM assembly line and compare it with the level of trust in a Volvo assembly team, I believe we could see how trust, ideation, and knowledge communities are intimately linked.

QUESTIONS HAVE MORE VALUE THAN ANSWERS

In the economics of knowledge, questions provide both direction and power for the search. Nobel Laureates frequently say that their breakthroughs came with a fresh question, not an answer. Questions open the human mind. Answers resolve the ambiguity and extinguish the fire of intellectual inquiry. Indeed, if questions are so critical to the capacity to create and develop human knowledge, we wonder why our public educational system focuses upon memorization and static answers rather than the art of questioning.

Illustrating a contrast with the typical western education, the distinguished Chilean biologist Humberto Maturana was recently asked how his schooling influenced his innovative thinking. He replied that he had attended an experimental high school in Santiago where half the students' grades were based upon the quality of their questions, not their answers. How can we expect a workforce trained to score well on SAT examinations to know how to formulate powerful questions? The economic productivity of knowledge communities will depend upon their collective capacity to articulate powerful questions and have the fortitude to remain in ambiguity until the fresh ideas appear.[1]

The ability to formulate powerful questions is also not taught in schools. And yet, the single greatest waste of knowledge-worker time in business today is conversations where the wrong question is being debated. By "wrong question," I mean either 1) the question lacks power; 2) the question contains unquestioned assumptions; 3) the question constrains the imagination; or simply, 4) the question misdirects the conversation towards an unproductive topic. How often have you found yourself talking about the features needed in a new product when the important question is the capability of the sales force? The economics of knowledge dictate that discovery begins with powerful questions, and our workforce has been trained to answer the wrong question.

MYTHS, MODELS AND METAPHORS: THE FOOD GROUPS OF THE KNOWLEDGE COMMUNITY

Sometimes I find it useful to look backward in order to look forward. Aboriginal people on all continents had extensive knowledge, honed with precision and passed to later generations by oral traditions. Western thinking arrogantly ignored and systematically destroyed many of those assets. Now pharmaceutical companies are scrambling to understand the wisdom of traditional, natural remedies. How were those traditional perspectives created and perpetuated? Their basic technologies were myths, models, and metaphors.

Storytelling and the associated myths represented then the way people constructed and explained new perspectives—new knowledge. We still do it, but we label it concept selling, public relations, or spin control. Speaking persuasively of new perspectives is a treasured asset in the knowledge economy.

Mental models consciously or unconsciously shape our view of the world. Fundamentalist religious groups have robust mental models that explain the status quo. An ability flexibly to try on alternative mental models and to go beyond what is given as gospel is the hallmark of a productive knowledge worker.

Metaphors are the means by which we create new meaning. How many times have you listened to someone describe a new phenomenon by saying, "It is like X?" We weave new concepts out of more familiar ones through the art of metaphor. Metaphor can be used creatively, but at the same time it can also serve to limit our thinking. "Knowledge is power" is a common metaphor that strongly supports the mindset of not exchanging ideas and perspectives with others. That can limit the quality and power of your ideas in the knowledge economy, which is why *Smart Business* opens with "Why Knowledge *Shared* Is Power."

Elliott Jaques writes eloquently of the concept of cognitive complexity in his book *Requisite Organization.* His claim is that those professionals who have the capacity to hold several dimensions of ambiguity at the same time are also those who will invent the future. As a line manager in the knowledge economy, I urge you to take a fresh look at the professionals you hire for your knowledge community. Are they fluent with myths, models, and metaphors? Can they easily move from one mental model to another? Are they comfortable with ambiguity, or do they need black-and-white clarity? One criterion for hiring the new knowledge worker is "does not need to wait for instructions."

KNOWLEDGE COMMUNITY LEADERS
MAKE MEANING, NOT DECISIONS

Our traditional view of leaders is based upon John Wayne movies. The leader is the powerful male who makes bold decisions and tells us what to do. In contrast, the essence of a knowledge community is its ability spontaneously to integrate the perspectives of the community and generate the optimal course of action—often different from the choice any individual might have made. The knowledge community leader is someone skilled at building the *context* for creative thinking and action. Building context requires the leader to make meaning rather than make decisions. Making meaning—answering the questions of purpose, creating coherence out of the chaos of today, and providing a compelling vision of tomorrow—is the work of the knowledge community leader. In contrast, simply making decisions can collapse the energy and imagination of the knowledge community.

The distinction in productivity between knowledge communities led by decision-makers and those led by meaning-makers can be immense. Are your knowledge community leaders capable of creating the context for productive knowledge creation and application? Perhaps you should be selecting leaders with different criteria.

BUILD COLLECTION SYSTEMS
INSTEAD OF DISTRIBUTION SYSTEMS

In the Industrial and Information economies we worried a lot about building distribution systems. The concern was to get the product from the factory to the customer. In the Knowledge economy, distribution is trivial. The Internet has linked the whole world together. In addition, knowledge communities thrive on new perspectives, particularly those which can improve their offerings to customers. Therefore, the economics of knowledge dictates that we think in terms of creating collection systems that allow for the instantaneous sharing of the new perspectives. Collection systems allow us to listen to the needs and concerns of customers. Collection systems allow us to tap into the global flow of creative ideas and fuel the imagination of our knowledge community.

How have you designed the collection systems for your knowledge community?

IN SUMMARY: COLLABORATIVE ADVANTAGE
REPLACES YESTERDAY'S COMPETITIVE ADVANTAGE

After years of searching for the ultimate competitive advantage, we may be surprised to find that this represents "wrong-minded" thinking in the knowledge economy. A more useful objective in the knowledge economy is, How can I share, collect, analyze, and reanalyze new ideas fast enough to be a thriving viable business *and* support the overall economy? The links between individual businesses and their more personalized knowledge communities to the overall knowledge economy are much closer than those found in the industrial economy. Isolationist firms will not remain viable in the knowledge economy. If ideas, new perspectives, collection systems, questions, metaphors, and meaning are the building blocks of the economics of knowledge, then constructing a walled city could cut us off from the much-needed commerce in conversation. Collaborative advantage is fundamentally different from competitive advantage. Rather than attempt to create an unfair economic advantage over anyone else, collaborative advantage seeks to build a sustainable win/win economic position. Using a metaphor, competitive advantage is akin to waging war, collaborative advantage is more like constructing an ecosystem.

Strategic alliances appeared on the business scene ten or more years ago, and today they are commonplace. Some organizations now list their alliances as major assets. That is the theory of collaborative advantage beginning to manifest itself. Intercompany communities, such as InterClass itself, are proliferating in support of collaborative advantage. Companies who organize themselves according to the principle of collaborative advantage will have a head start in the knowledge economy. Line managers who pay attention to the principles of knowledge economics summarized here may have an opportunity to thrive. Ignore the phenomenon of knowledge communities at your peril. After all, it is your future.

Company Contributions:
How Legacy Companies
Practice Smart Business

Whenever
a scout bee discovers
a rich food source, she recruits
nestmates by a waggle dance. Other bees
attending these dances learn the distance, direction,
and odor of the flower, and can translate this information into a
bee-line flight to the flowers.

—Nobel Laureate

Karl von Frisch, *The Dance Language and Orientation of Bees,* Belknap Press
of Harvard University Press, Cambridge, MA, 1967

In an economy
where the only certainty is uncertainty,
the one sure source of lasting competitive advantage
is knowledge.

—Ikujiro Nonaka

The Knowledge-Creating Company

KNOWLEDGE COMMUNITIES IN ACTION

Learning and knowledge are on the verge of "crossing the chasm" and becoming an essential part of the mainstream business community. This could, of course, wind up being a fad or the latest management program of the month. When I see great companies like Motorola or AT&T—which have embraced basic ideas of learning and knowledge—falter, lose their path, and incur unnecessary costs, my heart sinks. Is this subject really so dense and difficult that ordinary men and women—managers, front line workers and top CEOs—can't get it? I think not.

When education made the shift from church and family to state and federal government, there were untold protests and outcries. In the 1870s, for example, the Michigan National Guard had to be called in to quell riots against using tax money to support public high schools. Any shift of this magnitude entails endless social, political, and economic adjustments.

Now that business is becoming the major player in learning and knowledge during the information and knowledge age, there are bound to be disruptions and disappointments. I believe these are temporary setbacks. The main reason learning and knowledge will grow in importance in the commercial world is that it is in the business self-interest to do so. To say that "knowledge and learning is a fad" is akin to saying a hundred years ago that "machinery and automation are only temporary trends."

Science and medicine have grappled—successfully so—with learning and knowledge for centuries. It will take decades before business learns to transform itself to operate profitably, sustainably, and wisely—but change it will. In a world still grappling with issues of race, gender, cultural and ethnic diversity, environmental degradation, economic disparities, and other problems of global and local importance, we've got lots of learning to do.

My experience has taught me that reality is far more interesting than hypothesis. The future of business in the knowledge economy comes down to ordinary people doing extraordinary things. I've had the privilege to know and work with many such men and women, especially, though not only, through InterClass. I invited a number of them to share their views and perspectives on knowledge, learning, leadership, corporate cultures—any or all of the unfolding chapters in this story of building knowledge communities that can transform your organization.

These contributions come from executives on the front line in their different companies, industries, countries, and different responsibilities. What ties them together is their responsibility to make a return for their company and their commitment to make a difference in the world we live. Their words and insights tell volumes about knowledge communities—their power, potential, and future prospects—with reality, authenticity, and diversity.

In terms of my blessing of the honeybee, the authors below are like the scout bees who are returning with their wisdom to the hive to tell the rest of us where the flowers are. I invite you to forage with them.

Xerox: Documents Convey Knowledge

Dr. Priscilla Douglas, Principal
Xerox Professional Services
Knowledge Management Competency
The Document Company, Xerox

INTRODUCTION

My company, Xerox, is interested in knowledge: where it resides, how it is created, shared, and used to transform organizations. We define knowledge as information that is actionable. We view Knowledge Management (KM) as a discipline that creates a thriving work and learning environment. The aim: to foster the continuous creation, aggregation, use and, reuse of knowledge, and, to apply it to the pursuit of new business value.

Our commitment includes research and design in knowledge ecology at Palo Alto Research Center (PARC) and Grenoble; communities of practice at the Xerox-founded Institute for Research on Learning (IRL); the endowment of the first-ever "knowledge chair" at UC Berkeley's Haas School of Management (Ikujiro Nonaka); and appointing a director of knowledge initiatives (Dan Holtshouse). Our commitment to expediting services, software, and knowledge tools to market led to the creation of Xerox New Enterprises, a portfolio of entrepreneurial companies that includes dpiX, Inxight, InConcert, Documentum, PlaceWare, and Visual Recall.

FROM "THE DOCUMENT COMPANY" TO A KNOWLEDGE-BASED BUSINESS

Core competency in the document and its many uses led Xerox to reinvent itself as "The Document Company" in 1990. Some people scratched their heads: What exactly is a document, and why is Xerox the document company?

Documents are information structured for human comprehension. Our corporate vision for 2005 anticipates the declining role of paper as a storage medium for documents. We expect that people will store and locate documents electronically, print them, use them, and then recycle.

Our approach to understanding the workplace is unique. It begins with the social aspect. The workplace—how people really work and use document technology to enhance their personal effectiveness and organizational productivity—is our market. By studying work practices and the role of the copier in the workplace, we discovered the social and technical document life cycle: create, distribute, store, and retrieve. The process also includes editing, annotations, input from others, and much more. We also discovered that sticky notes don't produce a high-quality copy!

The diverse mixture of member backgrounds at PARC and IRL (anthropologist, artist, computer scientist, engineers, linguist, social and behavioral scientist) was a radical idea when the members first came together in the 1980s to study work practices and to rethink learning. Now that the "knowledge revolution" is under way, it is clear that the ideas and innovation developed in the research communities have influenced our approach to being a knowledge company.

FROM COPIER TO COMPUTER

Digital technology and globalization are changing the rules for customers, competition, and competencies. With scan, fax, and network capability, the Xerox copier is now a powerful computer. A digital document can arrive on a desktop as a piece of paper, a CD-ROM, an Internet site, or a computer file. Hundreds of pages can be compressed and printed on a business card. A scanned document can be translated from Portuguese to Japanese.

Access to digital technology has unleashed the talent and innovation at PARC—the home of the first computer (ALTO), the GUI, Ethernet, and the laser printer—and the ideas of early adopters within the corporation.

COMMUNITIES OF PRACTICE

Documents are containers that allow readers to construct their own understanding, that is, create knowledge themselves. Researchers at IRL describe how knowledge is "dynamic, shaped by a social setting, and inherently creative." Documents are social, rich in contextual clues. They come to life—take on meaning—by being used. Software collaborative tools make it possible to capture and share tacit knowledge, but where does tacit knowledge reside? It resides in work routines and in-groups of people who do the work.

Jean Lave and Etienne Wenger, former senior research scientists at IRL, call those groups "communities of practice." By distinguishing those informal groups, Wenger allowed us to "see differently" to understand where and how learning and knowledge is created and disseminated within groups and communities. Working together, IRL and PARC researchers developed a methodology that they call *phased interactive learning* to understand how learning occurs and knowledge becomes shared within communities of practice.

A pivotal study began when a PARC anthropologist was asked to gather information about customer service representatives so that a training course could be developed to enhance their productivity. A particular concern was the service reps' routine of meeting in the middle of the day to talk.

After careful observation, a breakthrough occurred when the researcher discovered that the "water cooler" talk allowed the service reps to swap their ideas. He noticed that the reps kept two sets of books: an official Xerox manual in pristine condition and a second copy—often in the format of a personal notebook—that was dog-eared and worn. Why? The reps were a community with agreed-upon work practices, *and* they were generating knowledge through storytelling.

By observing the way those people gathered and shared their field experiences collectively, PARC researchers began to develop a tool to preserve and share knowledge within a work group. Tested initially in Denver, the solution was a bit cumbersome: two-way radio headsets with a dedicated radio frequency known as a "knowledge channel." The reps could talk, answer each other's questions, identify problems, and share new solutions. The project had a limitation: No one *documented* the knowledge they created. This led to Eureka.

According to the Chief Scientist and Director of PARC, John Seely Brown, Eureka! "challenged the way Xerox thought about the nature of work, the role of the individual, and the relationship between the individual and the company. It was a shot in [the knowledge] revolution."

EUREKA: KNOWLEDGE TRANSFER INSIDE XEROX

Eureka was redesigned to be an electronic "knowledge refinery." Now, customer service reps submit their "tips" to an Intranet bulletin board. The tips are validated by their peers, posted, and made available within their community. Technically, Eureka is a relational database of hypertext documents available online via the

Intranet. It can also be viewed as the distributed publishing of local community know-how. In practice, Eureka! is an electronic version of war stories told around the water cooler—with the added benefits of a user-friendly search engine, an institutional memory, expert validation, and corporatewide availability. It is a way to grow both intellectual capital and social capital simultaneously, the latter stemming from the contributions of the more central members of the community of practice.

Currently the service engineers receive more than 25 million customer requests for support annually. The 19,000 service engineers have portable laptop computers, electronic manuals, and the ability to diagnose products remotely. Drawing from a real-time knowledge base, the Customer Service Engineers rapidly identify existing solutions or create new solutions that can be immediately shared within the global service community. According to Vernon A. Zelmer, Vice President, Worldwide Customer Services: "Knowledge Management and the associated intellectual capital is an area of clear competitive advantage for Xerox Service. The depth of potential is just beginning to be exploited."

"SWAGGER"

An array of research projects supporting work processes and practices was under way long before "knowledge management" became a general topic within Xerox. PARC and IRL researchers often engage in internal "community service" for the parent company. The development of Eureka! underscores the role the parent company has played as a convenient laboratory for innovation and the diffusion of new ideas.

Speaking in Rome at a conference on knowledge management, Xerox Chairman and Chief Executive Officer Paul A. Allaire said a sense of urgency exists within businesses to find an "explicit and systematic way to manage knowledge in the firm." The urgency within Xerox was magnified with the appointment of G. Richard Thoman as President and Chief Operating Officer.

With the advantage of being from the outside, Rick Thoman helped accelerate the flow of innovation to the marketplace as knowledge products, service, and solutions. He has recognized the intellectual capital and innovation resident within Xerox and encourages us to "swagger," in other words, to market our "know-how." Tools and services that capture how we really make sense of information are truly the "mother lode" of knowledge. They in turn will generate new services and technology that will continue the "spiral" of knowledge and possibility.

CAPTURING THE KNOWLEDGE IN
COMMUNITIES OF PRACTICE: DOCUSHARE™

Within Xerox, research and engineering are conducted worldwide. The Wilson Center for Research and Technology in Rochester, a member of this worldwide community, was constantly challenged in its efforts to share data and access to information to work collaboratively. It wanted to end the lengthy practice of working papers and documents, getting comments, and returning them to the author.

The Wilson Center developed a tool for researchers called AmberWeb, an Intranet-based, collaborative tool used to access documents. An example of a community-based design, AmberWeb allows members to access repositories of shared documents and databases. All sorts of file formats exist in harmony, so anyone can post information with security, and access is determined locally, not by a distant web master. As a result, researchers collaborate on documents in real time.

News travels fast. Within eighteen months AmberWeb listed more than 10,000 internal users. More importantly, users of AmberWeb began to reveal themselves as distinct communities of practice. Internal success led to the introduction of collaborative software marketed externally as DocuShare.™ DocuShare is a community-maintained knowledge management tool based on a standard web browser. Users post and share collections of information in any format. It's simple, and you don't have to know HTML.

As a result, our external customers have been quick to adopt DocuShare. For example, the Canada Communications Group provides printing services to the Canadian government from seventy locations. Michael Monette, Vice President of Strategic Planning and Development for the company, states: "With the new approach that DocuShare allows . . . employees are empowered." The ease of use eliminates the need for management oversight and concomitantly reduces cost. Another testimonial: John McCabe, Assistant Superintendent for Curriculum and Technology,[1] states that "DocuShare represents a breakthrough technology for us and the forty-seven school districts and 80,000 students we serve . . . the beauty is in its simplicity."

XEROX KNOWLEDGE INITIATIVE

In two or three years, KM will be the prime basis for a sustainable competitive advantage. Companies will use their corporate database to achieve competitive advantage in products, systems, and delivery of services. KM based systems are fundamental to capturing the learning that is occurring within the corporation.

—Ajit Laroia, Director, Corporate Business Strategy

It is no surprise that Xerox's 1996 planning sessions to define its strategic vision for 2005 included a Knowledge Work Initiative led by Dan Holtshouse. Early on, the initiative was designed to assess whether KM was a fad or had merit for Xerox. His team concluded: "KM is an emerging business focus, that is, an opportunity for new products and services; KM is strategic for Xerox since the document is so inexorably linked to knowledge . . . we feel this is a natural fit for Xerox." More important, the team discovered that customers view their unique knowledge and intellectual property as a strategic asset.

The question was, "How do we leverage knowledge assets internally and deliver value to customers?" Through extensive market research the team identified ten domains generic to knowledge management:

- Sharing knowledge and best practices
- Instilling responsibility for knowledge sharing
- Capturing and reusing experiences
- Embedding knowledge in products, services, and processes
- Producing knowledge as a product
- Driving knowledge generation for innovation
- Mapping networks of experts
- Building and mining customer knowledge bases
- Understanding and measuring the value of knowledge
- Leveraging intellectual assets

Holtshouse is an internal and external proponent of knowledge. Within Xerox his "knowledge horizon" web site provides a calendar of events, case studies, and news. In addition, Holtshouse sponsors learning events throughout the year. Interest in knowledge extends to product planning, marketing, and manufacturing. Every method of communication is being used: DocuShare sites expand, courses proliferate on the electronic learning site, senior managers hold satellite broadcast and conference calls to bring together worldwide organizations. Some organizations have active communities of practice. It seems we are off to a good start!

XEROX, KNOWLEDGE, AND INNOVATION:
PROJECT JUPITER AND PUEBLO

New knowledge always begins with the individual.

—Ikujiro Nonaka

Innovation is everywhere; the problem is learning from it. Where employees confront problems, deal with unforeseen contingencies, or work their way around breakdowns in normal procedures. The problem is, few companies know how to learn from this local innovation and how to use it to improve their overall effectiveness.

—John Seely Brown, Chief Scientist, PARC

Knowledge is embedded in all human activity. The impetus for knowledge may be curiosity. The quest for knowledge stems from vision, intuition, and the desire to create or invent. Knowledge begins with an idea, an intuition, or a gut feel often sparked from where the rubber hits the road. Ideas gain momentum when they are spoken within a group that shares similar beliefs and practices—a community of practice. Sometimes an idea is absorbed so quickly by a community that which individual introduced the idea is forgotten.

Tacit knowledge made explicit gains currency and momentum; it is shared and actionable. According to Danny Bobrow, Senior PARC Researcher, "Knowledge services are really document services framed for communities of practice." The more we characterize communities of practice, the more easily we can develop tools to support them. At the same time it is important to respect the essence of tacit knowledge. Susan Anderson, Manager of Work Practices and Co-Development, argues that "some tacit (if not most) tacit knowledge needs to stay tacit—that's why we need a combination of documented materials and apprenticeship to create and/or transfer expertise." The bottom line: Ideas and innovation come from individuals during the course of their daily routine.

A former PARC Computer scientist, Pavel Curtis, led a research team called Jupiter, which is now a Xerox New Enterprise Company, PlaceWare. Building on his ground-breaking work on computer-networked MUDS (multiuser domains) and MOOS (multiuser object-oriented programs), he is creating a virtual place with physical reality. For example, e-mail becomes a virtual world when users can "see" what a person is doing prior to sending e-mail. If the intended receiver is on the telephone, an "agent" has the intelligence to interrupt for an emergency. The receiver establishes rules to define when s/he is "interruptible." For tech weenies, early adopters, and members of the "Net Generation," this technology will significantly enhance the ability to create and share.

A community called Pueblo is in its embryonic stage in Phoenix, Arizona. PARC researcher Danny Bobrow's team created a school-centered learning community for people of all ages. This virtual world brings teachers, scientists, senior citizens, and children together. A teacher involved in the Pueblo project captures the value of this learning space: "When faculty have time to play, they can create; when they plan and systematically design curriculum, nothing happens. While this may not be obvious to a planner, it is surely obvious to those of us who surf and hit those breaking waves to get to the bleeding edge of innovation."

SUMMARY

Knowledge is embedded in social activities; its importance and meaning are determined by and within a local context. Documents are socially constructed and provide a convenient way to share information and in some instances knowledge. A core value at Xerox is to recognize the social nature of work and acknowledge that ideas and innovation occur *everywhere* in an organization. Understanding and respecting where and how people work—communities of practice—allow us to develop tools that harvest, preserve, and facilitate the sharing of knowledge.

The research and development communities within Xerox have been way ahead of the curve of the corporation. The move to digital products, software, and solutions has widened the portal to our parent company. Ideas and innovations flow from researchers to Xerox professionals to our customers. Together we are developing solutions and technology that help people do what they do naturally and more effectively.

By following the flow of documents in the workplace we have observed and captured the flow of knowledge. Our knowledge initiative will allow us to share with our internal and external customers as we continue to learn about knowledge. With the strength of the parent company, supported by the collective resources and spirit of PARC, IRL, and the myriad companies that constitute Xerox New Enterprises, it makes sense that we are not only The Document Company but also a knowledge-based company.

A Personal Note

After watching Xerox for years, my background in organizational behavior and marketing led me to join the Office Document Products Group, to participate in the revolution already in progress.

I immediately discovered that "Xeroids" are special and create a unique, sharing culture that values diversity. A simple request, like a presentation for a customer visit, sent via VMAX or e-mail, elicits information from virtual strangers everywhere in the company!

I rely on a virtual team of senior professionals who represent the education market. The team formed four years ago and has survived countless reorganizations. It continues to ensure that the customer's voice informs our pricing, product, and solutions strategies. It is quite a phenomenon—a true community of practice.

Ordinary People Doing Extraordinary Things: Knowledge Communities at the Front Lines

Helena Light Hadley,
Director, New Business Ventures,
Marriott International

INTRODUCTION

In an industry of rapid growth, enormous change, tough competition, and high turnover, Marriott keeps approximately 120,000 service workers focused on the customer.

In our lodging businesses,[2] Marriott customers are not just satisfied (as much as 90 percent satisfaction reported), they also keep coming back. Repeat business is a key indicator of satisfaction.

In our senior living business,[3] residents and their families are extremely satisfied with the levels of service and care provided. Satisfaction surveys give the business high marks from residents, families, and employees.

Turnover in the front line ranks can be as low as 30 percent or as high as 85 percent in some areas. How does Marriott provide a high and consistent level of service to its customers when that service is, for the most part, provided by an entry-level, highly diverse front line service worker?

J.W. Marriott, Sr., was able to grow his nine-seat root beer stand in 1927 to the company it is today largely because of his belief in people, a focus on customers, and his passion to deliver quality products at a fair price. That quality and the consistency existed because of the systems and processes created. They may have been called recipe cards, standard operating procedures, or inspections back then. That thinking has been embedded in the organization, and today we recognize the need for systems that are flexible, fast, and responsive and allow our "people" to think and act in the "moment of truth." To do so consistently, requires a front line that is prepared with the best information at the right time and supported by management. We want trained, involved, and empowered associates running the business.

DEFINING THE KNOWLEDGE COMMUNITY AT THE FRONT LINE

Knowledge communities at the operational level consist of housekeepers, food servers, certified nursing assistants, engineers, and front desk clerks. They are at the bell stand, behind a buffet, changing a bed, fixing a light. They work mornings, afternoons, and nights every day of the year and possess a common interest: "Take care of the customer," which aligns employees throughout the business.

Employees in each functional area, whether in a hotel, conference center, senior living community, or distribution center, have prescribed tasks and objectives. They are also keenly aware of the interdependencies those tasks have with regard to the overall products and services the customer expects, and all that requires teamwork by all departments.

TOOLS USED BY THE FRONT LINE KNOWLEDGE COMMUNITIES

If companies need to be prepared to provide knowledge-based products and services in the future, does that mean the hotel room of the future will be able to determine your every need without your having to ask? Will the room sense the temperature you require? How hungry you are? What kind of foods you prefer? Perhaps. In fact, the industry is creating customer databases to track your preferences so they can be shared with any of the hotels in the chain you use.

But one thing we shall continue to count on is that you have human needs, and to that end we will treat you and interact with you as a human being. That high touch is the foundation of our hospitality, which can be delivered only by a well-informed and well-trained employee.

What does Marriott do at the front line to foster the information and knowledge exchange? How does Marriott maintain such a highly motivated and aligned work force amidst constant change? There are several different approaches that have been adopted:

Preshift Lineup

Prior to the start of every shift, there is a method to communicate current events to the employees. At the front desk it may include reports on problems reported from the previous shift, volume of "check ins" expected during the current shift, promotions, and special and unique reservations. In one of our assisted living communities, the preshift exchange is vital. It is an opportunity for one shift to pass on current information about resident needs and daily community as well as corporate events.

Fifteen Minutes of Daily Training

Marriott holds the belief that training and learning are continuous and not dependent solely on formal, organized events. In full-service hotels, monthly calendars are published by the Operations' function and sent to every hotel in the system. Each week of the calendar has a training theme, such as "Safe Food Handling." Each day of the week, a specific related topic, like "Associate Hygiene," "Food Storage," or "Cooking Hamburgers Safely," is listed. The shift leader will include a brief presentation of the topic using a training format designed for short exchanges.

White Boards

White boards have been used extensively in many of our operations to post events and notices, important process issues, and even employee recognition. Many hotels have used white boards to display department performance and process flow charts showing improvements or problems that are being studied by the department. When clustered around the white board in standup meetings, there is a lot of energy and a high amount of knowledge exchange. White boards tend to be hung in areas where there is high traffic and visibility for the employees.

Electronic Note Boards and Best Practices

Technology is becoming increasingly important in the transfer and access to information that will enable cost-effective distribution of key business content as well as speed up decision-making. Marriott uses a variety of technology-based tools that facilitate "just-in-time" learning and decision-making. For example:

- Lodging engineers have been using a Lotus Notes database to post maintenance and repair issues for a number of years. It has served as a valued resource for this geographically dispersed group with highly variable levels of experience.
- Our corporate internet strategy is facilitating the development of web pages focused on special interests for associates at our corporate headquarters. The vision is to have inter/intranet access to every unit around the world. Employee use of this technology will be dependent on computer access.
- Training is available through internet, intranet and interactive CD-ROM technology for employees at all levels.

Feeding the Employee Cafeteria Line

The best time to exchange knowledge or to be receptive to learning is at the moment the worker has a question and is motivated to receive the answer lightening fast—"microwaved." Finding the answer in a book or manual is frustrating. It is impersonal and dispassionate, and it requires you to be sedentary—something our line workers are unaccustomed to. Whether or not technology is available, other "low-tech" resources are necessary:

- Managers and supervisors have open-door policies and encourage interruptions.
- Some units have newsletters.
- There are several processes that are used to communicate corporate announcements, including paper-based bulletins, leaflets, videos, and magazines.

STORIES OF FRONT LINE KNOWLEDGE COMMUNITIES AT WORK

There's Got to Be a Better Way . . .

A group of housekeepers was observed clustered around their department white board. The process under discussion was defrosting and cleaning the in-room refrigerators. The department manager effectively led the group to identify the process and obtain best practice suggestions from the employees. Because some of the housekeepers were relatively new, that was a great opportunity for them to learn from the more experienced employees how they have been effective and efficient in this task. Documenting this approach on the white board and fostering a verbal exchange is a method that works best for these front line workers, as opposed to providing them with a written manual. This method also serves as a form of recognition, since it provides an opportunity for the experienced workers to display their knowledge.

How Many Towels Does It Take to Prepare for This Group?

One hotel had created a magnificent guest problem and special request tracking system. When put to extensive use over a period of time it began to provide employees with data that could assist them in predicting (anticipating) customer needs. Members of one business group that frequented the hotel tended to travel with their families for the convention. As a result, the demand for additional in-room towels was high. That put significant strain on the housekeeping staff, who not only had to clean rooms but also had to return to those rooms to fill the special requests.

The next time the group was booked at the hotel, the director of rooms and related services, upon reviewing the database, decided to have the housekeepers preset the reserved rooms with additional towels. That action virtually eliminated the special request calls and enabled the housekeeping staff to be less reactive and to focus on other unique needs of their customers.

RECAPTURING CUSTOMERS

Marriott has a passion for formal and, more importantly, informal recognition of its employees. Mr. Marriott personally calls the company's top six salespeople every month. That kind of action from the very top of the organization causes an impressive ripple effect. General managers will personally write letters to their employees who have been singled out as providing extraordinary service to our customers.

Residents in our senior living communities include our employees on the holiday lists. Hugs abound. That kind of human interaction unleashes a personal power that effects productivity but, more importantly, customers relations. In his recent book *Turned On*, Roger Dow, Vice President and General Sales Manager of Marriott Lodging, cited one of Marriott hotel's room service captains who told the following story when he received the annual award for the best sports salesperson in the entire company:

> You've probably guessed that I'm not a salesperson like all of you. . . . I'm a room service captain. What I do have is a relationship with all the sports teams. When a team comes to town, I work twenty-four hours a day to take care of their every wish. I know what every player, every coach, and every manager likes as their special order. Sometimes they even call me before they get to town and request special snacks and treats.
>
> Last year, a competing hotel offered rooms to teams for four dollars less than we were charging. Half the teams went to that hotel to take advantage of the lower prices. Whenever a team that wasn't staying at the Marriott came to town, I took the day off. I'd call one of my friends in the other hotel to find out what time the team was scheduled to arrive. Then I'd go over in full uniform and wait for that team in the lobby.
>
> One time, the Dodgers came to town, Tommy Lasorda led the team into the competing hotel, and I was standing there waiting for him. Tommy smiled, shook my hand, and said, "Smitty, what are you doing here? Are you with this hotel now? This is great! So are we."
>
> "No, I'm still at the Marriott."
>
> "What are you doing here, then?"
>
> "Well, I just wanted to welcome you to town, wish you good luck against the

Braves, and tell you that I'm bringing over your special order from Marriott after the game tonight."

He asked me why I would do such a thing, and I told him that first of all, his new hotel's room services closes at eleven P.M.—if the game went extra innings, he'd miss his late night snack. "But more importantly," I said, "I just want you to know that even though you can't afford to stay with us any more, we still love you."

Smitty went on to say that the Dodgers, and every other team that left, came back to Marriott the very next year.[4]

THE HEART OF THE HOUSE

The ingredients to such success at the front lines starts with selecting the right people for the right job. The selection process is rigorous. Applicants may participate in three different interviews that would include employees who might be co-workers, managers, and executives at the unit level.

Many Marriott businesses are also using an instrument that assists in identifying people who have a predisposition to provide great service and will be happy, thrive, and contribute to the work environment. Marriott doesn't just look for experience, it looks for people with hearts. We can teach people technical skills. If they have the right attitude, a service attitude, then with proper technical training our employees become great service performers.

The Marriott culture has always been a very family-like culture filled with persistent, almost tenacious workers. Perhaps this comes with the recognition that as a 365-day, 24-hour operation . . . well, how close to life can you get? Joys and sorrows are shared. Friends are made. Both good and bad conflict exists, all as a part of everyday occurrences which cannot thrive safely without a strong value-based culture.

We recently conducted an informal benchmarking on business ethics training. The companies we contacted wondered why we were conducting the study, since they viewed us as a company whose business conduct already stands on a sturdy platform of honesty, trust, and integrity. While that is true, we also never take any of our positive attributes for granted and will always look for ways to do things better.

To improve and keep getting better continuously means always to be open to learning and sharing. It is not easy for us to accept that we don't already know it all . . . and therefore we rarely give ourselves the time to pause for formal training. Our preference is to learn while under fire. Training is happening all the time, and generally not in a formal way—on the job.

Early on, a newly hired associate is introduced to the concept of learning as a "process." Marriott's Employee Orientation is a ninety-day process, not a four-hour program. The process is designed to coordinate with the hierarchy of a new employee's needs when starting with the company.

We begin the process of celebration and recognition with the orientation. In Senior Living Services, certificates, mugs, or pins are provided at the completion of the ninety days of orientation. We also formally recognize hire date anniversaries. Whenever you gather a group of Marriott employees together, it will not be uncommon for each and every one to be able to quote their start date with the company.

BARRIERS TO FRONT LINE KNOWLEDGE COMMUNITIES

There are obvious barriers to creating this powerful front line community. Choosing the wrong people or the right people for the wrong reasons is one. But perhaps the most damaging barrier is poor leadership. Leadership that does not develop, nurture, or trust its employees will choke their vitality. Leadership that commands and controls every movement, every thought, stifles the spontaneous interactivity needed to build lasting relationships with our customers.

Controlling the information available to the front line is also deadly to its being a knowledge community and fulfilling its purpose to serve the customer with fervor, commitment, and passion.

OUR SUCCESS IS AT THE FRONT LINE

Without a front line that is passionate and fully service-oriented, our customers would not be satisfied nor loyal. Marriott's core business competency in the management and development of a diverse workforce can be stated simply:

- Find, attract, and select the best people
- Orient them with great care to the business and to the culture
- Train and retrain
- Provide opportunity for career growth and development
- Communicate, communicate, communicate
- Design and provide systems and operations that enable a full focus on the customer
- Recognize, compensate, reward, and celebrate

This "spirit to serve" strategy has kept Marriott going for more than seventy years.

People, Systems, Training and Development: Learning and Knowledge at Saturn

Gary High,
Director, Human Resource Development,
Saturn Corporation,
and Group Director of Education, GM North American Car Operations

OVERVIEW

Saturn's approach to learning sprang directly out of the company's founding vision and has evolved to support the concepts and strategies that constitute that vision. Perhaps the best way to understand Saturn's knowledge community is to trace its evolution—to examine how and why the company started, how and why learning was integral to the founding vision, and finally how structures and processes evolved through specific, practical efforts to implement that vision and its component strategies.[5]

LEARNING AS FUNDAMENTAL TO SATURN'S VISION

Saturn was created in response to a serious illness if not a near-death experience in the American automobile business. General Motors was losing market share and was not at all competitive in the small car segment. The old way was failing, and the need for change was clear. But what kind of change?

To find out, GM brought together a unique task force of unionized car builders, middle managers, international union representatives, and senior GM executives to examine the landscape and to make recommendations. Sharing their diverse expertise and perspectives, the "Group of 99," as they came to be called, researched best practices in the world's finest organizations and together created a vision for a "new way" that involved sweeping changes on both the union and the management sides of the house.

From the very beginning, knowledge and learning were recognized as essential enablers of change. Saturn's approach to learning emerged as a strategic initiative integral to the vision for the new company. We recognized that if we really wanted something to be different, we must start with a vision, but we must also give people the knowledge and skills to make that vision work. (It's interesting to note that the vision itself was possible only as the result of an intensive learning process based on the research and shared knowledge of the 99.)

To get a feel for some Saturn fundamentals, including the importance of knowledge and learning, let's take a look at some excerpts from *Concepts of the Saturn Organization—Phase II,* a seminal document published in 1984.

> Saturn's success is assured by and dependent on all its employees working together as true stakeholders in the business with individual opportunities to continually acquire and apply new knowledge, skills and abilities. . . . [The] organization structure . . . provides the framework within which people are encouraged and allowed to work in a manner consistent with our philosophy in achieving our common goals and objectives.
>
> All jobs and responsibilities in this organization differ from those in a traditional organization. Decisions are made by consensus, authority does not lie with any one person, and individual behavior emulates the philosophy with social skills being extremely important to success. The proper blend of technical knowledge and abilities with these social skills, then, describes important ingredients of a . . . Saturn employee.

If people are given the responsibility and authority to meet shared goals—to "own" the business—they must have the tools to do a good job of it. Education helps *deal people in* by equipping them with the skills and knowledge they need to accomplish their tasks, to be players in the business, and to make *all* the Saturn strategies work.

What Kinds of Learning?

What kinds of learning would be needed? And what would be the structural requirements of a "knowledge community" that would foster that learning? Let's start by looking at the strategies we were trying to support. What, specifically, must the learning help us *do* in this new organization?

First, we must be able to function effectively in a team-based culture based on a new kind of partnership between union and management, a culture in which broader participation is required of all team members. That would require knowledge of the organization's Mission, Philosophy, and Values; of the basic principles of the partnership with the UAW; and of how this organization differs from those previously experienced by Saturn team members. Our five-day new hire awareness program was designed to begin to address these needs. Then, in addition to knowledge of Saturn's precepts, we would need the interpersonal skills necessary to succeed in the new culture—skills in such areas as consensus decision-making, conflict resolution, listening and assertion, problem-solving, and making presentations. Courses were developed and made available in those areas.

231

Part of Saturn's vision was to be a "flat" organization, with a broadening of responsibilities for individual team members. We believe that involving the whole person in his or her work offers greater job satisfaction, fosters a feeling of ownership and commitment, and ultimately produces stronger business results for the team and the organization as a whole. In a large GM plant it was not uncommon to have upwards of one hundred job classifications. At Saturn we have three predominant classifications and four smaller populations. That requires each team member to have a wider range of skills, not only for rotating production and maintenance tasks but also for a variety of business management tasks. There are educational implications in both areas. Let's look first at production and maintenance.

Saturn realized that there was no chance of survival—we would be dead in the water—if quality was not consistently world-class from the get-go. We realized we had a lot of people from different locations and backgrounds coming together to build a newly designed product with newly purchased equipment in a situation where each person was required to perform a greater number of production tasks than had ever been required in the past. We could not just throw folks onto the line and expect them to "pick it up" as best they could. Thus we developed training programs with key input from the workers (members, as we call each other) themselves.

GM had some rough experiences with "advanced technology" in the early 1980s. By spending big money on technology without fully considering the human element, we ended up with big, expensive plants that didn't work. Saturn was committed to using state-of-the-art technology to achieve its business goals. But, having learned from the past, Saturn was also fundamentally committed to "the integration of people, technology, and business systems." We created committees to protect and support each of the various technologies we were using—to make sure our workforce would be ready in such areas as "Lost Foam" (a stretch technology for casting engine parts), CNC (computerized machining), and robotics. To support sustained learning in essential technologies, we put a variety of technical labs in our training center.

In addition to working on the assembly line, members of our manufacturing teams are responsible for what we call the 30 Work Unit Functions. These include team management of quality, safety, training, material flow, ergonomics, and other off-line responsibilities. Performing each of those functions requires an array of knowledge and skills for which training is identified and then either sourced or developed. Our teams are all responsible for playing a key role in the hiring process, so interviewer training is an early need. Team members participate in sourcing equipment, so negotiating and time management skills are needed.

There is a broader dimension of learning that is also critical if we are all to share effectively in the business. Team members must be exposed to information that will enable them to understand the market, to perceive what is necessary on *all* fronts for the business to be successful, and to build a broad view of job security with an understanding of how they can contribute to it. We are all taking a course now called *Spotlight on the Competition,* which helps us understand how we compare with other car makers in many different areas of our business. The class examines such topics as hours of labor per car, advertising style, and financial health. It also helps us understand larger trends and directions so we can see where the auto business has come from and where it's headed. We need to understand the *relevance* of what we are doing. We need to know *why* we must do certain things to run the business successfully.

Saturn is committed to a free flow of information so that its members can intelligently participate. Information-sharing and communication go hand in hand with training to foster the learning that will enable us to succeed. Using such tools as a daily newsletter and regular internal television broadcasts accessible throughout the plant, our Corporate Communications team devotes at least as much energy to internal communications as to public relations. "Free flow of information" is a stated principle in our Memorandum of Agreement (the document that defines our unique partnership with the UAW). It is considered an essential principle of consensus decision-making, because all stakeholders must understand the issues, the data, and the various perspectives if consensus is to be achieved. Information-sharing within and among our business teams is a way of life. Meeting minutes from all levels of the organization are distributed and made easily accessible to team members; verbal communication via a network of representatives flows daily between the work units and other levels of decision-making.

Along with this flow of information must come the skills to manage it responsibly. *Decision-making* training helps us understand the organizational structure and how we can effectively participate in the information flow and communication networks that are the lifeblood of consensus decision-making within that structure. In the *Information and Product Security* class we learn how to handle sensitive information and learn *why* we must handle it carefully.

STRUCTURAL EVOLUTION

These specific examples have provided a glimpse of some of the many areas of learning we needed to focus on to support our strategies. What are the structural requirements of a knowledge community that would accomplish all this? We did not have predefined structural requirements. (Nor would we pretend to be able to recommend specific structures to other organizations.) Our structures evolved to meet the needs and to get things done—form followed function.

Saturn views itself as a system of interdependent participants and is philosophically committed to involving, and meeting the needs of, those participants—including customers, team members, suppliers, retailers, and neighbors—as it pursues its organizational mission. To do so, it promotes a matrixed organizational structure designed for stakeholder communication, information-sharing, and involvement in consensus decision-making. Coordinating and guiding that structure is a governing body consisting of corporate officers from the different functional areas. That body is called the SAC, which stands for Saturn Action Council. Fanning out from and feeding into that governance is a relatively "soft" and fluid structure that manages day-to-day business by involving the appropriate organizational stakeholders to make decisions. The structure of our knowledge community evolved to meet the needs of the stakeholders in implementing the SAC's strategic direction.

The SAC's early decisions in support of learning and information-sharing included the following:

1. A master central training budget and a centralized training function (called People Systems Training and Development, or PSTD)
2. Significant training budgets in the various business units
3. A risk system that tied a percentage of compensation to completing a yearly goal of 5 percent of each team member's work hours spent in training
4. Yearly individual training plans (ITPs) for each team member
5. A benefits system offering funds for continuing education related to Saturn's business
6. A corporate communications function charged not only with public relations but also with internal information-sharing and business communications

Many of the early learning needs came from Manufacturing and Engineering. PSTD began to forge a partnership with those primary stakeholders and, through consensus decision-making, began to build the structures and processes that would enable them to identify and best respond to the needs. PSTD viewed the internal Saturn business units as customers and designed its own business to meet their needs. The business units viewed PSTD as a resource and a supplier. And there was a further dimension to the relationship: All parties were (and are) business partners in achieving Saturn's shared goals.

A significant training budget and staff were established in each manufacturing business unit to plan and implement training specific to the area. In support of the business units, PSTD's central training functions evolved to include managing the scheduling/tracking system, tracking risk and reward, teaching most of the Saturn-wide classes, offering training development services to the business units, producing materials for classes, and administering tuition assistance.

We established a biweekly meeting (called TNET, for "training network") to coordinate the activities of our evolving matrix of training stakeholders. Not surprisingly, the network quickly grew to involve all of the other functional areas within Saturn, including Purchasing, Finance, Corporate Communications, Marketing, and the Service Parts Organization. While TNET serves as a communication hub, the daily work is done by training resources in each of the various functional areas; and their work is supported by daily communications through myriad contacts outside of TNET.

As noted earlier, Saturn perceives itself as an interdependent system that also includes its retailers and suppliers. So the matrix soon expanded to include retailer and supplier training in much the same way as it originally emerged to support internal business units.

All of our research told us that the car buying experience had to change. It had long been one of the biggest areas for improvement in the auto business. How to change it? Again, first establish a vision for it, then give people the tools to implement the vision—including knowledge and skills.

Our retail partners saw the difference in culture at Saturn and wanted to be a part of it. They worked together with Saturn's Sales, Service, and Marketing team to identify education needed for the different roles within a retail organization (owners, sales consultants, service and parts people, and administrative staff). The franchise agreement was crafted to include access to and payment for training developed and delivered by Saturn. As with our internal training, the end users were included as stakeholders and subject matter experts in identifying and developing content. They were also a part of all decision-making related to delivery.

Though the retailer training organization has evolved somewhat independently of Saturn's internal training, we are closely connected through TNET and have consistently shared facilities, instructors, developers, and course content. Our retailer training has been part of our knowledge community almost from the beginning and has enabled Saturn to revolutionize the way cars are sold—much to the relief of the car-buying public.

More recently we have established a curriculum for our supplier partners.

SAC
Strategic
Direction

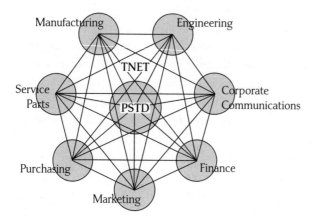

Though the particulars differ, this effort has been approached in much the same way as our others: by involving the stakeholders and doing what needs to be done to meet their needs in support of Saturn's mission. Saturn University, as our supplier training is called, came together as a joint effort of PSTD, Saturn's Purchasing team, and the suppliers themselves.

The learning network has now grown beyond our internal business units, retailers, and suppliers to include the larger business world around us. Saturn Consulting Services (SCS) is a business within a business that began in response to requests from outside companies, including other GM divisions, to learn about Saturn. This internal group, whose budget comes only from the money it generates, develops and markets (for delivery both on-site and around the world) programs about Saturn's culture. Not surprisingly, SCS shares facilities, expertise, and people with all the other neighborhoods in Saturn's learning community.

The latest breaking part of the unfolding structure is Saturn's role in the development of General Motors University. This new educational system, serving all of GM, is headed by Saturn's former president, Skip LeFauve. Its staff also includes several former Saturn team members from both training and organizational development. Saturn, through SCS, is evaluating and developing programs for

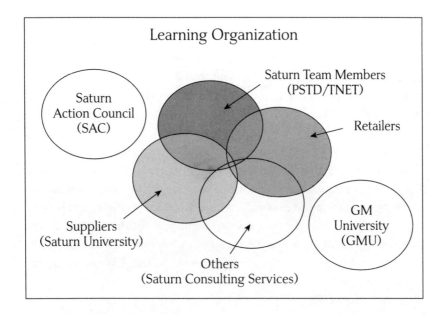

GMU, again drawing on the rest of Saturn's knowledge network for content and resource support.

IN CONCLUSION

We wanted our dollars spent *on* education, not just *in the name* of education. Traditionally in GM, every cost center had a relatively small line item for training, which tended to be used for everything but training. That is why our first move was a large centralized budget rather than a little bit in a million different places. But, as we've seen, the central training function does not hold the power of central governance over training. It is one of the many co-owners of Saturn's learning community, a community that has evolved in a very decentralized way in some respects, but one that is glued together by shared goals and decisions.

The overriding principle has been to stay focused on the "why" of the knowledge community—to support the organizational vision rather than to focus parochially. Our structures and processes evolved to serve the needs of the greater organizational community. We didn't try to keep training in a box; we didn't encumber ourselves with territorial concerns. We viewed training as a means to an end, and the different parts of the organization have worked together to use this "means" best to achieve their individual *and* shared goals.

On a Personal Note . . .

I would like to thank Russ Barenberg, the Saturn team leader for training development, for helping me collect my thoughts and write this article. Russ is a world-
class musician who accepted contract-writing and training development work at
Saturn ten years ago simply to supplement his income. His skills and abilities have
grown over the years so that he now leads a dedicated team of professionals in his
current capacity.

Russ replaced Eleanor White, a wonderful lady who came to Saturn as a car
builder or "operating technician," as we call them. Turns out that Eleanor was a
schoolteacher with a master's degree who went to work for General Motors because she couldn't support her family on her teacher's salary. We brought her into
the training group, gave her the opportunity to grow in both instructional design
and leadership skills, and watched her grow to lead the team Russ currently leads.

You see, Eleanor got real good at that design and leadership stuff and now
leads that function for General Motors University.

Where does it all end?

The Manager's Core Work in the New Economy

Peter Henschel,
Executive Director,
Institute for Research on Learning

BEYOND THE BUZZWORDS

In these crazy, on-the-edge times of accelerating change and unnerving uncertainty, it is not enough to rely on "empowered high-performance work teams" to
succeed. Nor do the buzzwords and platitudes around "knowledge management"
and "empowerment" give us much insight. What the new realities demand is a
deep understanding and belief in the ways people actually and naturally learn and
to act based on one's understanding.

The manager's core work in this new economy is to create and support a
work environment that nurtures continuous learning.

Was it not ever thus? Even if so, our organizations rarely give this the attention it deserves. Now, more than ever before, it's an imperative, and will be so "for
the duration."

In this brief essay, I shall lay out some of the principles that should serve managers well as they explore their new roles and responsibilities. I believe these principles can help us breed the innovation and unbridled creativity that will make all the difference in the competitive world in which we live and work.

In the past we often substituted training for real learning. In fact, the behavior one sees in the field would suggest in many cases that managers often think training leads to learning or, worse, that training *is* learning. But classroom models of training that happen episodically are not how people really learn. They are only part of the picture. Asking for more training is definitely not enough—it isn't even close—and often obscures what's really needed: lifelong, continuous learning *in* work and *at* work.

At the Institute for Research on Learning (IRL) we study learning in all of its facets and we design for effective learning. We do that work in a participatory design approach with myriad partners, both in the world of K-12 schools and in the world of work. In the area of workplace learning—my focus here—we do collaborative research and design with lots of partners, mostly from the corporate world. Those partners include Xerox, Hewlett Packard, Steelcase, and some major financial services companies. But half our work is also in our schools, with support from foundations and the federal government. Out of all our projects, we have evolved a set of enduring principles of learning that we consistently recognize in all of our work.

FROM APPRENTICESHIP TO "COMMUNITIES OF PRACTICE"

Shortly after our founding in 1987 by a generous multiyear grant from the Xerox Foundation, IRL began to examine various models of apprenticeship, up close and personal.

We discovered that apprenticeship is actually quite widespread, is usually deemed to be successful, and—very important—usually works because it requires becoming a member of a cohesive, informal community that goes beyond one master or mentor. Wanting to become "one of them," to be accepted into a community, is a powerful dynamic of apprenticeship. Further, we came to understand that newcomers learn best as they become members of these communities. Moreover, they continue to learn as they, in turn, teach, mentor, and participate "in the practice." Continuing to learn, we discovered, is an equally powerful prerequisite for continuing membership in those communities.

Out of that early work, IRL researchers developed a term, "Communities of

Practice," that has now gained recognition and encouraging acceptance in the business literature. The Institute is proud to have coined the term, to see it spread, and to work with our partners on practical applications of the concept.

"Communities of Practice" are simply those highly informal groups of people that develop a shared way of working together to accomplish some activity. Usually such communities include people with varying roles and experience. Every organization has them. Though they don't appear on "org charts," they are the largely invisible network of people who get the real work done. They are also the place where people tend to learn the essentials of their jobs—just as apprentices do—by participating in them. One might even say that a community of practice is like a super apprenticeship system that continually feeds even the most knowledgeable members the new ideas and feedback critical to continuous lifelong learning.

Much of what individuals know depends on their local environment. What an organization knows, however, is what's embedded in and among its communities of practice. Recently much has been made in business literature of statements like "if company X only knew what it knows," referring to the difficulty of capturing what many individuals know. That does not surprise us, since we have come to understand that much of what any of us know is "tacit knowledge" embedded in the practices we share with others. So, if we want to know what our organization knows, we should start by identifying our communities of practice and see them as the wellspring of what the organization *really knows.*

That is one reason why preserving the integrity of these informal communities is so important. The worst effects of downsizing and reengineering come from their complete disregard for communities of practice. The fact that training deals only with explicit knowledge while the value is often in tacit knowledge is another reason training can get at only part of what is understood to be effective.

There is another dimension to the community idea that is seldom discussed but critically important: Learning is powerfully linked not just to motivation but also identity. *What we choose to learn is often a function of who we are and who we wish to become. Not* wanting to be like "them" can be enough to keep someone from learning. That fact seems to hold true whether we are talking about company apprentices, high school gangs, or seasoned software engineers.

If those social dimensions of learning are as powerful and enduring as they appear to be—and our work strongly supports such a contention—then this is important news for organizations. Most organizations implicitly know they need to be continuously innovative through continuous learning. However, again, training alone does not even come close to addressing the challenge.

SEVEN PRINCIPLES OF LEARNING

From our extensive fieldwork in myriad workplaces and educational settings, IRL has developed a set of Principles of Learning that we believe are important guideposts for organizations. These are not "tablets from Moses"; rather, they are evolving as a "work in progress." However, it is already clear that they have broad application in countless settings. Think of them in relation to your own experience.

- *Learning is fundamentally social.* While Jim Botkin speaks in this book of learning as the process of acquiring knowledge, it actually encompasses a lot more. Successful learning is often socially constructed and also requires even slight changes in one's identity, which makes the process both challenging and powerful.
- *Knowledge is integrated in the life of communities.* When we develop and share values, perspectives, and ways of doing things, we create a *community of practice.*
- *Learning is an act of participation.* The motivation to learn is the desire to participate in a community of practice.
- *Knowing depends on engagement in practice.* We often glean knowledge from observations of, and participation in, many different situations and activities. The depth of our knowing depends in turn on the depth of our engagement.
- *Engagement is inseparable from empowerment.* We perceive our identities in terms of our ability to contribute and to affect the life of communities in which we are or want to be a part.
- *"Failure" to learn is often the result of exclusion from participation.* Learning requires access and the opportunity to contribute.
- *We are all natural lifelong learners.* All of us, no exceptions. Learning is a natural part of being human. We all learn what enables us to participate in the communities of practice of which we wish to be a part.

As an IRL trustee, Paul Allaire, Chairman and CEO of Xerox, once said, "To do things differently, we need to see things differently." As managers think about what to do differently, it helps to see through the new lenses the above principles provide. The challenge for each of us is to put on the new eyeglasses and look through them at the realities we face every day.

COMMUNITIES OF PRACTICE IN PRACTICE

Some examples in practice that IRL team members have observed:

- These principles help us understand why kids on a street corner can learn to run all aspects of an illegal drug business but, somehow, cannot learn math in school. Their identity is wrapped up in the first venture, their engagement absent from the other.
- The seven principles also help us understand why co-location alone does not necessarily help a software team "cohere" and learn together. If its members have not developed a community out of which a new practice develops, no amount of physical or organizational rearranging will make a difference.
- When a new technology requires both sales and service teams to learn "the new stuff" well and faster, it may not be enough to gain the knowledge; it may also require a change in professional identity in order to succeed with customers or other technicians.
- When a well-designed business process or a new system fails in its implementation, it may be because developing new practices, based upon a whole community's understanding of the old ones, was not part of the strategy.

All these examples make clear that training is not equal to learning. They also show that learning does not always go in stages, especially when we are exposed to rich environments in real-life situations. Also, simply specifying skills or competencies does not usually provide what people really need to know—and will learn—even if they are placed in the right environment. The principles also help us understand that much of what we often see as "low-level" work is not as routine or as low-level as it may seem. There are essential connections being built, strengthened, and honed among different members of the community.

LEVERAGING COMMUNITIES OF PRACTICE:
THE MANAGER'S NEW CORE WORK

What does all this mean for those who are in positions of coaching, shaping, and leading in the world of the new economy we are now in?

- The new work of managers is all about creating the enabling conditions for continuous learning, which is best done by supporting the informal communities in which it most effectively happens. That requires less control, more listening, more facilitation, and an enormous degree of support for policies and practices that, without the benefit of the lenses of the seven principles, may not appear to be efficient.

To accomplish the above, managers will also need to shift their focus, perhaps changing their own identities as well. The shift needs to be

- From teaching and training to coaching, mentoring, and ultimately continuous learning
- From selling only product to learning from customers
- From an infatuation with building innovative pilot projects—which seldom cross community boundaries—to building on existing pockets of innovation with explicit support to expand what's already working
- From "delivery" to natural "spread" of ideas and innovations

It all boils down to some eternal truths, which many of our corporations need to remember or learn for the first time:

- Listening, observing, and understanding existing practices and informal communities are a prerequisite to effective management, change, and management of change.
- It is necessary to think of the whole environment in which learning needs to take place—the cultural, facilities, professional, and intellectual aspects—as one designs and enables continuous learning.
- Facilitating greater, richer opportunities for those with whom one works is necessary to learn through the communities that already exist. Learning across communities and from one another requires special support and deep understanding.
- Supporting every opportunity for learning and honoring the power of informal learning is absolutely essential.
- Take risks and learn from them. Remember the eternal truth of healthy organizations: "It is far better to seek forgiveness than to ask for permission."

These principles and their implications are essential foundations for helping all of us cope, survive, grow, and thrive. To understand more deeply the issues addressed in this book, start by identifying and supporting the communities of practice that exist in your own organization.

If we do not pay attention to the new management work—and what it demands of us—we face the reality expressed by Intel's CEO, Andy Grove: "There is at least one point in the history of any company when you have to change dramatically to rise to the next performance level. Miss the moment, and you start to decline." The truth of that statement is shown over and over in *Smart Business*.

Finally, the author expresses his boundless gratitude for all of the work and insights of IRL and its people that informed his perspective in this essay.

Peter Henschel
Executive Director
Institute for Research on Learning
66 Willow Place
Menlo Park, California 94025
E-mail: peter_henschel@irl.org
Website: http:/www.Irl.org/

From Monopoly to Modernity
Fragile Autonomy in the New Swedish Postal Service

Gösta Hägglund, Deputy Senior Director, Human Resources, Sweden Post

WHY CHANGE?

Sweden Post has been in the market since 1636. We are considered a natural part of the Swedish society, we have good quality in what we do, and we have a good reputation—mostly. Even in the late 1980s Sweden Post was at ease with its letter monopoly, its 65 percent share of the parcel market, and its 50 percent share of Swedish banking for utility and other payments. Those figures could have given us the feeling that we were "in control of the market." So why change? Because in the 1990s we could see the use of e-mail influencing the letter, the letter market was deregulated, and competitors like Federal Express, DHL, and local courier services threatened to put us out of business if we didn't act.

PRIMER ON SWEDEN POST

Known locally as POSTEN, Sweden Post (the Swedish post office) is number 20 on the list of the 100 largest businesses in Sweden.[6] It is also the largest employer, with the same number of employees in Sweden as Volvo has. Like many European national postal services, it is also one of the country's largest banks for certain financial services: Swedes, when they pay their phone, utility, and other bills, don't send checks; either they go themselves to their local post office, or they put all their instructions to pay in the "yellow envelope" and send it to the "Postgiro." Besides banking and letters, Sweden Post is also in the parcel delivery business like United Parcel Service [UPS] in the United States, and it runs the largest Internet web site for electronic shopping in Northern Europe. It includes products for some 1,000 companies, such as those that provide books, dishwashers, jewelry, train tickets, underwear, and CDs.

REDEFINING THE BUSINESS

Some years ago Sweden Post took some strategic decisions about the markets in which we work. We no longer work in the market of letters; we are in the market of messages. We are not in the market of bank-counter transactions; we are in the market of payments. We are not in the market of delivering parcels but in the market of logistics. Our business concept is: *Through Sweden Post, everyone will be able to reach everyone else with messages, goods, and payments. Sweden Post shall also generate added value on behalf of its customers by creatively combining its own resources with those of others.* We see electronic communication as a means to enhance our value in fulfilling the needs of our customers. That comes close to the knowledge business Jim Botkin describes in Chapter 3.

Concerning letter distribution, the postal administrators in most countries do what they can to keep their monopoly, hoping that customers will stick to sending letters instead of using more modern techniques. Sweden has decided to let go of its monopoly here and also to make Sweden Post a limited-liability company,[7] albeit one owned solely by the Swedish state. Instead of receiving subsidies from Parliament,[8] we have to earn all the money we spend on our different services, and a little more to invest and give back to our owners (the state). And we have to earn it in full competition.

Those are, of course, normal business conditions, but that is still one of the problems we have to deal with, similar to AT&T after its 1984 divestiture. Not every one of our 45,000 employees then wanted or now wants the postal service to be like any other business. Imagine the old situation when most of our employees got their jobs in the postal administration: Public service, monopoly, secure employment, good working hours, and so on. And today we know that customers—most of them other companies—won't use postal services unless they are dependable and efficient enough to justify the price. So like most industries, we have to get used to the fact that things will keep on changing and, in response, find the right services, prices, and quality, and the right size of the company. That means downsizing. And downsizing means employee dissatisfaction, loss of knowledge and motivation, changes in age structure, and so on.[9]

PUBLIC REACTION

At the same time the public is not totally satisfied with the results of Sweden Post's working in full competition. For example, on one hand the in- and out-payments over the counter have fallen by three-quarters in the last decades.[10] On the other hand, the public demands the same number of post offices, the same business opening hours, and so on. And of course the public does not want a rise in postage to cover the cost of the post offices. Should we raise the postage, there is always the possibility of building up the alternate use of electronic mail!

To give one more example of the fragile situation: Many employees, those with the strongest feeling that things were "better before," strongly agree with public opinion. They do not yet talk about giving better service to our customers; they prefer to be a monopoly that serves the public on its own terms.

WORKPLACE OF THE TWENTY-FIRST CENTURY

Our basic idea to cope with the situation is what we call "The Workplace of the Twenty-first Century." Our aspiration is to create approximately 1,500 autonomous units whose independent business plans ensure that the creativity of personnel produces the best possible solution for the customer. If successful, the result will be "the small Business as part of the big Organization."[11]

If employees are expected to take responsibility and are allowed and able to make the decisions that satisfy customers, that would maximize customer satisfaction, employee satisfaction, and profits. To be able to take such responsibility, employees have to know enough about the business situation, competitors, technology changes, P&L statements, customers, and so on. To make that kind of information real, to instill feelings of responsibility, and to see your contribution to the whole, you have to belong to a smaller unit, where you plan, keep informed, follow the results, make your own decisions, and suffer or enjoy the consequences. Easy to say, hard to do.

STATUS REPORT

- You have to change the organization into these smaller profit centers (this is

being done). Today most of these many small units report to some 250 lead-ers, who in turn report to a member of the executive team. No more levels.
- You have to give all employees a chance to get the information they need (this is also being done: We have a very efficient knowledge management so-lution, where all necessary information can be found).[12]

Though we don't use the same terms as those in this book, we are talking about 1,500 entrepreneurial knowledge communities, building new knowledge businesses, and served by a knowledge management system.

But those organizational and technology changes aren't enough. For better or for worse, former middle managers are now suddenly leaders. They can either give support, encourage their employees, help find solutions, trust people, and let go, or cherish their power, stick to old rules, move people away for failed experi-ments, take care of their own P&Ls, and, in so doing, perpetuate the old leader-ship styles the new Workplace Program sought to transform. The cadre of 1,500 new leaders, whether they act in the first way or the second, believe they are doing the right thing for the company!

FRAGILE AUTONOMY

The situation is what I refer to as "fragile autonomy" for the newly autonomous managers. To be successful, they have to be secure in their beliefs and actions. Who can convince them that nowadays it is okay to trust people in situations that before were strictly controlled? In the past, middle managers were promoted partly because of their knowledge of the rules, routines, and regulations. To change, they have to be very confident in their superiors to be able to show confi-dence to their subordinates. But . . . do their bosses really think this trusting peo-ple will be all right? Well, according to experience, it's no use trying to influence one or two layers of management only. So it all ends up at the top level again. And that is where Sweden Post started serious work to develop an earnest dialogue on values, both corporate and personal. The name of our development effort is UPP—"up" with an extra p.[13]

UPP is all about sharing:

- shared knowledge about the situation for Sweden Post
- shared values
- shared enthusiasm for the task to take responsibility for Sweden Post.

UPP is a seminar program in four steps: UPP1 is on vision and values; UPP2 is on in-formation technology; UPP3 is on leadership that, in our way of thinking, similar to

PIPSA's, includes music, arts, and literature in addition to the usual knowledge, information, and training. UPP4 is a further individual development program, depending on background, situation, and individual needs. All together, the UPP1-uPP3 parts of the program entail 16–20 days of full-time effort.

One of the most novel aspects preceding the program was our CEO's decision to hire a young doctor of economics, who "lived" in Sweden Post for a year to find "the soul" of Sweden Post, as a business anthropologist would. Ulf Dahlsten, CEO and President of Sweden Post, has personally met all 1,500 managers during the seminars. He himself spent half a day at every seminar; his fellow member of the executive team spent two days at every seminar. For readers interested in the specifics—especially of UPP1, which focuses on values and is the greatest challenge of the four segments—please feel free to contact me via e-mail, gosta.hagglund@posten.se.

Culture change is never quick, ours included. And it is fragile. You don't need much interference to send a signal to the organization that the newfound autonomy is not for real. What is most important for the executive team and other top managers in Sweden Post is to get good feedback from the organization, to get mutual reinforcement from one another, and to get good support in keeping their hands off the change dynamics they have initiated.

Creating Intellectual Capital in the *Mind*facturing Era
A Learning Cells Approach

Dr. René Villarreal, CEO and CLO,
PIPSA Industrial and Commercial Group

People in the industrial world who mistakenly believe developing countries compete based on their cheap labor—as opponents of the North American Free Trade Agreement argue—had better take another look. PIPSA, the Mexican newspaper state monopoly since 1935, has privatized its management over the last decade, opened itself to free trade and competition, and transformed itself into an intelligent enterprise based on learning and knowledge. Its goal: to transform the business from *manufacturing* to *mind*facturing and to develop world-class productive knowledge workers.

PIPSA BACKGROUND

PIPSA Grupo Industrial y Comercial comprises four enterprises: its trading enterprise, Productora e Importadora de Papel, S.A., located in Vallejo Industrial Park,

Mexico City, and three paper mills—Fábricas de Papel Tuxtepec, in Tuxtepec, State of Oaxaca; Mexicana de Papel Periódico, in Tres Valles, State of Veracruz; and Productora Nacional de Papel Destintado, in Villa de Reyes, State of San Luis Potosí. PIPSA is currently one of the top 150 enterprises in Mexico.

With its creation in 1935, PIPSA became the newsprint monopoly in Mexico. That lasted until 1990, when the domestic market was opened to unlimited imports with a 15 percent import duty. Since NAFTA took effect on January 1, 1994, the duty is being reduced year by year, slated to be eliminated altogether in 1999.

Opening of the borders and elimination of import duties, together with price fluctuations of the newsprint and raw materials used in its manufacture, have presented new and stronger challenges for this group of enterprises. We are meeting them with transformations in our organization based on concepts of intellectual capital.

SUSTAINABLE COMPETITIVE ADVANTAGE

There are three new forces driving us:[5]

- **Knowledge** (*mind*facturing) where intellectual capital is the strategic factor.

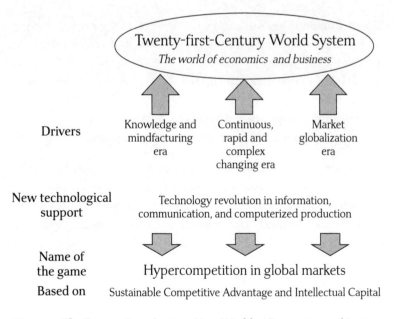

Figure 1. *The Twenty-first-Century New World of Economics and Business*

- **Change** that is continuous, rapid, and complex[16]—which generates uncertainty and reduces predictability.
- **Globalization** in production, trade, finance, communications, and information, which has resulted in the opening of economies and interdependency of business. (This means both new opportunities and threats, along with external turbulence and vulnerability not only for enterprises but for entire countries.)

These new drivers are built on three technologies (see Figure 1):

- **Communication technology,** which allows and intensifies long distance communication
- **Information technology,** which manages great volumes of information in real time
- **Computerized design and manufacturing technology,** which allows flexibility with precision and speed in production.

The name of the new game is "Global Hypercompetition." It has its own rules and demands new skills of its players. Just entering into the game of Global Hypercompetition is not enough. You have to stay in the game, improve your position, and reach the goal. The goal is sustainable competitive advantage, and it comes in three parts:

- **Basic Competitive Advantage** (BCA): This is the entry ticket to the Global Hypercompetition game, and it implies a product with internationally competitive cost, quality and service
- **Revealed Competitive Advantage** (RCA): This is reflected by your market share
- **Sustainable Competitive Advantage** (SCA): This allows the maintenance and improvement of the enterprise's competitive position in the market.

In this new game, the source of sustainable competitive advantage comes from innovation and productive knowledge (*conocimiento productivo*), produced by intellectual capital as the new strategic factor of production, not by the endowment of the traditional factors of production, namely physical capital and labor.

INTELLECTUAL CAPITAL AS KNOWLEDGE CAPITAL

In our way of thinking, intellectual capital has three main elements: human knowledge capital, systemic capital, and organizational capital (see Figure 2).

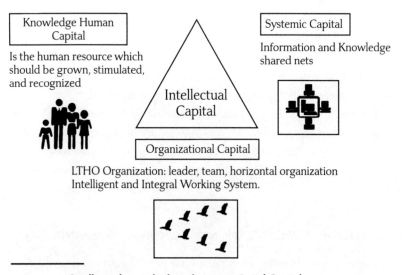

Knowledge Human Capital		Systemic Capital

Is the human resource which should be grown, stimulated, and recognized

Information and Knowledge shared nets

Intellectual Capital

Organizational Capital

LTHO Organization: leader, team, horizontal organization Intelligent and Integral Working System.

Intellectual capital is based on trust: Social Capital

Figure 2. *The Elements of Intellectual Capital*

Human knowledge capital is people with creative and learning capacity; *systemic capital* (technology) is the shared network of information and knowledge of the company; and *organizational capital* is the new LTHO organization: *l*eader, *t*eam, and *h*orizontal *o*rganization. Thus, intellectual capital is made up of people, technology, and organization.

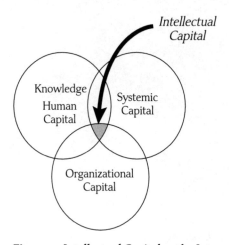

Figure 3. *Intellectual Capital as the Integration of Its Elements*

If the elements of intellectual capital are people, technology, and organization, then its real value is the overlap among them (see Figure 3). That overlap indicates the degree to which human capital is based on systemic capital and also how well they are embedded in an organizational environment that promotes communication, reduces bureaucracy, and increases productivity.

Analyses of competitive advantage conducted by Morgan Stanley[17] show that the common denominator—regardless of industrial sector—is strong management. The key to strong and entrepreneurial management is obtaining the optimal integration of the three elements of intellectual capital—people, technology, and organization.

THE INTELLIGENT ORGANIZATION OF CONTINUOUS LEARNING

PIPSA's approach to a learning organization is based on "collective learning organisms" called learning cells[18] as a process of organizational learning: The Intelligent Organization of Continuous Learning (IOCL).

The raw material for productive knowledge is information, which is relatively cheap, abundant, and accessible in the new era of the knowledge and information revolution. The main output of intellectual capital is productive knowledge or innovation. Therefore the new challenge is to create intellectual capital.

Learning and knowledge management at all levels of the enterprise (worker,

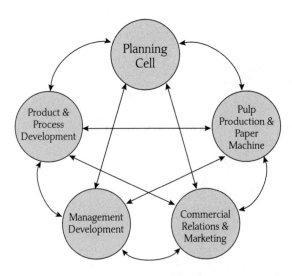

Figure 4. *Interactive Operation of the Learning Cells*

team, and organization) are the hallmark of the Intelligent Organization of Continuous Learning (IOCL). Learning and knowledge management are not only operational tools but the basis of a new organizational model built on continuous learning and the creation of productive knowledge. Thus the IOCL is not only a new form of organizing work. It is also a new organizational model for sustainable competitive advantage.

LEARNING CELLS OF PRODUCTIVE KNOWLEDGE

In PIPSA we call our knowledge communities "learning cells" (*células de aprendizaje*) that are the means to create productive knowledge. Learning cells are groups of workers joining together for the specific purpose of developing productive knowledge.

Inside learning cells, knowledge is created and transferred among members in two ways: person-to-person transfer (tacit to tacit) and codification of knowledge (tacit to explicit). Once knowledge is codified, it becomes part of the organization's knowledge wealth. That knowledge crosses the cells' membranes, or borders, and becomes an asset available to all members of the organization, supported by PIPSA's Intranet, our information and knowledge shared network. PIPSA integrates the organization's local net with the mills via satellite.

The Learning Cells operation made possible the development of several products like uncoated free sheet and specialities like hi-brites and telephone directory paper, even though our paper machines were designed to produce only newsprint. All these improvements were developed during a short period of time.

THE KNOWLEDGE WORKER IN THE *MIND*FACTURING ERA

In the knowledge and *mind*facturing era, the handicraft worker of the manufacturing era has become obsolete. Today knowledge workers are required—not only to work but to learn, create knowledge, and apply that knowledge to work. That constitutes a virtuous circle, which adds value to the enterprise.

PIPSA knowledge workers perform with a WLCA formula:

- *W*ork in an organized manner and efficiently
- *L*earn continuously and productively
- *C*reate productive knowledge to achieve innovation
- *A*pply productive knowledge in their tasks

Not only does the WLCA formula transform a handicraft worker (*manufac-*

turing) into a knowledge worker (*mind*facturing), and not only does it create value for the enterprise through productive innovation, but also the workers themselves benefit. They open their creative working potential, are enriched by new knowledge and skills, increase their capacity to be employed in other firms, and participate in the increase of the productivity of the enterprise.

VIRTUAL CENTERS OF LEARNING DEVELOPMENT AND PRODUCTIVE KNOWLEDGE

In order to develop the workers' intellectual skills, provide them with specific knowledge, and create a shared knowledge net, PIPSA has negotiated with its unions the trade-in of its training centers for Virtual Centers of Learning Development and Productive Knowledge. These centers are virtual in the sense that the whole enterprise has been constituted as a development center for all workers through their participation in learning cells. We use a new approach to learning that we call "learning to undertake."[19] It consists of learning to learn, learning by doing, and learning by interacting.

Former paragm		New paradigm
Cheap hand labor	**Competitiveness factor**	Productive hand labor
Low wages and salaries	**Strategy**	Investment in human capital with a learning approach
Adversary	**Enterprise–workers relationship**	Cooperative
Zero-sum	**Economic approach**	Positive-sum
Enterprise as a working center	**Scope**	Learning and participatory community

Figure 5. *The New Corporate Culture of Productivity for the Twenty-first Century*

Operation of these centers is performed by a small team. Its main function is to link cells, to promote their functioning, to manage long distance education, and to be the connector with outside sources of knowledge. The small team acquires both internal and external trainers, whose job includes teaching specific knowledge, supplying course information, and performing knowledge management. Thus these learning cells transform the entire enterprise into a learning community.

A NEW CORPORATE CULTURE OF PRODUCTIVITY

To use the new potential opened up by intellectual capital, we had to eliminate obstacles from the old paradigm like beliefs in cheap hand labor and a zero-sum relationship between enterprise and workers. That required investment in knowledge human capital (see Figure 5).

Achieving the new productivity will require new entrepreneurial cultures from labor unions and government—the three actors of the process in society—that recognize and allow creation of intellectual capital and productive knowledge or innovation.

ACCOMPLISHMENTS

The intellectual capital created by knowledge workers organized in learning cells has allowed PIPSA to maintain its revealed competitive advantage (RCA)—it has 80 percent of the internal newsprint market in Mexico and exported more than 70,000 tons to the United States in 1998, making a total sale of 400,000 tons in a free market open economy (no custom tariffs) with the competition of large international enterprises such as Canada's Abitibi, and the United States' Bowater.

In addition, the sustainable competitive advantage (SCA) is indicated by the fact that PIPSA has the number one position in the national newsprint market, and no doubt it has the basic competitive advantage (BCA), since it offers internationally competitive costs, quality, and price.

One key element has been the work that PIPSA has done with the scenario planning cell, working with a collaborative philosophy called "the flying of the geese." When geese fly, they do so in "V" formation, flying higher and farther, and increasing their flying rate by more than 70 percent.

Viewed from another perspective, the key strategic cells have been the process technology cell and the new products development cell. They have allowed us to work under our own *multi-process, multi-product,* and *multi-abilities* workers approach.

The process technology cell has been able to maintain competitive costs together with international quality while facing the market's raw materials volatility by using three different material processing technologies in the same production line: mechanical wood pulp, pulp of recycled papers, and chemical pulp from bagasse of sugar cane. The technology optimizes the mixture according to the economic conditions relating to the offers and prices set by the market.

In order to face efficiently the turbulence of shorter and increasingly deeper cycles of the newspaper market, the new products development cell has achieved the production of other kinds of special and noncoated papers—such as bond paper and telephone directory paper—getting 8 percent of the bond paper market and significantly participating in telephone directory paper. All this has been done with the same physical assets (machinery) with practically no new investments (financial assets) but based mainly on the development of intellectual capital.

CONCLUSION

Successful business in the twenty-first century—"smart businesses," as Jim Botkin presents them in this book—demand that their participants master the drivers that create and control the twenty-first century world of economics and business. That can be achieved by knowledge developed inside the enterprise—at the microeconomic level—by learning cells and through intelligent organizations that create, use, and accumulate intellectual capital (Knowledge Capital) as the strategic business factor that creates productive knowledge or innovation, the source of sustainable competitive advantage in the knowledge and mindfacturing era.

To Be a Business Innovator:
Building a Corporate Culture for Renewal

Berth Jönsson,
Senior Partner, SMG North America,
San Francisco and Stockholm

INTRODUCTION

Big corporations have grown to what they are today because they have been successful in serving their customers in the past. Yet success is probably the worst enemy to renewal of a mature company. There are many examples where companies have been too slow to respond to market needs or have been too obsessed by what they are doing successfully, so they have neglected to innovate and invest in new technology, in new products and services.

It takes visionary and skilled management to lead an organization to reap the harvest from current successful offerings and simultaneously provide a number of initiatives that secure new products for the future. To give attention and recognition to two very different sides of the business requires excellence in leadership. Leaders must understand how to manage both knowledge and different subcultures at the same time.

The predominant issue in business today is no longer continuous improvement but continuous renewal. It is a matter not of change in general terms but of real and timely adaptation to the external environment.

In technology-based companies, the need for innovation is evident. Technical inventions drive the business. The need for renewal and innovation is, however, becoming increasingly vital for any company that has to compete in a free market. Information technology impacts all walks of life and organizations. The creativity by which companies use IT, bundle products and services together, partner with others, and so on, is all part of the new business logic. The need for innovation must not be confined within the walls of the company itself. The ability to work with partners, customers, contractors, and distributors so as to maximize added value is crucial.

SMG North America, a San Francisco-based consulting firm specializing in IT and telecom companies, believes that a firm's "Knowledge Capital" is its key asset for competitiveness and future growth. Sometimes that is referred to as the "Intangible" asset. It is vitally important for a firm to nurture this asset and make the "intangibles" measurable and therefore visible.

When the Swedish mobile phone manufacturer Ericsson decided to move heavily from fixed telephony into cellular, it moved its engineers to a new site far away from the traditional R&D center and close to a university campus. That was one of the most fundamental conditions for success: to create an environment with no constraints left over from the old organization, so as to enhance creative thinking and to explore and experiment freely.

When Volvo decided to develop new production technology and work organization in the early 1970s, it gave its first project team plenty of leeway to think and plan freely. The pioneering Kalmar plant was located five hours' drive from the main plant in Gothenburg.

Similarly, when GM started the Saturn project in the 1980s it decided to give the people in charge more freedom to think, study, and experiment than was common within GM. Saturn acquired a unique status as an independent company to allow new ideas to flourish.

Those cases have some common denominators. They are guided by a clear vision that stimulates employees to commit themselves and to use all their creativity at work.

An organization that has innovation as its main objective will succeed only if certain forces are at hand:

- **Management** must be visionary and must have the capacity to communicate its vision and values, to nurture a spirit of creativity, to fight red tape, and to minimize formal control systems. Management needs to develop leaders rather than managers. Personal responsibility must go beyond formal job descriptions. Knowledge and problem-solving are more important than position.
- **Leadership** on all levels needs to be part of the team, to encourage new ideas to flourish among associates, but it also needs to communicate its own ideas to stimulate the process of new thinking. Leaders should be willing to take personal risks.
- **Individuals working together** with others freely, without formal boundaries, must at the same time have the freedom to develop and suggest their own ideas.

MANAGING INNOVATION

Based on many years of work within companies that have successfully renewed themselves through an innovative organizational culture, SMG has developed a model called "Managing Innovation." The key parameters of the model are:

1. Enterprise objectives
2. Competence and knowledge
3. Values and incentives
4. Organizational forms and processes

A company or a product or technology can be described in terms of the life cycle curve, like any living system. It goes through the early stage of invention and adaptation to the environment, followed by the later stages of growth, market adaptation, retention, maturity, and finally ending up as a laggard compared to competition.

The difference between the phase of innovation and that of maturity is easily conceived. The dilemma most companies that have reached maturity face is how to renew themselves and find the right *timing* for new products and offerings. The mismatch in terms of life cycles often has to do with *managing innovation* and getting the timing right. The issue is how to optimize a possible cash cow that can be achieved during the phase of growth, particularly early maturity, and the need for continuous renewal at the front end of innovation. It takes many ideas and trials before a product is ready for the market. If one out of ten ideas makes it to the market successfully, the batting average is pretty good.

The focus of innovation has to shift as products and technologies mature. It is not enough to be innovative only in terms of products; the whole business system has to be aligned to the particular position of the product. If a new product is well received in the market but there are deficiencies in the sales and marketing system or in product support, launching of the product may well fail. Consequently we are looking for consistency within the *whole business system* as well as consistency within any given subsystem, be it R&D, Product Planning, or Sales & Marketing.

SMG has spent a lot of time thinking through the dimensions of corporate cultures that would enhance the different phases of the life cycle curve. We designed a survey instrument and asked an expert panel to assess the position of a particular company. Once the instrument is applied within an organization, it will demonstrate

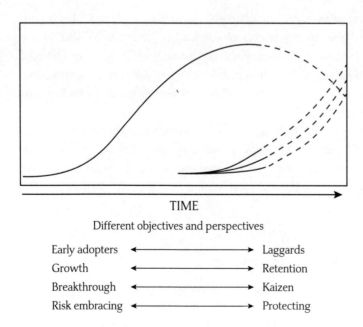

TIME

Different objectives and perspectives

Early adopters	←	→	Laggards
Growth	←	→	Retention
Breakthrough	←	→	Kaizen
Risk embracing	←	→	Protecting

How Do Companies Manage the Front and Back Ends Simultaneously?

the stage of development on the life cycle curve and the degree of consistency between the underlying parameters by which the corporate culture is defined.

The key findings of the panel demonstrate the differences between three phases of development: (1) startup, (2) growth, and (3) maturity. The focus of this essay will be on "*early adopters,*" which are primarily the "startups" that are about to make it to the market and companies that just proved themselves by beginning to grow successfully in the market.

1. ENTERPRISE OBJECTIVES

Focus on the Business Mission

The early stage is dominated by an almost "religious" belief in an idea. Management has the ability to communicate a vision and a business mission explicitly to the employees, which sparks a lot of energy within the company and a strong belief in the idea.

Bill Gates's early vision for "information at your fingertips" had a powerful impact on employees. People shared the vision and interpreted it into their own job context. The development of the vision toward the "Super Highway" concept and connecting people electronically has further inspired people to contribute to the business.

A vision communicated to customers has in many cases had a dual effect. Sometimes the empowerment of employees has been extraordinary. That was the case when Jan Carlzon of the Scandinavian Airline System (SAS) communicated his vision about service and of how each and every employee would contribute to it. Moreover, he lived what he preached. Employees often met him at the front line helping customers.

The sooner the early adopters become market-focused, the better. 3M is among the companies that strongly emphasize speed as a key success factor. Only an explicit business mission, communicated and translated into many individual tasks, will make a company's culture revenue-driven.

2. COMPETENCE AND KNOWLEDGE

Basic and Differentiating Competencies

There is a lot of self-confidence among early adopters. Trust in their own ability to master today's ideas and projects as well as the future business is typical for this culture. People have a good sense for how a company will be uniquely positioned in the market through its products and technology. People feel tightly connected to that business because they see how their skills contribute to the market position. The company is not necessarily more focused than other companies, but it is likely to be faster and more flexible. There is an awareness of key resources needed to solve tasks. Whether those resources are available inside or outside the company is of less importance. The early adopters trust that their external network is at hand as well as their ability to attract skilled people to the company.

When Ericsson Radio Systems developed the broadband technology for mobile telephone systems, there were no given solutions to numerous technical problems. In most cases it could not go elsewhere to find the one right solution. Yet management was able to compose an appropriate team of people from inside (80 percent) and outside (20 percent). It knew what it needed to accomplish, and so that's what it did.

3. VALUES AND INCENTIVES

Work Styles and Culture

People's inner drive to fulfill the idea—their idea—is a cornerstone of the innovative organizational culture. People have fun at work, and the border between serious work and play is very thin if not invisible. Passion for the challenges at work and play go hand in hand. People thrive on uncertainty and flux. Confrontation in terms of ideas is a common phenomenon, which helps to stretch the thinking and to promote problem-solving.

At Intel it is a well-known fact that constructive conflicts between individuals are encouraged. They are looked upon as natural in the functioning of groups. Out of the many conflicts and challenges grow new creative solutions to problems. Most of Intel's leading-edge technical solutions have emerged out of this culture.

When Microsoft tries to find a new approach to a product, several work groups or individuals may tackle the problem at the same time. The notion is that those parallel processes will lead to confrontations and to a superior end result. There is less concern for duplication of efforts. People are given difficult logical tasks in order to exercise the brain. The concept of creative and logical problem-solving is part of the "play."

3M emphasizes speed through concurrent development. Failures from work experiences are a large part of learning and the building of knowledge. Accumulation of knowledge is the foundation for value creation.

Risk Tolerance and Management Style

Intuitive thinking is the engine behind many breakthrough ideas. To invent, by definition, is to create something new, something no one else has done before.

There are no customers for such ideas until what they can do can be demonstrated. Who asked for the Sony Walkman before it was invented? Intuition and a strong belief that this little machine would help people to enjoy music (and more) in any environment drove this idea.

Early adopters often come up with ideas that at a first glance appear to be crazy. It is not until we actually experience the product that we as customers can evaluate it and put a value on it. Who asked for stickers before they were invented? Today there are stickers used everywhere, in homes and workplaces. 3M is one of the best known companies for continuously introducing new products. More than one-third of 3M's revenues stem from products that did not exist four years earlier. That ratio has been sustained for the last fifty years.

Among early adopters you definitely do not lose face if you come up with a new idea that no one has heard of before. On the contrary, you are encouraged to take "personal risks." The role of management is to encourage personal risk-taking among employees and for themselves.

Remuneration

When a company is successful through its innovative work culture, people will see the connection between their contribution and business success. Ownership of ideas and ownership in terms of value added in the market have to go hand in hand. Thus the remuneration system has to be designed on the principles that people get a stake in the company and can share in the returns that they helped to create.

That being said, there will always be a struggle for fairness. Fairness has to continue stimulating a true loyalty to ideas and a vision instead of encapsulating people in a system that builds on material drivers solely. This balance is not easy to strike over time.

4. ORGANIZATIONAL FORMS AND PROCESSES

The notion of being able to predict inputs and outputs at work is foreign to early adopters. Rather, it is flexibility that counts. The nature of work will change frequently and in many cases daily. People not only must be willing to change but must look for those changes to bring them variety and new challenges at work. This also calls for flexibility in terms of internal processes and support systems.

It becomes utterly important that system developers are tightly integrated into the product and business processes. There is no legitimacy for systems that are not integrated into the overall business idea.

The informal and collegial atmosphere that dominates the early adopters is a prerequisite for the underlying drivers that characterize those organizations. There is also a deeply felt respect for other people with complementary skills that contribute to the whole. It is foreign to management to recruit people in a streamlined fashion. Management is instead focused on composing a team that together can solve the task because its members have different backgrounds and experiences.

Knowledge in its broadest sense is the key for successful early adopters. Position has no role or extremely little role in reality. By contrast, long-term position is gained through knowledge and skills.

Typically it is a good idea—an interesting idea or a challenging thought—that catches the ears and eyes of management and colleagues. The organization is idea-driven. People react to good ideas, not to who offered them.

At 3M management counts among its key drivers to innovation their organization of multidisciplinary teams composed of engineering, marketing, and financial personnel. People with great ideas and diverse backgrounds contribute most to the end result.

CONCLUSIONS

This essay has tried to capture the key drivers for renewal and innovation based on many years of experience and SMG's research. The focus in characterizing successful change has been on *early adopters,* who grow and prosper through continuous renewal.

Because our clients are telecom companies, innovators and early adopters all, they provide stark evidence that knowledge is the core for all growth in the new economy. They are extreme cases, certainly, but they provide useful object lessons for older, more traditional organizations.

Understanding Scientific Knowledge Communities:
A Model for R&D Managers
Derived from Work at Los Alamos National Laboratory

Dr. Heidi Ann Hahn, Senior Executive Advisor, Laboratory Director's Office,
Los Alamos National Laboratory
and
Dr. Rebecca R. Phillips, Research Director,
Motorola University[20]

OVERVIEW

Knowledge communities in science, like those at Los Alamos National Laboratory and other national research labs, are beginning to interact with those from business. But they don't follow the same rules as knowledge communities in business, or elements present in business knowledge communities may take different forms in scientific knowledge communities. For example, take knowledge sharing. While the very essence of science is sharing of knowledge with a broad spectrum of peers, business tends to share more with partners but less with competitors; however, even in science (particularly in knowledge communities spanning many institutions) competitive relationships and a lack of shared objectives can create barriers to knowledge sharing. Overcoming such barriers and maximizing the output of new scientific knowledge—especially of the breakthrough kind that shifts paradigms—can be a significant management challenge. The model described in this essay shows the complex and conflicting tensions that an R&D manager must understand in order to manage a scientific knowledge community successfully.

BACKGROUND

Los Alamos National Laboratory was born at the beginning of the scientific heyday of the United States at a time when the role of basic science in national security and prosperity was a matter of national consensus. The presence of a threatening Communist Russian adversary was enough to create support for science throughout the Cold War. As part of this, both basic and applied scientists at LANL were provided with broad guidance and adequate funds to conduct the research to support the build up of the nation's nuclear arsenal. They were then essentially left alone to pursue their research. For many years that "hands-off" approach was successful in ensuring the nuclear superiority of the United States and preserving an uneasy global peace that ended a cycle of ever-increasing carnage in wars through the first half of the century.

With the antimilitary sentiments during and after the Vietnam conflict, questions regarding the size of the nation's defense and national security apparatus began to emerge. With the end of the Cold War, critics of defense-related activity became more vocal, and there were also increasing questions about growth and accountability within basic and applied science. That, in addition to pressure to reduce the federal budget deficit, has resulted in several years in which there was reduced spending for research to support ongoing weapons responsibilities. Not only did total dollars decline, but changing requirements for the conduct of research operations also changed the balance of costs, so that a smaller part of the research dollar went to the research itself and a greater percentage went to infrastructural and operational considerations.

This picture has changed considerably by the national recognition of the need for a stewardship program to assure the safety and reliability of the nation's remaining stockpile indefinitely, without nuclear testing. However, at the time we initiated the study that led to this model, Laboratory scientists were being encouraged to pursue "dual benefit" activities—those that maintain their ability to answer science-based questions regarding the enduring nuclear stockpile while also meeting the needs of industrial partners or nondefense government sectors—in order to compensate for the decline in funds.[21] However, some people questioned whether industrial competitiveness was a mission compelling enough to justify basic science. Writing in *Scientific American*, Cohen and Noll stated "We believe the new competitiveness rationale will not succeed in reinvigorating the national R&D effort. [C]ompetitiveness is not a politically powerful substitute for the cold war in forging a durable, bipartisan coalition for supporting R&D at the generous levels typical of past decades."[22]

Despite such potential pitfalls, there was a trend to link funding of basic research to industrial competitiveness. The fundamental debate, expressed by Williams in "Research and Recession," is: "If we [scientists] allow ourselves to be prioritized solely by what we perceive as research likely to lead to identifiable wealth creation, then I believe it is likely that we may well make a number of errors of choice, and may indeed stifle creativity in many areas of science."[23] It was that concern and others that ultimately led us to build a model[24] to elucidate how one might better manage research to nurture its long-term vitality despite increasing pressures for near-term utility.[25]

Over the course of about a year, we interviewed many of the Laboratory's scientists and R&D managers in order to understand the impact of those pressures on the life of the scientific knowledge community. We found that scientific enterprises require two distinct types of management: (1) management of the research itself and (2) management of what can be called a "relationship chain."[26] Success in managing both aspects is necessary to maximize knowledge development, sharing, and adoption.

MANAGEMENT OF THE RESEARCH

R&D managers typically decide what work will be done, decide who will do the work, and, in collaboration with a funding agent, articulate the desired results, i.e., they make investment decisions, assign personnel, and set objectives. They also negotiate to varying degrees how much the product can cost and when it must be delivered.

The basic dynamic in a manager's portfolio of activities is the research characteristics (shown as vertical bands in Figure 6) mapped against the expected outcomes (shown as the top horizontal band) and contextual factors of funding and skill levels (shown as the lower two horizontal bands). Each band, whether vertical or horizontal, represents a continuum. For example, the ends of the top horizontal continuum are "breakthroughs" versus "directed outcomes." And the ends of the lower continua are "flexible use" to "constrained use." These continua do not imply direction, i.e., breakthrough is not more closely related to technical-administrative work products and interactions than to the one-many dimensions.

We identified five major research characteristics, which are represented as the five clusters of vertical bands shown in Figure 6. From left to right, these are:

Continuum 1: Technical to Administrative (Interactions and Work Products)
Continuum 2: Basic to Applied
Continuum 3: Theoretical to Experimental (Projects and Infrastructures)
Continuum 4: Long Duration Versus Short Duration (Objectives and People)
Continuum 5: One to Many (Projects, Disciplines, People, and Objectives)

This may seem like a lot of characteristics and clusters, but the complexity represents the actual situation as best we can identify it. We speak of all of the continua together as a collection of "tensions" to be managed.

It is important to realize that no one end of any continuum is more "right" than any other; rather, balancing of the tensions and managing the movement along the continua to produce optimal results are the objectives. Interestingly, the vertical tensions of the five project characteristics shown in our model are quite similar to the four great dilemmas of learning Jim describes in Chapter 6,[27] suggesting that learning and knowledge creation may follow parallel paths.

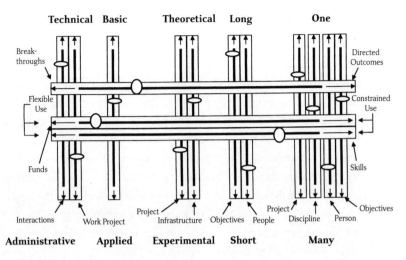

Figure 6. *Management of Research in R & D Knowledge Communities*

Research Characteristics

In designating the five research characteristics we show in the model, we had to wrestle with the following set of issues:

- Scientists do not often describe their research as either purely basic or purely applied. However, they do view the time dimension of particular projects as pulling them in one direction or another. Thus the model shows, for example, that projects of long duration generally exist at the same end of the continuum as basic projects.

- There exists a positive feedback loop between the basic and the applied, where resolution of applied problems can lead to paradigm shifts in the thinking of basic researchers.[28] Similarly, basic research in one field often capitalizes upon technological breakthroughs in other disciplines.

- The time dimension of research projects has two primary components: (1) time available to achieve objectives and (2) length of time personnel are assigned to a project. Although the two components may be related, it does not follow that they are fully correlated: A project of long duration may have many short-term objectives and require cycling of numerous personnel. Short projects potentially limit the scientist's ability to delve into an area in depth. And projects having too many short-term objectives may stifle creativity and curiosity by not allowing scientists to explore avenues of interest not related to the near-term goal in the most (apparently) expeditious way.

267

At the same time, a short project or a project with many short-term meaningful milestones may be rejuvenating because of feelings of accomplishment resulting from quick successes.

- For the "one-to-many" dimension of research projects, there are as many as four primary components: (1) the number of projects to which an individual is assigned; (2) the number of people assigned to a particular project; (3) the number of disciplines represented on a project team; and (4) whether there is one or more than one objective of the whole effort. Funding cuts are forcing scientists to dedicate fractions of their time to numerous projects, thereby diluting their efforts on any one activity and precluding the kind of concentration that may be required for scientific breakthroughs. However, multiple assignments across related projects can also be valuable where they require scientists to broaden the scope of their thinking.

- Similarly, declining budgets are resulting in an inability to sustain large research projects that demand contributions from many scientists. Smaller projects, particularly those that support only one or a few investigators, may stifle opportunities for intellectual exchange and cross-fertilization of ideas, especially in cases where projects are too small to allow multidisciplinary participation.

Expected Outcomes

- Research programs vary in the degree of directedness of their outcomes. Projects with directed outcomes have specific scientific objectives and may also emphasize the production of publications and presentations as well as garnering peer recognition, citations, and awards. On the other end of the continuum are curiosity-driven projects, which may lack specific expectations regarding objectives but in which breakthroughs are anticipated. Here, terms like "revolution in the field" or "paradigm shift" are used to describe the hoped-for breakthroughs. Paradoxically, though, one can never really plan for breakthroughs—the more a researcher aims for them, the more elusive they become. Rather, this end of the spectrum represents the freedom to explore intriguing aspects within a scientific domain without being explicit about what one is seeking.

Contextual Factors

- Related to the notion of freedom to explore are the final horizontal dimensions depicted in Figure 6, namely, the degree to which availability of both funding and skills is constrained. Unlike the other factors described above, these two are not so much related to a particular research project as to the organizational context in which all research projects exist. R&D managers must be aware of those factors but are not able to exert much control over them.

- Funding here refers not to specific funds available to perform project work[29] but to the more intangible perception of organizational wealth versus organizational poverty. When scientists perceive organizational wealth, they feel free to purchase state-of-the-art equipment, for example; to attend conferences to exchange information with their peers; and to buy such services as computer support. The degree of organizational wealth or poverty is less a financial issue than a cultural one of how, by whom, and for which purposes money is spent. When scientists perceive a culture of organizational poverty, the effects can be paradoxical. On the one hand, "necessity is the mother of invention." Some degree of deprivation can result in creative solutions to research problems. On the other hand, however, "a wolf at the door" can threaten access to necessary tools and relationships needed to raise scientific productivity.[30]

- Similarly, skills as used here refers not to whether a project demands cross-disciplinary skills but to whether the organization can provide them when the demand arises. That will depend on whether the right skills exist within the organization, whether project management systems are flexible enough to free them up when faced with higher-priority demands, and whether the systems in place facilitate crossing of internal boundaries by staff to meet skills demands.

MANAGEMENT OF THE RELATIONSHIP CHAIN

In addition to managing the research itself, the task of R&D managers also includes managing a set of relationships among end users, funders, trustees, and scientists. These are shown in Figure 7. The manager's task is to align the wants and needs of the various parties with respect to the research itself or vice versa. The position of the parties on the diagonal is notional—depending upon the personalities of the players and the nature of the research itself, certain members of the relationship chain may be more closely or more loosely aligned.

Let's take a closer look at who the players are. Our relationship chain identifies four distinct parties to the relationship: the scientists, the trustees, the funders, and the customers or "end users."[31] The chain that exists within the knowledge community is shown as the diagonal line on Figure 7. By overlaying the main graphic in Figure 6 with the diagonal relationship chain in Figure 7, we mean to convey the notion that the relationships crosscut all the other dynamics involved in scientific management.

Scientists represent the individual researcher or experimenter and his or her collaborators. Not all the scientists in our knowledge community need exist within the same organization; they may be drawn from any combination of government or industrial R&D laboratories, application centers, or academic institutes. The critical feature in identifying a scientific entity within the knowledge community is that the entity actually participates substantively in the research program.[32]

Scientific staff varies in different organizations. It may include the senior researcher, student assistants, and technicians, all of whom contribute knowledge at different levels. This subgroup is not treated in any detail in our model; rather, we focus on how the collective interacts with other members of the relationship chain. However, it is not difficult to see that the R&D manager's task includes both the management of the internal team and its interactions with the entire knowledge community, internal and external.

Trustees are often scientists in their own right and experts in a particular scientific discipline. They usually have stature in the knowledge community at large and play a complex and vital role. Like others in the chain, trustees have the possibility to relate with the other three; indeed, the trustee is the most likely member of the relationship chain to interact with *all* other members, even if he or she may be involved in competitive projects. The trustee advises the funders regarding the merit of particular investment opportunities, reassures the end user of the value of the research, and supports the integrity of the scientists with emphasis on con-

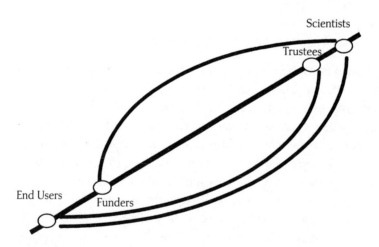

Figure 7. *Management of the Relationship Chain in R & D Knowledge Communities*

tent knowledge. Like that of the funders, the trustee's knowledge contribution tends to be more strategic than tactical, looking at how a project fits with an overall portfolio, looking ahead to future research needs, and assessing the quality and relevance of work in progress. Usually trustees refrain from dictating the details of a particular piece of research.

Funders, those who pay for the research, may be within or outside the organization. They might be the consumers of the research, but not necessarily. Although funders may have technical competence, their knowledge contribution is likely to be in understanding market niches and the direction of an overall research agenda, rather than in the technical details of a particular piece of research.

End users are those who consume, apply, or use the product of the research experiments. For example, anyone who buys a transistor radio could be considered an end user of transistor technology, but not a funder: transistor technology breakthroughs were paid for long ago. Broad and indirect knowledge contributions of end users are most influential in creating a demand for new knowledge from the other members of the relationship chain. Interestingly, end users are often anonymous to the other parties in the relationship chain and are likely to exert influence not as individuals but as part of an aggregate, such as by participating in market research or customer feedback surveys.

Several features of this relationship chain pose challenges that are more prominent in scientific than in other knowledge communities. They include a lack of shared business objectives and a presence of competitive relationships that intensify the barriers to knowledge sharing. Each of these is discussed briefly below.

Because the parties to the relationship chain do not all belong to the same organization, they often do not have a shared business objective. Indeed, for some types of R&D there may not be an explicit business objective at all. What parties do share, however, are values that commit them to the scientific enterprise and that bind the relationship chain together. Having shared values is important but sometimes tenuous: It does not necessarily produce agreement on the correct path to follow. The fact that members of the relationship chain come from different organizations can exacerbate the challenge to share knowledge, especially when information is proprietary or organizations are competitive.

Members of the relationship chain bring with them different forms of knowledge. Ensuring that participants limit themselves to sharing *relevant* knowledge is a challenge. For example, a scientist who was once technically proficient but is now an administrator (perhaps now interacting in the role of funder) may try to shape the scientific approach to the problem. While such people may add great value in positioning where the research fits in a broader scientific portfolio, they may be less qualified to comment on state-of-the-art scientific details. Curbing the desire to contribute such knowledge, however, is difficult without appearing dismissive. Managing a relationship chain where some members control funding levels but others influence where the funds are directed is an especially challenging balancing act for an R&D manager.

In some cases there are multiple R&D managers, each trying explicitly or implicitly to manage some aspect of the chain. That can further complicate arriving at common objectives, which are to encourage each player to bring relevant knowledge to bear; to minimize situations in which power dominates knowledge; and to foster a sense of shared purpose and direction. In addition, the managers of relationship chains must recognize and adapt to the different "latencies" that the various parties may have with respect to the adoption of innovation—that is the speed at which various parties will accept and endorse new scientific ideas.

IN CONCLUSION

The utility of this R&D manager's model is in framing conversations among the various participants, especially regarding optimal "settings," which we show as elongated circles on the various dimensions. Using the model as a common point of reference, parties can talk about where they personally fall along each continuum. The model helps them note preferences and patterns, matches and mismatches, and personality-driven versus business-driven goals. Thus, R&D managers can better understand the human resources responsible for the creation and sharing of knowledge.

Such conversations can occur at different points in the life of a research project. At the start of a project the model can be used to focus on negotiation of the research agenda. Later, when communication problems among parties in the relationship chain most commonly occur, exploration of the model can point to areas where different participants have different objectives. In fact, because of the dynamic nature of scientific research, one would expect the "optimal" settings to change over time. Thus, even when no problems are perceived, the model can serve as a tool to focus progress reviews. Using the model to discuss progress and future directions could allow the parties to come to a common understanding that is not just a current snapshot but also a moving set of guidelines to keep a project on target in the future. Participants can engage in a dialogue around milestones that are expected to occur in the future that would indicate the need for a change in settings along the way.

Although we have not yet done so, the model outlined here could be computerized; as such, it could also serve as a training exercise for people charged with managing knowledge communities in both the scientific and the business world.

Acknowledgments

This book could never have evolved without the patience, understanding, and support of many people and institutions. First I want to thank InterClass and its members and staff for sharing their ideas and time with me following our norm of "hard on ideas, soft on people." I especially want to thank my Inter-Class partner and Chairman, Eric Vogt; the Vice President for Finance, Joe Weber; and Administrative Assistant Angelica Yozzo, who managed the community during my periods of writing.

I thank Free Press Senior Editor Bruce Nichols for his excellent work, astute intelligence, and skill in editing. President Paula Duffy and I have something in common: the allergies to bees and shellfish. Thanks, Paula, for your empathy.

Ehama Institute and its founders, RainbowHawk and WindEagle, have been an inspiration to me and gave support immediately after my anaphylactic attack to help me understand the significance of what I experienced. May you and your community walk in harmony and beauty.

I want to acknowledge the Club of Rome and its founder, the late Aurelio Peccei, who introduced me to the power of learning and the potential of knowledge. I am also grateful to CoR's current President, Ricardo Diez Hochleitner, a valued supporter of global learning; thanks as well to the CoR Secretary General, Bertrand Schneider, who keeps creating new international forums for these topics.

George Kozmetsky, founder of the Institute for Creativity and Capital at the University of Texas in Austin, where I am proud to be associated as a Fellow, has been a supporter, especially on topics of entrepreneurship. The late Tom Eliot, who as President of the Salzburg Seminar in Austria and former Chancellor of Washington University in Saint Louis, and his wife, Lois, were for many years my mentors in matters of international intellectual development.

In the business world, there are so many to thank. That you're acknowledged in a list redoubles my thanks for ideas you've contributed over nearly ten years of quarterly InterClass meetings involving more than two thousand managers from nearly thirty different companies.

CLAUDE BALTHAZARD, Senior Consultant, Learning Org. & Leadership Development, CIBC

SUSAN BLOUCH, Director, Training & Organizational Development, CSC Consulting

DAVE BOGAN, Chief Information Officer, CSI/CSC

RUTH BOULDES, Manager, Retail, Processes & Development, Chevrolet

JOE BUDA, Director, Human Resource Programs, Otis Elevator

LINDA BURGESS, Senior Consultant, Organizational Change Management, CSC Consulting

JIM CHESTER, Director, Core Values Implementation, Chevrolet

JIM CHRZ, Area Manager, Dealer Development, General Motors

RAUL CICERO, Strategic Planner, Finance, PIPSA

WENDY COLES, Director, Learning Organization, General Motors

MICHÈLE DARLING, Executive Vice President Human Resources, Prudential Insurance Company

STEVE DENNING, Program Director, Knowledge Management ITS, World Bank

PRISCILLA DOUGLAS, Marketing Manager, Public Sector, Xerox

LEIF EDVINSSON, Director, Futures Centers, Skandia Insurance

JEFF FARR, Director of Training, KPMG Peat Marwick LLP

NORM FRIBERG, Manager, Human Resources Development, Volvo Cars of North America

ERNESTINE FRYE, Manager, Education and Development, Prudential Insurance

CLIFFORD GILPIN, Division Chief, World Bank

PHIL GOLDSTONE, Special Assistant, Science & Technology, Los Alamos National Laboratory

JOHN GRECO, Senior Vice President, Marketing & Technology, RR Donnelley Financial

REBECCA GRUBER, Principal, Consulting & Systems Integration, CSC Consulting

GÖSTA HÄGGLUND, Deputy Senior Director, Human Resources, Sweden Post

HEIDI HAHN, Group Leader, Los Alamos National Laboratory

TONY HAIN, General Director, OED, General Motors Corporation

BRAD HALL, Division Manager, Knowledge Communities, AT&T

JUNE HANSON, Vice President, Learning, Prudential Insurance

SCOTT HAWKINS, Analyst, Intellectual Capital, Skandia, AFS

BRIAN HELWEG-LARSEN, Principal, Professional Skills Training

PETER HENSCHEL, Executive Director, Institute for Research on Learning

BRITT-MARIE HESSELBÄCK, Associate, Customer Focus Institute

GARY HIGH, Director, Human Resource Development, Saturn Corporation

OVE HJELMERVIK, Project Manager, Exploration & Development, Statoil ASA

JAN HOFFMEISTER, Vice President, American Skandia

LILLEMOR HOLM, Internal Consultant, Leadership Development, Volvo Car Corporation

TARIQ HUSAIN, Manager, Learning & Leadership Center, World Bank

DOUG IZARD, Director, Tax Knowledge Management, KPMG Peat Marwick LLP

GAIL KILGOUR, Senior Vice President, CIBC Leadership Centre, CIBC

JAN LAPIDOTH, President, Customer Focus Institute

DICK LEIDER, President, The Inventure Group

HELENA LIGHT HADLEY, Director, New Business Ventures, Marriott International

BRUCE MCBRATNEY, Vice President, Management & Org. Development, RR Donnelley

DON MCCREESH, Executive VP, Human Resources, CIBC

BILL MCELWEE, Human Resources Director, Business Markets Div., AT&T

JOHN MIDDLETON, Division Chief, New Products & Outreach, World Bank

JAMIE MILLARD, National Practice Director, Organizational Change Management, CSC Consulting

BRUCE MOORHOUSE, Manager, Corporate Communications, 3M

CHUCK NEWCOMER, Manager, KM/Vehicle Sales & Service, General Motors

KATE O'KEEFE, Director, Executive Education, Honeywell

INGMAR PERSSON, Vice President, Sweden Post

REBECCA PHILLIPS, Research Director, College of Leadership & Transcultural Studies, Motorola University

BOB PORTRIE, President & CEO, InfoMation Publishing Corporation

ROCÍO RAMOS DE VILLARREAL, Senior Adviser, PIPSA

JOANNE RAYNES, Vice President, CIBC Knowledge Based Business, CIBC

JULIE RICHMAN, Project Leader, Saturn University, Saturn Corporation

PASCHA SACHS, Sr. Research Scientist, Institute for Research on Learning (IRL)

STEVE SASS, President, Sass and Associates

RUTH SAUNDERS, Principal Economist, IFC-World Bank

MARK SCHLEICHER, Director, Knowledge Management, Motorola University

MARY LEE SCHNEIDER, Sr. Vice President, Technology, RR Donnelley & Sons

BARBARA SHELHOSS, Vice President, Marketing, InfoMation Publishing Corporation

CAROL SILK, Vice President, Prudential Insurance

ALBERT SIU, Vice President, Human Resources, AT&T

ANN SKUDLARK, Technology Manager, AT&T Labs

HUBERT ST.-ONGE, Vice President, People, Knowledge & Strategies, Mutual Life of Canada

SUSAN STUCKY, Associate Director, Institute for Research on Learning (IRL)

RUTH THOMPSON, Consultant, EDINP, World Bank

JERI THORNSBERRY, Career Coach, AT&T Alumna

WAYNE TOWNSEND, Managing Consultant, General Motors University

TOM TREZISE, Global Vice President, Marketing, RR Donnelley Financial

NANCY TUYN, Director, TCE & Organizational Learning, Chevrolet

SARAH VANDER ZANDEN, President, Vander Zanden Inc.

FERNANDO VÁZQUEZ, Chief Learning Officer, PIPSA

RENÉ VILLARREAL, President/CEO, PIPSA

BILL WADT, Special Assistant, Deputy Laboratory Director, Los Alamos National Laboratory

ETIENNE WENGER, Research Scientist, Institute for Research on Learning

JOHN ZITELLI, Director of Training, CSC Systems & Integration, CSC Consulting

For their suggestions and inspiration, I would like to thank my friends and co-authors Stan Davis, Jana Matthews, Mahdi Elmandjra, and Mircea Malitza, as well as friends and professional associates Tom Davenport, Amy Edmondson, Mary Ann Hedin, Judy Jacobs, Larry Prusak, Ev Rogers, Peter Senge, Syed Shariq, Bill Ury, Jim Utterback, David Warburg, Scott Aarenson, Sami AlBanna, and Alan Webber.

I was aided immeasurably by Naomi Bauer with her acute skill in evoking images and accuracy in the organizational learning domain. Many thanks again to Angelica Yozzo, who has cheerfully and efficiently assisted me throughout this project.

Finally, my friends and family were overly patient. George Pandapas, who came to see me in the hospital after the bee sting; Ken Brill and his wife, Margot Brill Wygant; Charlotte Pollard, Mimi Chase-Trujillo, and all my friends in New Mexico. Special thanks to my talented artist friend, Gary Lund.

My two sons, Alexander in San Francisco and Christopher in Boston, have been a constant source of inspiration, as has their younger generation.

During the most hectic part of the writing, I went to Felecia and Tom's wedding, where I introduced myself to their guests as the SOMOB—the Significant Other of the Mother of the Bride—Karin Bartow, whose support, patience, and love have been a blessing to me.

Thanks to all of you.

NOTES

INTRODUCTION: THE WISDOM OF NATURE

1. I used a film entitled *Koyaanisqatsi* as the basis of a series of lectures from which many of these ideas are drawn.
2. The word "courage" can be read as the French word for "heart" (coeur) plus "rage" = courage.
3. www.jbotkin.com/smartbusiness

1. WHY KNOWLEDGE SHARED IS POWER

1. A seventh is the Client Business Managers Community, which is responsible for all six technical offerings.
2. Everett M. Rogers, *The Diffusion of Innovations,* Fourth Edition (New York: The Free Press, 1995).
3. Instead of arranging its keys as QWERTY, which was done to slow down typing so the mechanical keys wouldn't entangle, Dvorak put the most common letters AEIOUTN where they are most easily accessible. Even though this method is approved by the American Typewriter Association, it has never caught on, because too many typists are invested in the familiar if inefficient keyboard.
4. James M. Utterback, *Mastering the Dynamics of Innovation* (Boston: Harvard Business School Press, 1996). Page 162.
5. I am indebted to Jim Utterback's scholarly telling of the story of the "Ice King," which includes the tale of snob appeal of American ices—"just as we witness today with bottled waters," he writes. The purest ice came from Wenham Lake and was sold to British Lords and Ladies until Norway renamed its Lake Oppengaard "Wenham Lake" before the introduction of international copyright laws. More amusing still (historical reality is always better than modern fiction), Utterback continues "The British Lords and Ladies most likely did not realize the extent to which teams of horses strained on the surface of pristine Wenham Lake, doing what horses do in abundance. Ice compa-

nies, in fact, had a job category for young boys whose sole duty was to pick up after these horses."

6. See Leonard M. Adleman, "Computing with DNA." *Scientific American,* August 1998, pp. 54–61.

7. Geoffrey Moore is not to be confused with Gordon Moore, author of "Moore's Law" which was cited above and is well known in the silicon-based computer world.

8. Geoffrey Moore, *Inside the Tornado* (New York: Harper Business, 1995).

9. The waves to wisdom model is a reimaging of the "Four Steps to Wisdom" model developed by Stan Davis and me in Stan Davis and Jim Botkin, *Monster Under the Bed* (New York: Simon & Schuster, 1994).

10. Technically speaking, "knowledge" is a noun and "knowing" is the verb—unlike its relative "learning," which is both a noun and a verb. Nonetheless, most writers (including me) use the words knowledge and learning to encompass BOTH a content part (noun) AND a process part (verb). Another challenge is a split between those who see knowledge as a belief on which to base action versus those who see knowledge as an ecology that needs to be nurtured. The former use the metaphor of computers and information processing, while the latter use the language of biology and ecological processes. A holistic view, to which I aspire, honors both perspectives.

11. Thomas H. Davenport and Laurence Prusak, *Working Knowledge* (Boston: Harvard Business School Press, 1998). Reported in *Knowledge, Inc., the Executive Report of Knowledge, Technology & Performance,* vol. 3, no. 2.

12. McKinsey & Company, "Managing Knowledge and Learning," Harvard Business School Case Study 9-396-357, prepared by Christopher Bartlett.

13. Create or discover? A provocative point of dialogue is whether any of us can create knowledge or whether we only discover knowledge that's already there.

14. Glatzmaier's work was published in *Nature* magazine and received an avalanche of publicity. The description and goals are in the InterClass report "Innovation, Speed, and Cycle Time."

15. You can learn more about them in the paper in the Appendix of *Smart Business* contributed by Peter Henschel, the Executive Director of IRL and former deputy mayor of San Francisco. Further elaboration can be found in Etienne Wenger, *Communities of Practice* (Cambridge, U.K.: Cambridge University Press, 1998), written while he was at IRL. Communities of practice are also discussed by Xerox Chief Scientist John Seely Brown in the *California Management Review* special issue on Knowledge and the Firm, where he refers to them as the place where personal identity emerges through community membership.

16. I usually avoid the word "collaboration" because for French speakers it connotes "collaboration with the enemy," referring to France's World War II experience.

17. For a good discussion of this process, see Stan Davis and Bill Davidson, *2020 Vision* (New York: Simon & Schuster, 1991).

18. I am indebted to Leif Edvinsson, former Intellectual Capital director of Skandia in Stockholm, for sharing his views on the role of intellectual capital in boosting Skandia's revenues and income. Author of *Intellectual Capital,* Leif is recipient of the Brain of the Year Award from the United Kingdom.

19. Quoted from www.torget.se.

2. THE KNOWLEDGE AGE—OPPORTUNITY FOR A NEW ENLIGHTENMENT?

1. The notion that bumblebees can't fly or that they violate aerodynamic theory is rooted in folklore. Recent scientific research as reported by Bernd Heinrich in *Bumblebee Economics:* "It used to be thought that insect flight could be understood on the basis of fixed-wing aerodynamics, when in fact the wings of many insects, including bumblebees, operate more on the principle of helicopter aerodynamics—the action of the wings of bees is essentially like that of reverse-pitch semi-rotary helicopter blades. . . . Although the idea that bumblebees theoretically can't fly is erroneous, there is some truth in it: bumblebees indeed cannot fly if their muscle temperature drops below 30°C."

    However, folklore to the contrary, bees are capable of seemingly tireless flight. Bees are never "out of breath" no matter how vigorously they exercise. They never have a problem of getting all the oxygen they need and getting rid of carbon dioxide. This is because bumblebee physiology is such that gases (like oxygen) are moved by passive diffusion. They also have internal mechanisms to keep their muscle temperature high.

2. Thomas S. Kuhn, *The Structure of Scientific Revolutions,* third edition (Chicago: University of Chicago Press, 1996. First edition, 1962).

3. Adam Smith, *The Wealth of Nations,* 1776.

4. Priestley and Lavoisier did their breakthrough work during the period known as the Enlightenment, the roughly hundred-year period that began with the French philosopher Montesquieu (b. 1689), included the American Revolutionary War of 1776 and concluded with the outbreak of the French Revolution in 1789. The German philosopher Immanuel Kant gave the Enlightenment its motto: "dare to know." Two American names closely associated with the Enlightenment are Benjamin Franklin and Thomas Jefferson.

5. Variations of these names are Information Age, Information Society, or Information Economy (same for Postindustrial and for Knowledge). I use "age" to refer to an epoch, "society" to refer to social issues, and "economy" to refer to economic issues.

6. Dating the Industrial Revolution of course depends on which part of the world is considered. Leaders of many countries in Africa or other parts of the developing world would argue that their countries have not yet experienced an industrial revolution, or even an agricultural revolution. Whether they have or not, they are experiencing an information revolution. Some tribal groups in Africa see the Information Highway before they see an automobile highway.

7. Stan Davis in *2020 Vision* reasons our current economy will last until 2020, by which time biology will take over. Leif Edvinsson in *Intellectual Capital* sees 1995 as an inflection point marking a halfway station. Building on what they say, the mid-1990s is a time when Windows 95 became the PC standard, web browsers outsold word processors, and more PCs were sold than TVs.

8. See Stan Davis and Chris Meyers, *Blur: The Speed of Change in the Connected Economy* (Reading, MA: Addison Wesley, 1998).

9. Gary High, whose paper is among the contributions at the end of the book, properly protested when I pressed him for a description of his responsibilities at Saturn that I would use in the form of a title.

10. The value of a computer is proportional to the square of the number of connections it makes (or literally to the number of other computers to which it connects).

11. William Strauss and Neil Howe, *Generations: The History of America's Future, 1584–2069* (New York: William Morrow, 1991). Also by the same authors, *The Fourth Turning* (New York: Broadway Books, 1997).

12. In their follow-on book *The Fourth Turning*, the names change slightly: Prophets, Nomads, Heroes, and Artists.

13. You actually have to look at the exact birth years. For most people it will be great-grandparents. But if you were born to relatively old parents, it may be grandparents. For children from a lineage of very young parents, it could be great-great-grandparents.

    Generation Next (born 1961–81) look to earlier counterparts like Martha Washington and Paul Revere. The Millennial Generation (born 1982–) look to Abigail Adams and "Uncle Sam" Wilson.

14. Alfred Sloan, founder of General Motors, was born in 1875; Henry Ford, founder of Ford Motor Company, in 1863. Pierre Du Pont, who transformed his family's company into the hierarchical, multidivisional giant of the present day, was born in 1870. The Missionary idealist generation comprises those people born between 1860 and 1882.

15. Wilbur Wright was born in 1867, Orville, his younger brother, in 1870.

16. Some people from places like New York or Boston are surprised to learn that Navajo Indians in the Four Corners part of the United States live in "Navajo Nation," which is larger than Connecticut.

3. WHAT'S THE KNOWLEDGE BUSINESS IN YOUR BUSINESS?

1. The Hartness case is described in *FAST Company,* 1998.

2. I want to acknowledge Gary Hamel, from whom I have learned much in his talks, his award-winning *HBR* articles, and his contribution to John Seely Brown's *Seeing Differently* (Boston: Harvard Business School Press, 1988, 1997).

3. See, in *The Smithsonian* magazine, December 1997, the story of my friend and colleague Bill Ury, co-author of *Getting to Yes.* The story recounts his efforts to mediate the Russia–Chechnya conflict. One of Bill's main techniques in conflict resolution is to drop the adversarial idea that each side start by demanding more than it really wants or expects, and then narrowing down the difference between the two extremes. While this may work in a bazaar, it's disastrous for serious conflict resolution. Instead, Bill searches for interests the two sides have in common and works to create a shared understanding of what each side needs to come to an agreement. This approach is entirely consistent with the concepts of learning and knowledge described in *Smart Business.* Had our roles been reversed in life, Bill would have written *Getting to Knowledge* and I would have titled my work *Smart Negotiating.*

4. See Andrew Klein, "WallStreet.com," *Wired,* February 1998, pp. 90ff.

5. Much of this material comes from internal industry reports and from published reports in *Business Week* and other business trade journals.

6. Stan Davis and Jim Botkin, "The Coming of Knowledge Based Business," *Harvard Business Review,* September–October 1994.

4. KNOWLEDGE COMMUNITIES AS ENTREPRENEURIAL VENTURES

1. In summer 1998, AT&T and British Telecom concluded a "Joint Global Venture" that created the largest global telephone service in the world. This move came in response to the massive changes that created World Com and the failed MCI attempt to take over British Telecom. While the AT&T-BT agreement fell short of an actual merger, it had all the characteristics of a merger except for consolidation of financial statements and both entities kept their own names.
2. This is no small task for AT&T, which for 95 percent of its corporate existence was a domestic monopoly with international contact limited primarily to countries where copper cables came ashore (England, France, Japan, and Venezuela—in that order).
3. Mike Armstrong is AT&T Chairman, John Zeglis is AT&T President, and Sir Iain Vallance is Chairman of British Telecom.
4. In the chart CBM = Client Business Manager, DSM = Data Sales Manager, DSE = Data Sales Executive, and IP = Internet Protocol.
5. Utterback's conclusions are consistent with the findings of Michael Porter from Harvard and James Brian Quinn from Dartmouth.
6. Honeywell's is "Vision 2005," GM's is "Leadership 21," and the Army's is "Force XXI."
7. A similar study was carried out by the business historian Alfred Chandler in his 1990 work, *Scale and Scope: Dynamics of Industrial Capitalism.* In it he examines the world's two hundred largest manufacturing enterprises, firms accounting for some two-thirds of world industrial output from the 1880s through the 1930s.

5. MANAGE KNOWLEDGE SO YOUR CHIEF KNOWLEDGE OFFICER DOESN'T HAVE TO DO IT FOR YOU

1. At McKinsey, Brook Manville describes the evolution of the paradigm of knowledge management as follows: "Knowledge management was once about managing knowledge (information). It then expanded to include managing people with knowledge. It will increasingly mean managing in the knowledge economy," which is the focus of this chapter. From "What's the 'Management' in 'Knowledge Management'?" presentation, The Knowledge Management Conference, Boston, June 22–24, 1998.
2. Morten T. Hansen, "The Search-Transfer Problem: The Role of Weak Ties in Sharing Knowledge across Organization Subunits," *Administrative Science Quarterly,* forthcoming 1999, Morten T. Hansen, "Combining Network Centrality and Related Knowledge: Explaining Effective Knowledge Sharing in Multiunit Firms," Working Paper, Harvard Business School, 98–081. Morten Hansen is Assistant Professor in Business Administration at the Harvard Business School.
3. September 1994, 10th Mountain Division, which had gone into Somalia in December 1992. P 204 Gordon Sullivan.
4. Ikujiro Nonaka and Hirotaka Takeuchi, *The Knowledge-Creating Company: How Japanese Companies Create the Dynamics of Innovation* (New York: Oxford University Press, 1995).
5. Presentation at the Berkeley Second Annual Conference on Knowledge and the Firm.

See also Carla O'Dell and C. Jackson Grayson, Jr., *If Only We Knew What We Know: The Transfer of Internal Knowledge and Best Practice* (New York: Free Press, 1998).

6. Richard Rhodes, *The Making of the Atomic Bomb* (New York: Simon & Schuster, 1986), a Pulitzer Prize winner. The three who were key to the atomic bomb were Leo Szilard, Eugene Wigner, and Edward Teller. Teller was the one who persuaded the United States to build an even bigger bomb, the hydrogen bomb. See also the *Newsweek* extra, "The Power of Invention."

7. Antonio Damasio, *Descartes' Error* (New York: Avon Books, 1994). I have drawn heavily on this work for the incredible details and implications described. Many of the conclusions are also corroborated by Rosalind Picard at MIT, cited later.

8. Rosalind Picard, *Affective Computing* (Cambridge, MA: MIT Press, 1997).

9. Damasio, in explaining why this sad tale is worth relating, says, "Unwittingly, Gage's example indicated that something in the brain was concerned with unique human properties, among them the ability to anticipate the future and plan accordingly within a complex social environment; the sense of responsibility toward the self and others; and the ability to orchestrate one's survival deliberately, at the command of one's free will."

10. Daniel Goleman, *Emotional Intelligence: Why It Can Matter More Than IQ* (New York: Bantam Books, 1995).

11. The Army's After-Action Review system contains videotapes that show new soldiers the problems of crowd control. They are highly emotional and effective tapes because they are affective. They communicate the reality that soldiers confront.

6. LEARNING TO LEAD THE KNOWLEDGE REVOLUTION

1. Edward O. Wilson, *Consilience: The Unity of Knowledge* (New York: Alfred A. Knopf, 1998).

2. General Gordon Sullivan and Michael Harper, *Hope Is Not a Method* (New York: Time-Life Books, 1996).

3. J. Botkin, M. Elmandjra, and M. Malitza, *No Limits to Learning: A Report to the Club of Rome* (Oxford: Pergamon Press, 1979).

4. See Utterback, *Mastering the Dynamics,* Chapter 1, note 4.

5. Many Fortune 500s have their own universities. There's the Aetna Institute for Education, American Express Quality University, Apple University, Cigna, Disney University, Dow Chemical's Midland Learning Center, Eastman Kodak, First of America Bank's Quality Service University, General Electric's Management Development Institute, General Motors University, GTE, IBM, Intel, the Johnson Controls Training Institute, MasterCard University, Merrill Lynch, Motorola University, Nationwide Insurance, Pitney-Bowes's and Marriott Hotels' jointly owned Aberdeen Woods Conference Center, Procter & Gamble College, Bristol-Myers Squibb, Southwest Airline's University for People, Sun Oil, 3M, United Auto Workers/Chrysler National Training Center, and Xerox Document University. Even more are tracked by *Corporate University Review,* "the magazine about organizational learning and performance."

6. Botkin, Elmandjra, and Malitza, *No Limits to Learning.*

7. Positron Emission Tomography.

8. For fascinating and easy to read accounts of the latest brain research, see Ronald Kotulak, *Inside the Brain* (Kansas City: Andrews & McNeel, 1996).

9. One of my favorite poems, modernized for the millennium, based on *The Kabir Book: Forty-Four of the Ecstatic Poems of Kabir,* the fifteenth-century Sufi, translated by Robert Bly, 1993.

10. Herbert A. Simon, "The Architecture of Complexity," *Proceedings of the American Philosophical Society,* 1962. Recounted in T. Seeley, *Wisdom of the Hive* (Cambridge, MA: Harvard University Press, 1995).

11. Motorola material from *Business Week,* May 4, 1998, pp. 52–57. Quote from p. 54.

12. Boeing material from *USA Today,* May 6, 1998, p. 1 of Business Section.

13. Thomas Davenport, co-author of *Working Knowledge,* professor at Boston University, and director of the Institute for Strategic Change at Andersen Consulting.

14. Joseph Horvath, Senior Consultant, Knowledge Management, at the IBM Consulting Group, is knowledgable on AARs and CALL.

15. Brian Helweg-Larsen is a principal of Professional Skills Training, based in the United Kingdom. The Knowledge Puzzle is one of the simulations he developed to give business executives direct experience with the challenge of converting tacit knowledge to explicit and further diffusing the explicit knowledge to more distant parts of the organization. This process goes from individual learning to community learning, and from community to corporate learning.

16. Fons Trompenaars, *Riding the Waves of Culture* (London: Economist Books, 1993).

7. CULTURES THAT QUESTION ARE CULTURES THAT TRUST

1. If it's much higher than 50 percent, you may want to call in the corporate morticians. All big accounting firms have specialists in bankruptcy.

2. Interestingly, this approach is both at the root of the modern scientific process and also the source of ancient wisdom.

3. Chris Argyris, "Teaching Smart People to Learn," *Harvard Business Review,* 1991.

4. SOL is the Society for Organizational Learning, Cambridge, Massachusetts.

8. LEADERSHIP IS BUILDING YOUR COMMUNITY'S FUTURE

1. Thanks to Marty Gecek, director of the American Studies Center at the Salzburg Seminar, for verifying this information.

2. Gordon R. Sullivan and Michael V. Harper, *Hope Is Not a Method* (New York: Random House, Times Business, 1996). I wish to acknowledge General Sullivan and his book, which has strongly influenced my thinking on leadership. I met Sullivan at a meeting of Shell Oil, where he is on the Board of Directors.

3. From Senn–Delaney Leadership Consulting Group and from personal sources.

9. "NOT FOR TANGIBLE BUSINESS PURPOSES" AND OTHER PITFALLS

1. Sam Levinson comically observes: "We must learn from the mistakes of others because we will never be able to live long enough to make all the mistakes ourselves!"

2. Charles Lucier and Janet Torsilieri, "Why Knowledge Programs Fail," Booz • Allen & Hamilton, *Strategy & Business,* I 9, (Fourth Quarter 1997), Reprint 97402.

3. The same dynamics also explain why pilot projects fail to spread: They are seen as creations of someone else's community, which brings up the Not-Invented-Here syndrome for others.

4. CCL was cited by the *Wall Street Journal* as the top leadership program in the United States. Conclusion based on figures of public-enrollment executive-education offerings in the 1992 *Bricker's International Directory.*

5. A trust walk is a management training exercise where people walk through unknown terrain, one as the guide and the other blindfolded. It is done without mishap, and the blindfolded person gets to experience "what trust feels like."

6. In terms of elders, many companies treat employees who go to work for another company as traitors. They are excommunicated from their old community of practice. Other companies, however, have a different approach. KPMG sees departing personnel as sources of future business when they go to work in another industry. Arthur Andersen's education facility at St. Charles near Chicago mandates that once you've been through the Andersen orientation-training course, you are forever Andersen alumni/ae and always welcome back.

7. From John Seely Brown editor, *Seeing Differently: Insights on Innovation* (Cambridge: Harvard Business School Press, 1997). Gary Hamel's contribution is "Strategy as Revolution."

8. Adapted from Sue Hubbell, *A Book of Bees.*

10. A SMART BUSINESS ENGAGES THE KNOWLEDGE REVOLUTION AND GROWS FROM IT

1. Indeed, the research on CoPs is best done by consulting with business anthropologists. Like good social anthropologists, they resist attempts to mold or modernize something that has grown organically.

2. IRL uses these methods with its partner companies.

3. Margaret Mead, *Coming of Age in Samoa: A Psychological Study of Primitive Youth for Western Civilization* (New York: William Morrow, 1971). Margaret Mead taught at the opening session of the Salzburg Seminar and, in the context of the Club of Rome, I had the chance to meet her to describe my interest in learning. She had many questions and concerns about the role of business in learning; were she still alive today, she would be urging all of us to keep wisdom always present in our dialogues.

4. Actually, there *is* an AT&T HR Knowledge Community, which does just that.

5. IKE is a registered trade name of AT&T.

6. Leif Edvinsson, Michael S. Malone (contributor), *Intellectual Capital: Realizing Your Company's True Value by Finding Its Hidden Roots;* Thomas A. Stewart, *Intellectual Capital: The New Wealth of Organizations;* and Johan Roos (ed.), et al., *Intellectual Capital: Navigating in the New Business Landscape.* The original idea for intellectual capital is attributed to Erik Sveiby of Sweden.

7. Tom Davenport, "Knowledge Management in the Advanced Stages," InterClass Presentation, November 1998.

8. The National Education Association and the American Federation of Teachers.
9. The film is directed by Robert Redford, based on John Nichols, *The New Mexico Trilogy: The Milagro Beanfield War; The Magic Journey;* and *The Nirvana Blues* (1987).

AFTERWORD: THE ECONOMICS OF KNOWLEDGE

1. "The Art and Architecture of Powerful Questions," published at www.omegaperformance.com.

APPENDIX: COMPANY CONTRIBUTIONS:
HOW LEGACY COMPANIES PRACTICE SMART BUSINESS

1. Wayne—Fingerlakes BOCES, New York.
2. The Marriott lodging portfolio includes full service hotels, Fairfield Inn, Residence Inn, Towne-Place Suites, Courtyard, Conference Centers, Vacation Club International, Renaissance, and Ritz Carlton. With more than 1500 properties in more than fifty-four countries, Marriott plans to have two thousand lodging properties by the year 2000.
3. Marriott Senior Living Services currently has nearly one hundred communities that provide a range and continuum of care for senior citizens across the United States. Marriott plans to have more than two hundred communities by the year 2002.
4. Roger Dow and Susan Cook, *"Turned On"* (San Francisco: HarperBusiness, 1996).
5. When Jim Botkin asked me to author this article, I began to think about the many aspects of the Saturn education story that might be of interest to readers and in keeping with the flow of the book.

    I am absolutely convinced that the skill development of the entire Saturn family has been fundamental to our outcomes, not only in our most obvious result—the car itself—but also in such areas as teamwork, customer focus, and union–management relationships, which so critically support our car-building. And since the story can't be told in just a few pages, I struggled with how best to contribute.

    As Jim and I discussed the possible topics for my article, we kept bumping into the issue of governance of education at Saturn or, in the broader sense, "How did this whole thing happen?" I knew the topic had value, but as I wrote and rewrote I couldn't get comfortable that this discussion would appeal to the reader. But every time I left the topic to pursue my commitment to Jim from another angle, I found myself returning to governance and origin.

    And then it finally dawned on me. The importance of the topic is that many business imperatives and strategies to implement the imperatives never see the light of day because they get caught up in compartmentalized, organizational struggles that detract from rather than add to speed, customer focus, and execution of strategic plans. Thus this article is about how Saturn's approach to learning and knowledge was built in from the outset of the company's founding.
6. In Sweden the letter market is deregulated. That is the situation in only a few countries in the world. In the markets for payment handling and parcel and logistical services, on the other hand, competition has been tough for years. The evolution of electronic

means to communicate brings major changes. Sweden Post has come to meet more and more competition as customers change their behavior, needs, and demands: fax, e-mail, telemarketing, TV/radio advertising, new distributors, and so on.

7. The formal names in Swedish are Posten AB and Posten Sverige AB, or, in British English, Sweden Post, Ltd., and American English, Sweden Post, Inc.

8. As the U.S., Canadian, and Mexican postal systems still receive.

9. Saying that these are "normal business conditions" is right in one sense: normal for people in normal business. Many employees in Sweden Post have never worked in any other organization. The organization has to experience competition, deregulation, profitability demands, downsizing, technological change, new customer demands, and so forth at a pace that is very threatening for many. Some love it, though, and say, "At last!"

10. The decline continues at 13 percent a year!

11. This would be similar to the way companies like 3M in America or ABB in Europe are organized.

12. For example, both the information you might need to change working plans because of late aircraft, and information you need to keep updated on the company as a whole.

13. In Swedish: Utvecklings Program för högre chefer i Posten, something in English like Development Program for Upper-level Managers in Sweden Post, but I think up with an extra p gives the idea.

15. In the twenty-first century world of economics and current business, the paradigm "the bigger fish eats the smaller" has changed to one that says "the speedier fish eats the slower."

16. In other words, *ceteris paribus* ("everything else remaining constant") becomes *mutatis mutandis* ("everything is changing simultaneously").

17. Morgan Stanley, Inc., *Global Investing: The Competition Edge* (United States: Equity Research, 1996).

18. In Spanish: "células de aprendizaje."

19. In Spanish: "aprender a emprender."

20. Heidi Ann Hahn, PhD, is Senior Executive Adviser to Los Alamos National Laboratory's senior managers and also manages a group of human factors engineers and organizational psychologists, Los Alamos, NM, *hahn@lanl.gov.* Rebecca R. Phillips, PhD, is Deputy Director of Human Resources, Los Alamos National Laboratory, Los Alamos, NM, and Research Director, College of Leadership and Transcultural Studies, Motorola University, Schaumburg, IL, rrphillips@lanl.gov. Other primary researchers in original study were Phil Goldstone, PhD, LANL, and Bill Wadt, PhD, LANL.

21. Goodstein points out an interesting paradox here, however, namely, that those very industries (such as manufacturing) that could support scientific research, either politically or financially, are those most quickly being replaced by service-sector industries that have little need for a scientific infrastructure. D. L. Goodstein, "Scientific Elites and Scientific Illiterates," *Engineering and Science,* Spring, 1993, pp. 23–31.

22. L. R. Cohen and R. G. Noll, "Privatizing Public Research," *Scientific American,* September, 1994, p. 72.

23. P. Williams, "Research and Recession: Regeneration or Resignation?" *Physics in Business,* no. 6, 1994, p. 2.

24. This is not (or not yet) a computer-based model, though it could easily be a simulation put into a software system like Ithink.© Rather, our purpose was to provide a useful tool for shared understanding to enable better discussion among the various members of a particular knowledge community.

25. Management of business knowledge communities is hard enough, but under the special circumstances associated with R&D, managing a scientific knowledge community can be quite a delicate undertaking because often all parties in the relationship chain do not share the same view of the "ideal" outcome, products, or even set of research characteristics involved.

26. The relationship chain can be best understood as a specialized form of a knowledge community, whose members are both internal and external to the research organization.

27. Reading across the top of Figure 6, "Technical" corresponds to the dilemma of scale; "Long" corresponds to the dilemma of time; "One" corresponds to the dilemma of scope. The fourth dilemma of space (global versus local) is not shown on Figure 6 because Laboratory research is inherently supposed as national. The other two vertical continua on Figure 6, "Basic" and "Theoretical," do not correspond directly to any of the main learning dilemmas.

28. Omitted from Figure 6 for the sake of clarity.

29. We do not mean to imply that direct project funds are unimportant. They are an influencer for the time and one-to-many dimensions. They are, however, a part of the general context, having presumably been negotiated in the course of setting the overall research agenda.

30. The deleterious effect of organizational poverty is well documented in the industrial safety literature; see for example J. Reason, *Managing the Risks of Organizational Accidents* (Aldershot, England: Ashgate, 1997).

31. We use the term "end user" because sometimes the customer is the same as the funder; other times, they are two separate entities.

32. That is, the knowledge brought to bear is scientific/technical knowledge applied directly and in detail to the particular R&D project.

About the Author

Dr. Jim Botkin—known to friends as "Dr. Jim"—is cofounder and president of InterClass, the International Corporate Learning Association, a knowledge community of Fortune 500 companies seeking to improve its members' organizational learning and enhance their knowledge assets.

After a freak bee sting caused a near death experience, Jim Botkin became an ardent student of the ideals and practices that characterize successful innovations in legacy companies blinded by their very success. An expert on corporate learning and knowledge, he is an internationally known speaker and well-respected writer.

Dr. Botkin wrote the award-winning Club of Rome report *No Limits to Learning,* which has been translated into more than a dozen languages, and six other books on business.

A former Academic Director of the Salzburg Seminar, he is an Honorary Citizen of Salzburg, Austria, a past resident of Santa Fe, New Mexico, and a present Fellow at the University of Texas in Austin. He has taught at the Harvard Graduate School of Education, and his doctorate is from the Harvard Business School.

He lives and works in Cambridge, Massachusetts. You can learn more about Dr. Jim's work and interests at *www.jbotkin.com/smartbusiness.* Jim is listed in the national registry of *Who's Who.*